# COME TOGETHER
# RIGHT NOW

*Organizing Stories
from a Fading Empire*

Bruce K. Gagnon

*Foreword by Karl Grossman*

*Illustrations by W. B. Park*

Just Write Books

47 Main Street #3, Topsham, Maine 04086
207-729-3600 • www.jstwrite.com

© 2005 Bruce Gagnon

Library of Congress Catalog Card No.: 2005929157
Gagnon, Bruce
Come Together Right Now: Nonfiction/Bruce Gagnon
p. 262
1. Military—Non-Fiction.  2. Politics—Non-Fiction.
1. Title.

ISBN  0-9766533-5-4

ISBN  978-0-9766533-5-4

Printed in the United States of America

For the
Future Generations

# Contents

# FOREWORD

Bruce Gagnon is the finest organizer I have ever known. His stories constitute a picture of the United States of America in recent decades, and the idealistic, honest, hard-working, courageous journey of an American Radical.

*"The motives of the American Radical engaged in organizational work will be viewed by many people and organizations with suspicion, cynicism and hostility,"* wrote that earlier model of an organizer, Saul D. Alinsky, in his *Reveille for Radicals.* *"They will measure him with the only measuring stick that a materialistic society has taught them, one that is marked in units of selfishness, exploitation, money, power, and prestige. They will wonder and ask, 'What's in it for him?' 'What's his angle?' 'What's his cut?' 'There must be a catch in it some place—what is it?' 'People don't do things for nothing—what's he doing it for?'"*

"Basically, the Radical must meet this opposition by a simple honesty, and always remember that in the long run he is striving to make honesty a virtue instead of a stigma of stupidity. One of the most significant ways that he can do this is by the power of personal example."

Bruce has long organized through personal example.

I vividly recall going to his house in Orlando soon after meeting him. It was so simple: a photograph of that other great organizer, Cesar Chavez of the United Farm Workers Union, above a plain bed. A few pieces of furniture and books, and that was that. I rode with him in the pick-up truck he drove throughout Florida when he was coordinator of the Florida Coalition for Peace and Justice—a vehicle (one of the very few in Florida) without an air conditioner. Bruce, I said, you just have to get an air conditioner. He smiled.

This book explains (and it is tale very much worth learning) where Bruce got his values. He wasn't born to them. He came from a conservative background. As a young man he was a Republican for Nixon and joined the U.S. Air Force. But as the obscene Vietnam War raged on, he underwent a conversion and grew.

Always Bruce has been imbued with the notion that a good spirit flows in people, a spirit that can be connected with—not with sectarianism, not by speaking down, but by respecting the dignity of every person and being honest.

Significantly, in the peace and social justice movements—as in other sectors of American and world society—there are the lures of money and power. Big foundation grants and monies from individuals with specific agendas, cause some activists to lose their independence. Power corrupts some—even some whose mission is supposed to be serving the powerless.

I've known Bruce well for near two decades and never in those years has he deviated an inch from a path of integrity, selflessness—and an eye on the prize, that seemingly impossible dream for which all good organizers work.

A few months before he died (very much too soon), Cesar Chavez, for whom Bruce worked, appeared on a television program I hosted. He was at the height of his organizing successes, yet he was wearing simple clothes and sneakers. But with Chavez, it went way beyond humility in dress. Chavez's simple personal life and total commitment to the plight of farm workers shone through, as did his deep knowledge about the lethal pesticides used in agriculture causing widespread cancer among those who cultivate and harvest what we drink and eat.

In Bruce's life, this great organizer has represented more than a picture above his bed.

I first connected with Bruce in the 1980s while as a journalist I was investigating the use of nuclear power in space. In 1986, I broke the story in *The Nation* that the next mission of the ill-fated shuttle Challenger (which exploded after launch) would have involved lofting a plutonium-fueled space probe. Bruce saw the article. He understood that plans were afoot for a series of plutonium space shots from Cape Canaveral. So one day Bruce telephoned me, explaining that his people in Florida were on the "front line" in terms of the nuclear launches. He wanted information.

It didn't take long for Bruce to master the science—and the public health dangers—of sending nuclear material above our heads. And as a dedicated, highly capable organizer he rallied people to challenge this wrong-headed program. (His group became advocates of solar and other safe energy systems which can substitute for life-threatening space nuclear power).

First in Florida, and then as coordinator of the Global Network Against Weapons & Nuclear Power in Space, Bruce has traveled constantly around the world. He has been there slogging away, speaking straight to people (even nuclear rocket scientists with their vested interests), reaching out for that spark, that spirit.

Bruce has always emphasized that there is no shortcut, no magic bullet. At the heart of successful organizing is hard work, conversation, education, and creating a vision about which people can agree. And by personal example, Bruce motivates people and helps show the way.

Alinsky ended *Reveille for Radicals* by writing: *"Let it sound, then. Let it come, clear, strident, ringing, and heart-stirring. Let it come, the rallying cry of America. From the historical 'Don't tread on me' to the grim "Tyranny, like Hell, is not easily conquered,' to 'John Brown's soul goes marching on,' to 'You shall not crucify mankind on a cross of gold,' to 'Solidarity Forever!' These are a few of the battle cries of the American dream. Let the cry sound again, clearly, boldly, shattering the death-like silence of decay."*

That's what Bruce does for this new century in his moving and stirring and important book.

Karl Grossman
Professor of Journalism
State University of New York College at Old Westbury
Author, *The Wrong Stuff:*
*The Space Program's Nuclear Threat To Our Planet*

# PREFACE

*"Behold, a sacred voice is calling you;*
*All over the sky a sacred voice is calling."*
—Black Elk

As I travel, I frequently write reports about my trips and send them to our growing Global Network Against Weapons & Nuclear Power in Space e-mail list. People often tell me they enjoy reading them, that they feel hopeful when they read the stories about activists working hard to bring sanity, fairness, and justice to our world. Many have suggested I compile them into a book.

I always figured I was too young to write a book - not enough experiences under my belt. Some years ago, I wrote my life story up to 1974, the year I was discharged from the U.S. Air Force. I was never able to get beyond that point. The memories were too fresh; I felt they needed more time to jell.

Our dear friend and former neighbor Julie Netzer in Gainesville, Florida was the impetus for this book. Julie was a part of several campaigns I worked on while living in Gainesville and felt I should write a book about organizing.

There is a lot of talk today about reframing the debate. People are looking for what I call the "magic bullet"—one thing that will push the progressive community over the top and bring the wavering masses to our side. I don't believe in the magic bullet. Instead I believe in hard work. Of course, we could always do a better job of articulating our vision. I also think we could use more confidence, inspiration, determination, and learn lessons from successful organizing efforts. It would be great if organizing became a respected field of endeavor in our culture so that there were more of us doing this work on a full-time basis.

I have included in this book some early stories from my life to show my own conversion process. I began my political work as a know-nothing young Republican for Nixon in 1968. My years in the Air Force turned me toward the peace and social justice movements. It is possible for ordinary right-wingers to change. We make a mistake when we call people who don't agree with us "stupid" and write them off. If we try to connect to the good spirit in people first, we might be able to get past our political differences long enough to find common interests.

I've also shared some stories from my days working with the farm workers union and as a social justice organizer. I learned a great deal about how to organize during those years and those experiences motivate much of my work today.

From 1983-1998 I coordinated the Florida Coalition for Peace & Justice and in that job I began to learn about the space program. The creation of the Global Network Against Weapons & Nuclear Power in Space, in 1992, pushed me further into teaching and organizing about plans to move the arms race into the heavens.

Since my son, Julian, graduated from high school in Gainesville and headed off to college, I have been able to dramatically increase my organizing trips across the U.S. and around the world to promote the work of the Global Network. Since 1999, I've kept up a punishing pace of travel, sometimes as much as three weeks a month, in order to help create a global constituency to protect space from becoming the next battleground. I have included reports of many of these trips in this book.

Since moving to Maine in 2003 with my partner, Mary Beth Sullivan, I began listening hard to what people in my new state were talking about. The subject of jobs came up over and over again, and I began to look for ways to more fully integrate this issue into my existing peace work. In communities all over America weapons corporations are often the dominant employer. I began to raise the question, "How can we ever stop war if we don't deal with the jobs issue?" As well-paying manufacturing jobs leave the U.S. by the millions, there is little to replace them except for low-paid service jobs, or the high-tech jobs building weapons of war and mass destruction. It seems clear to me that the progressive community must begin to articulate a transformative vision for the conversion of the military industrial complex to peaceful production if we hope to change the current military and economic system in the U.S. In the latter part of the book you will find much more of my thinking around this important subject.

I use different writing styles in this book. I start with a narrative and then later on switch to reports from my trips. Sometimes I throw in an op-ed or a satirical piece I wrote for my blog. Along the way I put in a few diary entries. There are some articles I wrote for the Florida Coalition's newsletter *Just Peace* and from the Global Network newsletter *Space Alert.* I included a poem and even a play I recently wrote about economic conversion.

I am often asked what religion I belong to. I tell people I don't have one. However, I do consider myself a very spiritual person. My spiritual connection is to the Earth and all the living beings on this beautiful planet. My personal agenda is to protect life and to make the future better for coming generations. I want to see a stronger nation, not militarily, but instead a power that comes from a confident people who take care of the air and water, who educate their children, and who provide jobs that sustain and protect the Earth. To me nothing is more important in life than working for that kind of a future.

I think we have a mutual responsibility to ensure that we create a fair and hopeful nation that plays a cooperative and peaceful role in the world. The pro-space development *Mars Society* says we need to move off this dying, stinking, rotting planet, and they lobby Congress for the funds to "terraform" Mars so we can move our civilization there. I'm not interested in moving to Mars. I look around this amazing planet Earth and see such beauty. I wonder why we can't take care of things right here before we go careening off into the heavens planting the bad seed of war, greed and environmental degradation. I am not opposed to space exploration. I am just opposed to heading off into space with our current juvenile delinquent mentality. Let's slow down and head into space once we've matured a bit.

We need to come together right now here on Earth. I want to help. I hope you appreciate my stories and learn from them. The stories come from the people. I have learned that people are the same everywhere. They love their families, love food, and love to laugh. Love is what can move mountains.

*Bruce K. Gagnon*
*June 2005*

# INTRODUCTION

## THE MAKING OF AN ACTIVIST

*"Gramma said when you come on something good, first thing to do is share it with whoever you can find; that way, the good spreads out where no telling it will go. Which is right."*

—The Education of Little Tree

All I ever really wanted to be was a basketball coach, or maybe a baseball coach. But I never planned to become a political activist, to find myself jailed, spied on, organizing global campaigns, or getting caught in the middle of political power struggles. Thirty years of activism later, I am wiser and much richer having lived this life.

It all started while I was watching President Richard Nixon make his famous "secret plan to end the war" speech back in 1968. Something about the guy just convinced me he was an honest man with an honest plan to end the Vietnam War with an "honorable victory" for the U.S. It didn't matter that I knew nothing about Nixon and his years of crooked politics. I took the bait and was hooked.

I was a sophomore at Choctaw High School in Fort Walton Beach, Florida. This Panhandle beach town is home to Eglin Air Force Base where my stepfather was stationed. The school was conservative, the town was conservative, my family was conservative. It was natural that I too would become conservative. After all, we are what we are programmed to be. Right?

I volunteered for the local Nixon for President campaign and was quickly thrown into a public event working a booth with another high school student for "Tricky Dick." I took a few minutes and read Nixon's background information on his campaign literature and noticed that my co-worker had not. As people approached our booth my co-worker didn't have much to say but I was spouting off all the campaign rhetoric and sending folks off nodding their heads in agreement. "Yeah, Nixon sounds like the man." It wasn't long before I was regularly working with the campaign and soon was Vice Chair of the Okaloosa County Young Republican Club. And when Sen. Strom Thurmond (R-S.C.) came to town for a Nixon fish-fry pre-election event, I was given the "honor" of sitting next to him at the picnic table as a reward for my hard work. I remember asking Thurmond, in my most naïve way, what he thought of our fine candidate, this Mr. Nixon. He just looked at me like I was a damn idiot and gruffly cleared his throat. It was my first subtle lesson in how politicians crawl into bed with those they intensely dislike.

Nixon went on to win the election and one of the teachers at Choctaw told me I had talked him into voting for our new president. I felt pretty good about myself and was anxious for more.

The "more" would have to wait. My stepfather had been transferred to Vietnam, and the family stayed in Fort Walton. It was hard enough living on an enlisted man's pay with six kids when he was home. But he was gone to 'Nam, and I was soon waking up at 3:00 every morning to deliver newspapers out on Okaloosa island. The paper route was 50 miles long, spread out all over the beach community that was just beginning to explode on the barrier island. So, I'd fold my papers until 4:00 a.m. then hit the road in my parents' car and throw papers to the homes and bungalows on sand pit streets. Several times after I threw a paper, the car would swerve and I'd veer onto the sandy shoulder of the road and get stuck. It was hard to have to knock on the door at this pre-dawn hour and ask my customer to help dig my parents' car out from the sand. But, none of my customers ever cancelled the paper. I'd get done just in time to get off to school. After school, I went to work at a local hamburger place until closing at 11:00 p.m. All my friends were surprised that often on weekends, when they wanted to go to the movies, I'd say I couldn't because I had no money. "You've got two jobs, " they'd reply. But I was giving most of my earnings to my mother to help keep the family going in between meager military paychecks that were split between Florida and Vietnam.

I was also involved in Sea Explorer Scouts at the time. Our explorer crew had an old ocean-liner life boat, like one from the Titanic. We put a sail on it and tried to maneuver the boat out in the inter-coastal waterway. We were a rag-tag outfit that had loads of good fun camping and canoe racing throughout the region.

On one of those campouts I remember one of the older boys, more worldly now that he had graduated high school, talking about the Vietnam War. He told stories that he "had heard" about U.S. troops in Vietnam torturing Viet Cong, sewing their genitals in their mouths after capturing them. This was my first "anti-war" experience and years later after hearing directly from a soldier who wrote his mom telling her that U.S. troops cut the ears off Iraqi troops and stuffed them in the dead men's mouths during the 1991 Persian Gulf War, it confirmed for me the likely truth of those earlier tales.

In August, 1969, our Sea Explorers were undertaking a 50-mile survival hike through the Eglin A.F.B. bombing range. Our leader, a local radio personality named Dutch Van, split us into two crews. I was named crew leader of one and my best friend, Andy Schmidt, was made the leader of the other crew. The rules were that you could take anything you wanted but you had to carry it all on your back for the whole 50 miles in the hot and humid Florida summer. My crew met and mapped out a plan. No tents, no cooking gear, simple food— very little to carry. We were ready. I was very proud of how organized we were. When we arrived at the starting point we saw Andy's crew. They showed up with cook stoves, ice chests, big tents and tons of canned goods. How could they ever carry all of this, we wondered? The first thing the adults did was to load Andy's coolers in their cars for them. So much for the rules being even. Andy's crew grew weary and after the first day they began dropping out like flies. My crew hung in there and kept walking.

Eglin A.F.B. is known as the largest military base in the world. Long ago the Air Force took large parts of state forests and incorporated them into the base. The base is used for missile and bomb testing (the new Mother of all Bombs—MOAB was tested there) and to rehearse ground combat operations. While on the 50-mile hike we ran across a "Vietnamese village" used by the Army Rangers to practice jungle warfare.

Only two of Andy's crew finished the walk. Andy did not. My entire crew finished and I lost a big toenail in the process. This was one of the first times that I realized I could effectively organize people and I felt a tinge of leadership ability.

Aside from this "anti-war" campfire storytelling experience, there was so much support for the war in Fort Walton Beach that I never heard another word against the war or U.S. government policy again while living there.

Due to my two jobs, I didn't get much sleep at night. I slept in school. My teacher in Business Law was such a bore that I spent a whole semester asleep and got the grades (F) to show for it.

My football career at Choctaw High was short-lived. Our coach was a genuine crazy man. He used to take the whole team into a little room with padded floor and walls about the size of a standard bathroom. He'd make two guys go into the middle and beat the hell out of each other, all the while spitting chewing tobacco all over everyone else on the team who were crammed into the doorway. He would beat the two warriors in the padded room with his whistle strap. I got my elbow busted in my first entry into the padded room. You could poke your finger into the middle of the elbow bone and move the pieces around. He told me to put ice on it. When I got to the hospital they operated and put two pins in the elbow.

# TOUCHED BY THE GREAT SPIRIT

*"The seeds that you plant will sprout in the future."*

—Thich Nhat Hanh

I was born in Maryland to Kenneth Edgar Gagnon (a former chicken and turkey farmer) and Ruth Tarantino DiCapua. Before I was born they'd had two kids, Karen and Joan, and a divorce. They remarried before I was born. I learned years later that they had named me Bruce after Sir Robert Bruce the Scotsman, who coined the phrase "If you at first don't succeed, try, try again." I was the Great White Hope. Maybe having another child, a boy, would keep the marriage together?

My dad, born in up-state New York, had his chicken farm in Montgomery County, Maryland when he met my mother. No electricity. No TV. He was ten years older than she. A shy, bright guy who had studied agriculture at the University of Maryland. My mom had to leave home in Connecticut because she had gotten pregnant. Her social-climbing Italian immigrant family refused to allow her to marry the love of her life—a Jewish guy. She was sent to Washington D.C. to stay with her mother's brother, Arthur Tarantino. Uncle Arthur was a lawyer and had been an officer in the Navy during World War II. He was married to a French Canadian woman whose last name was Gagnon. Her brother, who lived not far away on a chicken farm, and was very shy around women, came over for dinner one night. Soon my mother and he were married. Now, the out-of-wedlock baby had a father.

Kenneth Gagnon put in electricity, rugs and a TV into the house for his new bride, Ruth. She quickly tired of the farm, however, and eventually got him to sell it. He went to work for the Agriculture Department in Washington. But he was unhappy. He was a nature boy. The family moved to Tampa, Florida, and Kenneth got a job working as a salesman for General Electric. My mother's sister would later tell me that he was a top salesman there. She said he was a nice, quiet guy who sat in the corner and read whenever the family got together. But Kenneth wasn't happy being a salesman. One day he came home and told mom that he wanted to go to Georgia and pick peaches. That was the last straw. She threw him out and moved herself and the three kids to Jacksonville Beach, near her brother David, who worked for Eastern Airlines. Soon thereafter, mom moved the kids again, this time to Orlando where she got a job working in the laboratory at a local hospital.

I never saw my father again.[1] My oldest sister Karen remembers that when he tried to visit us kids, my mother called the police and had him chased away. But I always felt close to him. It wasn't until my own son, Julian was born in 1980, that I began to realize just how much my father had impacted me spiritually during our two brief years together. One day before Julian could talk I was showing him a brick wall that was full of insect life. He understood everything I was telling him. It was then that I knew that parents speak to kids on a level beyond language and that we have influence beyond our imagination on the early child.

It was there in Orlando that I had my very first organizing experience, at the age of three. I was put in day care while my mother worked. Lunch was late in coming one day, so while all of us kids sat at the lunch table waiting I picked up my fork and spoon and began pounding them on the table chanting "We wanna eat, we wanna eat....." Soon the whole group of us were chanting, driving the day care workers crazy I'm certain. An organizer was born!

My mom was in a bind. She was a young woman with three kids and was particularly anxious about the future. In those days single parents were not supported by society. Orlando was a large military training center and she soon met a tall skinny guy named Wesley Stiles. Wesley was from Maine. Wesley and Ruth got married, and my life as a dependent of an Air Force enlisted man began.[2]

Wesley Stiles was the son of a paper mill manager from Rumford, Maine. He was a wild youth and joined the Air Force rather than face the law for his drinking and driving fast cars back home. Folks never talked about his history too much, but he was a serious rebel. He was also a gifted man, good at electronics, repairing cars, carpentry, plumbing and having a good time. Despite his own troubles he had a kind heart for others and used to bring single GI's home for Thanksgiving, Christmas and Easter dinners. It was always fun to have this company at our otherwise chaotic house. While Wesley was kind to others he was not always so kind to those of us inside his own home. He had a bad temper and when drunk, which he often was, one had to watch out for flying combat boots. His father was a drinker, too, and his own family had disintegrated when he was young. Wes had to live with his grandparents who were free with the switch and the belt on the young boy.

Wes struggled with his sensitive side and his macho, backwoods lumberman side. Once, when I was young, I got into an argument and punched a boy and knocked him out cold. I remember he landed in a mud puddle and I thought he might be dead. Wes thought it was great and proudly recalled the story now and then as I grew up. The incident probably had much to do with eventually turning me into a pacifist.

My mom was a born organizer. She always used "To Do" lists. When we moved, which we often did, she would have our new house in shape by the end of the day after the moving van had pulled away. She would direct the entire family—put this here, put that there. By the time we went to bed that first night in our new home it was as if we had been there for years. This was quite comforting as it made us feel like we had some semblance of security in an otherwise, at times, chaotic life. Despite being quite self-centered at times, mom could also be one of the most fair-minded people I have ever known. She always found a way to evenly divide what little we had between six hungry kids. She would go without in order to make sure there was enough for everyone else. Our house was full of contradictions.

Wes got stationed in Germany in 1959. I was 7 years old at the time. We were the only American family in the town of Landscheid in the Eiffel Mountains. I went to school on the nearby Spangdalem Air Force Base and spent all my play time with the German kids in Landscheid. I helped bring in the cows with bells around their necks at dusk, gather eggs from the chickens in the mornings, and on weekends would spend the entire day in the fields gathering hay by hand and piling it onto the horse drawn wagons with a pitchfork. I was in heaven.

We rented the upstairs rooms from a farm family, and we spent much of our time in the kitchen of the German family as they were some of the most welcoming people I have ever known. Kathryn and Alvis made us feel like we were part of their family and they shared meals with us and took care of us like we were their own. One day Kathryn asked me to go into her bedroom to get something for her that was on her nightstand. There, I discovered a framed picture of Adolf Hitler. I knew enough about recent history to know that Hitler was a bad guy and here, this German family I adored, had a picture of this evil man in their bedroom. At that moment I learned the world is not always black and white.

Wesley got transferred to Bruntingthorpe Royal Air Force Base near Leicester, and we moved to England after only 6 months in Germany. We did not live on the military base but instead rented a two-story house in a working class English neighborhood. I took the bus to the base each day for school and spent many hours playing soccer and cricket with the local English lads. They taught me all the fun things to do like yelling "dirty coppers" at the bobbies as they chased us down the street.

We often visited castles and I became a devotee of Robin Hood who stole from the rich and gave to the poor. The class consciousness of the British I experienced during those 2 ½ years in their country surely gave me a foundation that I have always appreciated. I also learned to love the British people's sense of humor. Maybe it came from having lived through an empire themselves. Any way you look at it the Brits taught me to laugh at the world, and at myself.

I was entering the fourth grade when we left England in 1962. After a vacation stop in Connecticut and Maine to visit family we moved on to Rapid City, South Dakota. We arrived in South Dakota in the middle of a blizzard. I recall our car sitting at a traffic light in Rapid City late that night in the blinding snow storm. As I pressed my face to the cold window glass of the station wagon I could feel the bone-chilling wind whipping through the old white wooden shotgun shacks just across the street. Who could live in those houses, I wondered? Those poor people in there must be freezing to death. My heart cried out in pain for them.

I was soon to learn it was Native Americans who lived in those shacks. Sioux Indians. So, this ten-year-old boy began frequenting the library with an all consuming desire to find everything I could about these Indian people.

Who were they? What had happened to them? What did they feel? Why were they treated this way? Who was their Robin Hood?

It was from these books I began learning about Native culture and that all life is connected, that the things that swim, fly, crawl and walk are all related in the web of life. An energy connected all of this life and I would lie in bed at night pleading with the Great Spirit to touch my heart so I, too, could escape the madness of my family and be part of this connection. The trips our family made to the Black Hills on our Sunday drives further connected me with these Native people. On our visits to Mount Rushmore I would stand apart from everyone and study the Indians who made a living getting their pictures taken with tourists. I would see Native people around Rapid City in the janitor jobs, sitting in drunken isolation, walking tiredly along the roads. I heard the jokes of the white people. I was profoundly moved. I felt the spirits of the Badlands and the Black Hills. I felt the spirits in the rocks inside Custer State Park. I smelled the spirits in the hot summer plains' sweet grasses. I heard the spirits in the howling winter blizzard winds. I felt the spirits in my bursting chest when I would push through the snowdrifts on my way to school each winter morning. Whenever I heard the drums and the high pitched singing of the people, their spirits would touch me deep inside. I felt I was at home at last. I continually prayed to the Great Spirit, begging to be part of "all my relations." I pledged that I would devote my life to the Mother Earth.

My best times with Wes were in the Black Hills. We'd wake up way before dawn and drive into the sacred paha sapa[3] with his 30/30 rifle. We'd track deer all day, wading through the snow, loving the outdoors and the beauty and silence of the winter. Never did I see Wes shoot a deer. Once we came upon a beautiful buck on the South Dakota and Wyoming border. We were on one side of the fence and the deer on the other. All Wes had to do was shoot it and drag it over the fence. No one would have known the difference. But instead he talked to the deer and we went our way. I was upset at Wes. I thought by shooting the deer he could show himself and others that he was a real man. It took me many years to realize that Wes did not go hunting to shoot deer, but that he, too, was on a spiritual journey. He had a soft side he rarely knew how to reveal.

During these years in South Dakota we were taught to hide under our school desks to avoid a nuclear explosion. The Cuban Missile Crisis was underway, and we were told that our base, Ellsworth, was a prime target because of the B-52 bombers stationed there. Wes had to leave home for days at a time, as the base was on alert, and I worried that I would lose another father. We survived, but one day in 1963, while at lunch in the school cafeteria we learned that President John F. Kennedy had not. He had been shot dead. The feeling of shock was enormous. Presidents were kings and were not supposed to die.

I was learning to be a patriot too. My voracious reading habits led me to the *We Were There* series of stories about American history. We were there at Lexington and Concord. We were there at the Alamo. We were there at Iwo Jima. America was the greatest. We were the leaders of the free world. I was hooked. I had gone from the Indians to the Cavalry. But, I still liked the Indians, too.

Wes came home one day and told us that we were moving again, this time back to Germany. I was shattered. I had finally found peace and my place in the world. Now we had to pull up roots again.

We moved first to Frankfurt, but within a few months Wes was transferred to Weisbaden A.F.B. We rented a second story two-bedroom apartment in downtown Weisbaden, just blocks from the train station. On my many walks through the streets of Weisbaden I began to see signs of anti-American feelings among the German people. Once the tires on our car were slit, and I often saw "Yankee Go Home" graffiti painted on the walls of buildings. I had not before thought about American imperialism or occupation, but I began seeing signs of it everywhere. Once, while playing baseball with my team on the base, I saw an old German man standing by the base fence with his face pressed up to it and his fingers clasped through the wire. He had a confused and bitter look on his face that said to me, "Take your strange game out of the middle of my neighborhood and go home!"

My ninth grade history class took a trip to a castle on the Rhine River, and I will always remember the guide telling us about the Roman soldier barracks that once was located on the very stone slab where we were standing. My first reaction was, what were the Romans doing so far from home? Later, that memory made me realize that it is unnatural for foreign troops to occupy a land and inevitable that in time they will have to return home. My later experience during the Vietnam War and the eventual crumbling of the Berlin Wall are testimonies to this truth. Occupation is a violation of the natural order and cannot stand over time.

From Germany we were to move to Fort Walton Beach, Florida where I attended high school during the period of 1967-1969.

In 1969, after Wes's return from Vietnam, he was given orders to move to Beale Air Force Base in northern California. So, we packed up. I was given the job of selling the family Rambler station wagon, and off we flew on a new adventure. My third high school in four years.

Beale was the home of the SR-71 Blackbird spy plane. Wes worked on the cameras of the planes that flew reconnaissance missions over "hostile" parts of the world like Vietnam, Russia, China, Korea and Cuba.

After my two years in Fort Walton Beach, Florida, northern California was a welcome experience. Everything that conservative Florida was, California was not. My new school, Wheatland High, was right in the middle of peach growing country and Mexican farm workers were the fruit pickers of choice. I began to learn about their migrant reality.

I made the varsity basketball team at Wheatland High, but had to miss the first game of the season because they needed a waiver to allow me to play because of my low grade-point average I had developed at Choctaw high school in Fort Walton Beach. I remember my coach asking me, "How in the world could you flunk business law?" I just shrugged my shoulders and said "I don't know", like kids do all the time when authority figures ask a question that is not intended to get an answer.

At Wheatland High, they talked about the war in Vietnam. Anti-war GI's came to speak with the classes. Teachers spoke out against the war. Girls at the school organized a sit-in protesting the fact that they could not wear pants. I had never seen anything like this before. In Fort Walton Beach, no one dared speak out about anything. Black students at Wheatland had "an attitude" and Afro hairstyles. They would argue with white students. In Florida, black students were angry over the killing of Martin Luther King Jr.. You could see the slow burn in their eyes, but they never verbalized anything. The culture in Florida said "no." In California, everything was "yes, yes, yes." I attended Wheatland High the year of the movie *Woodstock* and the Beatles album *Abbey Road.* It was the year my mind began to open even more to the reality of the world. My protected days were over.

# INTO THE MILITARY

*"You're going to have to change the priorities of your life, if you love this planet."*

—Dr. Helen Caldicott

It was clear to me, after I graduated from Wheatland in 1970, that I would have to make it on my own. My family could do little to help me financially. So, in January, 1971, I joined the U.S. Air Force and was sent to Lackland A.F.B. in San Antonio, Texas for my basic training.

But before that, I had a series of experiences that were to be the beginning of a seismic shift in my life. I had to report for my military induction physical at the Oakland, California center. Long lines of new recruits stood outside the induction center waiting for the doors to open. A middle-aged woman was working the line pleading with each of us not to go into the military. Her son had been killed in Vietnam, she wailed. Her mournful cries cut right to my gut and were followed by more appeals from a black man who had no face. No ears, nose, just holes in his head surrounded by a burnt, scarred face. That told us more about the horror of the war in Southeast Asia. Imagine that as your first image after joining the military.

Once inside the induction center, they lined up those who had been drafted and counted them off, 1-2, 1-2, 1-2, all the way down the line. The ones were going into the Army and the twos into the Marines. I was volunteering for the Air Force but will never forget that exercise, and the moans of those assigned to the Marines.

I was told I flunked my induction physical because of my old high school elbow injury that limited full extension of my left arm. I asked for a waiver and was told I would have to go to the Army hospital in San Francisco and be examined by the head surgeon. They gave me a bus pass and I set off on the day-long journey. Others who were on the bus told me they were trying to get waivers to keep from going into the service. I was reluctant to tell them that I had failed my physical and wanted a waiver to get in! They would have done anything to have the opportunity I had. This was my first up close experience with anti-war people and I was impressed by their kindness and humanity. One of them was going to claim he had flat feet and others claimed similar ailments. The guy with flat feet failed to get his waiver and I got mine thus allowing me to get into the Air Force. On the return trip to Oakland they congratulated me and I wished them well. I've often wondered what happened to the nice guy with the flat feet. I hope he made it ok.

Basic training was in San Antonio, Texas at Lackland AFB. Suffice to say I didn't enjoy it much, especially the parts where they try to break you down mentally. Some guys tried to kill themselves during basic training. One threw himself down the stairs. Another walked out in the middle of the rifle range when we were practicing with the

M-16 rifle. Crazy stuff like that. Begins to make you wonder where you really are and what you have put yourself into. My favorite moments in boot camp were when I was assigned to work on KP—kitchen patrol. There for a few hours I scrubbed huge cooking pots but I was able to have a slight respite from the insanity of our drill instructor screaming in our faces.

After basic training, I was sent to Keesler A.F.B. in Biloxi, Mississippi. I was trained to be a Personnel Specialist. The administrative skills I learned in this job came in handy as a peace activist over the years. To be organized in an office is a key skill to have when you are trying to run a peace organization on a meager budget with very little administrative help.

At Keesler, the U.S. was also training South Vietnamese pilots for the war effort. One story that was frequently told was about a Vietnamese pilot who had written a letter to the Keesler base commander thanking him for his training. He had returned to Vietnam, defected to the side of the communists, and was using his new skill to bomb U.S. troops.

After a couple of months in Mississippi, I reported to Travis AFB, in California for permanent duty. I checked into the "orderly room," the office in the barracks that makes room assignments and keeps the lid on barracks life. It was mid-1971. The clerk in the orderly room ran his finger down the long room list and shook his head. "Man, I only got one room left. But, we'll get you out of there as soon as we can. Sorry man, but we've only got one room left." He told me to grab my bags and follow him. Down the long dark hallway, last door on the left. I thought it might be a broom closet, maybe with a cot in it. Figured I'd be in there for a few days before they found me a real room. The clerk opened the door and in we went. Anti-war posters were all over the wall. A refrigerator, against barracks rules of course, painted an ugly dark blue sat in the corner. They had put me in with the leading anti-war organizer in the barracks. They were trying to keep him isolated as they attempted to build a case against him to kick him out. "Grab that cot man," the orderly clerk said as he again apologized to me and shut the door, leaving me in my new world.

My new roommate was from Beaver Falls, Pennsylvania, football legend Joe Namath's hometown. He even looked like Namath. Let's call him Joe. Joe had as much to do with my coming life change as anyone else in the world.

Joe wasn't too excited when he discovered this conservative, naïve, young Republican in his room. But we adjusted. A couple of nights a week there would be a knock on the door and white GI's would bring chairs into the room, arrange them in a circle, light some joints, and begin talking about the Vietnam War. I sat in the corner in sheer terror. Communists, pot smokers, cursing our government and our president Nixon. I didn't know what to do, but I stayed there and listened. Another night, the knock on the door would reveal black GI's from the cities, members of the Black Panthers talking about racism.

It didn't take long for me to begin to inch my chair into the circle in my new barracks room. The things these GI's were saying, even though much of it was new to me, made sense. I began reading their books and I began smoking their pot[4].

The Air Force wanted to kick my roommate out, but didn't have enough on him to warrant the bad conduct discharge they hoped to give him. The orderly room forgot all about getting me into another room, so I was left to continue this anti-war, anti-racism experience for almost a year before they finally threw Joe out of the service. He had been working in the base gym handing out basketballs and towels. He didn't have to wear a uniform, just a T-shirt that said *Base Gym* on it. In fact he was the only GI that I ever met in my 3 ½ years in the military who actually had no uniform. One day he squirted his supervisor in the face with a squirt gun and that was the end. He was court-martialed and given a General Discharge. And to his court-martial proceedings he wore *my* uniform. With my name on it. With my stripes. What a start for me in the military! Was the Great Spirit looking out for me or what?

Travis A.F.B. was a key airlift base for the Vietnam War. Troops from all over the U.S. were sent to the base to get on the planes for the trip to Nam. Supplies were also loaded on the huge cargo planes like the C-5A and C-141. On the return trips they brought back wounded soldiers to be treated at our base hospital, or the bodies of dead soldiers. Across the street from my office was the flight line and on most mornings I would see the body bags of dead soldiers lined up awaiting transfer to their home towns. Day in and day out this sight wore on my conscience. Even though I was not a foot soldier, I began to feel a greater sense of participation in the war and a greater feeling of responsibility. But what could I do? In one of my annual career briefings early on, I told my advisor that I felt I had become a conscientious objector. His response was that without a history of religious opposition to the war, I could not qualify for CO status. Years later, in the peace movement, I learned that I had other options at the time, but I believed what I was told and kept on, despite the moral dilemma.

There were regular protests at the front gates of the base with about a dozen people participating on the weekends. For days prior to a protest we would be warned that a demonstration was to be held at the base and that under "no circumstances" were we to go near the front gate. We were told that the Office of Secret Investigation (OSI) would be out at the gate taking pictures, and anyone caught attending could be court-martialed. I never went out to a protest, but began to wonder why in the USA, the land of freedom, we could not attend such an event. The contradictions were becoming ever more clear to me and I was beginning to feel like I was in prison. On one occasion, Jane Fonda and the famous band, Country Joe and the Fish, joined a large rally of more than 500 people at the gate. To this day I wish I had had the courage to attend.

The anti-war GI's took every opportunity to make life miserable for the "lifers." After a few months at Travis I began to identify myself as "anti-war" too. It was our credo that we should do all we could to make life in the military a struggle for all those supporting the war. It was the least we could do. We argued the anti-war position on the job, in the chow hall, and in the barracks all night long. We refused to get our hair cut. We gave officers a hard time. We tried to teach new GI's about the war. In my first year at Travis, there was a major GI anti-war movement. Most of those who had joined the Air Force did so when they got their draft notice, rather than going into the Army or the

Marines where they would have to be directly involved in combat operations. In the Air Force, they could work in an office or be far from the shooting war. A year after I got to Travis, the new recruits coming in were different. They had not been drafted but had joined because they needed a job—victims of the economic draft. They had less anti-war intensity about them because the draft, at that time, began to wind down.

We smoked a lot of "dope" in those days. Also, inside the body bags coming back from Southeast Asia were ample supplies of drugs. The drugs were then distributed on the base and beyond. We smoked in our rooms at night, trying to forget the boredom of military life and the war. Marijuana, Thai sticks, opium. It was everywhere.

There were serious problems on the base for the black GI's. They protested the egregious racism of the military structure which dealt with them so unjustly. While anti-war whites like me would be labeled and written up, the black resisters would some-times be jailed. In late 1971, after black GI's marched to the jail and tried unsuccess-fully to get some of their comrades out of the lock-up, a riot broke out. Newly elected Congressman Ronald Dellums (D-Ca.) held hearings on the base and the military brass denied all problems. The riots eventually got so bad that martial law was declared. The local county police were brought in with their dogs to help restore order in the barracks compound. It truly had become a prison camp! I'll always remember a knock on our door early one evening when black GI's, the same guys who came to our room for rap sessions, came to warn us to stay in our room as they had decided to attack any whites out in the barracks compound. That night serious fights broke out in the compound. I stepped outside and saw one white guy lying on the ground, bleeding. An ambulance siren could be heard in the distance. I was revolted by the violence. It seemed like violence was everywhere around me: the war, the bodies coming back from Vietnam, and now violence between black and white GI's on the base. I believe I became a pacifist that night.

Thousands of troops were sent to our base to get on airplanes to fly to Vietnam. Some would refuse to board the planes. One night, a GI sat on the curb and cut his penis off in order to avoid going to war. These kind of things get inside you, and I was never the same after that.

When the first prisoners of war were flown back to the U.S. from North Vietnam they landed at Travis. Virtually the entire base population was ordered to go out to the flight line to welcome the returning "heroes." I'll never forget standing there watching as POW's, who had their planes shot down while bombing North Vietnam, descended onto the runway to the cheers of thousands of Air Force personnel. A friend and I, refusing to cheer, called them killers loud enough to be heard by those around us. An officer standing next to us overheard our remarks and threatened to have us disciplined for our bad attitude. As usual, nothing came of the officer's bluster.

In the election of 1972 , while still at Travis, I volunteered to work for the local county Democratic party and the George McGovern presidential campaign. I had just read McGovern's book in which he spoke out against the war and against nuclear weapons and felt I had to do something to help. I pasted a McGovern sticker to my office typewriter and began promoting his campaign in the office, in the barracks, and by going door-to-door off the base in the evenings after work.

It wasn't long before I got into trouble at work for violating some military regulation that forbade GI's from political activity on base. But I persisted. In my door-to-door efforts in neighborhoods off the base I was troubled by how few voters showed support for McGovern. At some local Democratic Party events I watched in horror as the local political machine distanced itself from the ticket. The Watergate scandal had yet to take hold, and Nixon swept to victory. As I sat with friends watching the one-sided returns come across the TV screen on election night, the phone rang. Wes was calling to rub in the loss. He was proudly one of Nixon's "Silent Majority," the working class stiffs who thought the anti-war movement was a bunch of Communist bullshit.

By this time Wes had retired from the Air Force and moved the family to Orlando, Florida. After years of his drinking and abuse he and my mother were not doing well.

In early 1973 Air Force personnel headquarters in Texas called to ask if I'd like to be transferred to Hawaii. I thought the idea sounded good. When else might I get to go to Hawaii? So I said sure.

I was assigned to a special unit in Hawaii. We were a dispatch from Headquarters Command in Washington with a special task. We were to serve the U.S. Embassy Air Force personnel that were stationed throughout the Pacific Ocean region. Someone decided that we could better serve the Pacific personnel if we had an office in the Pacific rather than in Washington D.C. So, that meant we would not be serving the personnel on Wheeler A.F.B., where our office was located on the Hawaiian island of Oahu. We would have no walk-in traffic. We would handle all of our work through the mail and over the phone.

I quickly realized what this meant. We would have nothing to do. This was the most frustrating time in my Air Force stint. I had run into the wall of hypocrisy. I was told that I could not read books, magazines and newspapers. I was told that I had to look busy all day. My boss told me to read thick, boring, military manuals. Some people were really good at wasting time. They'd spend hours standing by the coffee machine in idle chatter. But I didn't drink coffee, which took away at least two hours of time-wasting possibilities.

One day, while suffering from intense boredom, I tried looking busy by paging through the personnel files of all the officers we were assigned to service. Most of them were assigned as aides to the embassy staffs in places like Jakarta, Indonesia and Bangkok, Thailand. As I read the job descriptions of these officers I was struck dumb: "Capt. Jones is assigned to serve as liaison between the host government and U.S. weapons contractors." In other words, they were salesmen for the military industrial complex, assigned to promote weapons sales in these Third World countries. This was guaranteed to create more regional instability and "justify" longer and greater U.S. military occupation of the "host country." And think of the jobs these "salesmen" could get working for the weapons contractors when they retired from the Air Force!

About this time *The Pentagon Papers* were released to the *New York Times*. Daniel Ellsberg, working for the Rand Corporation, started xeroxing copies of the secret Pentagon documents that outlined the history of U.S. participation in Vietnam. President Nixon went crazy. They were published in book form and I picked up the bestseller in the base exchange one day while wasting some more time not wanting to return to the office after lunch. Imagine how my bosses felt when they caught me, feet up on my desk, reading *The Pentagon Papers* in the office. Well, isn't this like a military manual?

Actually it was. The Rand Corporation had been given the job of documenting the official inside history of U.S. involvement in Vietnam. I read on. The United Nations had set up an election for Vietnam trying to end the years of French colonial rule and warfare in the country that had suffered one foreign invader after the other. [5] President Eisenhower and other U.S. "policymakers" were worried that Ho Chi Minh, the George Washington of Vietnam, would win the election.

The U.S. government had other plans. The CIA was sent in to disrupt the election. (Now this was not supposed to happen I thought. We were the ones who believed in democracy. Freedom. Elections, the will of the people.) One of the first things the CIA did was to forge a letter on Ho Chi Minh's stationary saying that once elected he would round up the minority Catholic population in the northern part of Vietnam and kill them all. The CIA disseminated the letter in the Catholic community, and its operatives began helping to whip up hysteria amongst the Catholics. Almost overnight the Catholics, with CIA support, began a mass exodus into the southern part of the country. U.S. TV crews were brought in and American audiences were shown the pictures of the poor Catholics running for freedom and religious liberty from the despotic Communist Ho Chi Minh. The next day, the U.S. Congress appropriated the first money for U.S. military advisors in Vietnam and we were in the war. The election was never held and we went after Ho Chi Minh and the Vietnamese people with a vengeance. The rest is history.

So here I am at Wheeler reading this book, telling everyone about it. In the barracks, in the chow hall, at work, no one wants to listen. By this time the war in Vietnam is beginning to wind down. "Big deal, Gagnon, the war is almost over. Why do you have to make a federal case out of it?"

I couldn't believe these people. I'd seen the body bags all lined up on the runway at Travis across from my office. A guy at Wheeler, who had done a tour in Vietnam, got drunk in the barracks one night and tried to jump out of the third story window to get the bad memories out of his brain. I helped coax him back inside. And these people at work wanted me to forget about it!

# TO COLLEGE—LEARNING TO ORGANIZE

*"You've got to do your own growing, no matter how tall your grandfather was."*

—Irish Proverb

On June 30, 1974, I flew from Hawaii back to Travis A.F.B. in California where I was given an honorable discharge from the U.S.A.F. after 3 years, 5 months and 6 days in the military. I felt like I was being released from prison. I had been given an early out for college and planned to attend Valencia Community College in Orlando. I was heading home to help my family. My mother had filed for divorce from Wes and needed help with my three younger sisters.

Of all the places I've ever lived in, Florida is my least favorite place. I am not fond of the weather nor do I feel at home in the transient, tourist-haven culture. I had hoped to move to either South Dakota or northern California when I was discharged from the Air Force, but once again duty called.

Valencia Community College was on the far side of Orlando. I had no car. I had to hitchhike to college each morning. There was virtually no public transportation in the city. I'd walk a mile down to the main road and try to catch a ride to the other side of the city by standing at the entrance to the east-west expressway. This was a shortcut through the center of the city and was the fastest way to get across town. Not long after I had begun taking this route, a local Sheriff's Department Deputy threatened me with arrest if I continued to hitchhike on the expressway. I stood by the side of the road as he zoomed away. I looked up to the sky and asked the Great Spirit how anyone could own a road. How could someone say I had no right to stand on this corner and ask for a ride? I wanted to fight back but knew he would be watching for me and would be eager to show me the extent of his powers. I felt like I was in the Air Force again.

Valencia was a pretty conservative place. Everyone was well-dressed and long hair was not in fashion. I, of course, had been dying to grow my hair long after spending the late 1960's getting direct orders from Wes to keep my hair short, followed by 3 ½ years in the Air Force taking orders to get a hair cut. I was ready to let my freak flag fly! And so I did. My curly hair grew wild for the next four years—in every direction. I loved it, but I stuck out like a sore thumb in Republican Orlando.

After two years at Valencia, I moved on to Gainesville to attend the university there. My first impression of the University of Florida was the clothes. The students were pretty well dressed and the disco was in style. They all looked like a scene out of John Travolta's movie *Saturday Night Fever*. By now it was 1976 and the backlash to the hippie days was well underway, especially in Florida. Political activity, which I was eager for after two quiet years in Orlando, was rare in Gainesville, too. So I settled in to do some serious studying in my chosen fields of political science and sociology.

The professor in one of my political science classes, was a big fan of Secretary of State Henry Kissinger. I, of course, thought him a murderer, so it was no coincidence that I got C's on all my papers. I realized that students who didn't tow the Kissinger ideological line would not make the good grades. Just to test this theory, I once spit out the Kissinger themes on a paper and got the ceremonial reward, an "A". I soon went back to my customary C since I couldn't stand to play this game. It was a real turning point for me as I began to view "higher education" as a funnel that screened out those with thoughts outside the mainstream. Once again I felt the constraining forces I had resisted while in the military.

One night in 1978 I was sitting on my bed studying for a geology exam just two days away. I was near graduation, only needing to fulfill a language requirement and two other required courses. There was a providential knock on the door and in walked the good Rev. Fred Eyster. He told me he was with the National Farm Worker Ministry. He had gotten my name from a friend. He was looking for volunteers to help organize on campus to get the lettuce out of the school cafeteria in support of the farm workers in California who were organizing a boycott. Could I come the next day and help pass out leaflets?

He was probably the nicest man I had ever met. I really was sorry, I told the Rev. Eyster, but I had this test in a few days and I didn't think I could help. We talked for a long time. He finally left.

The next day I skipped class. I went to the Student Union at noon to help convince my fellow students to boycott the iceberg lettuce. Normally, I was too shy to walk up and just begin speaking to someone I didn't know. But with a leaflet in hand, and this cause, I had a cover and was able to do it. In no time, I ran out of leaflets.[6] Soon the action was over. They invited me back the next day. I apologized saying I had this geology test the next day, and I was so close to graduation.

The next day I skipped the geology test and before I knew it I was standing in front of the student government arguing the merits of a lettuce boycott resolution. I watched in horror as the frat boys sat back and laughed and play-acted like important politicians. They were basically pompous rich kids in training to take over for their parents. Pass the reins of power. They declined on the resolution and we began a two-day fast on the steps of the Student Union. I did my first radio interview and felt the rush of excitement for taking a shot at the powerful arrogant bastards.

The staff of the United Farm Workers Union (UFW) soon offered me a job as an organizer with the union. I immediately quit college and was sent to Lakeland, Florida to work in the state office of the UFW. The State Director was a tall black man named Stephen Roberson. He spoke fluent Spanish and impressed me with his dedication. They gave me boring administrative jobs in the office for a week to test my abilities and my commitment. I was thrilled to be around dedicated people who earned a $20 a week stipend. They lived simply together in a house rented by the UFW and all drove old donated Plymouth Valiants, the reliable six-cylinder union mainstay.

I'll always cherish the memory of my first meeting with farm workers. It was held at the small union hall in Avon Park, right in the middle of the Citrus Belt. The dignity with which the workers carried themselves touched me deeply. Their desire to be treated humanely while they picked fruit and to be paid a fair wage seemed like a good place for me to begin my new life.

Once the UFW staff felt that I had "passed the test," I was interviewed formally by Dolores Huerta, the first Vice-President of the UFW and one of its original founders. She had worked with Cesar Chavez to build the union. Dolores was in Florida in February, 1978 for a series of meetings with the UFW membership that was scattered throughout the state. About 1,200 workers were under contract with the Coca-Cola company that owned Minute Maid Orange Juice. Dolores's message, reported in the UFW newsletter at the time was, "The UFW has had a contract with the Coca-Cola company since 1971. We should have a good working relationship with the company by now."

The UFW contract with Coke was good for two years at a time and the membership was in a constant state of preparing for and then negotiating a new contract. Even though there were over 100,000 farm workers in the state, the UFW staff and membership were focused on holding on to that one contract with Coke. It had been negotiated under threat of a national boycott of all Coke products by Cesar some years before. The union, battling daily in California for its very life, wanted to hold onto the Florida contract at all cost.[7]

Three other volunteers joined the staff of UFW in Florida at the same time I did. We were all sent to California for one month of training following our meeting with Dolores and acceptance into the union ranks. We were taught that the UFW was different from many unions in that this union belonged to the workers. What they said ruled. That was good enough for me.

The UFW headquarters "La Paz," is located in Keene, California, east of Bakersfield. It had been a sanitarium for people with tuberculosis in years past. A supporter of the union had arranged the purchase without the local agribusiness growers knowing about who it was intended for and then he sold it to Cesar and the UFW for $1. It was a big place with offices scattered throughout the facility. Sleeping quarters for those working at the headquarters were simple. A few of the older, higher ranking officials in the union (most of whom were former farm workers) were housed in trailers on the compound. Cesar, his wife Helen, and their family lived in a simple white wooden house with a fence around it. Nothing to brag about.

One evening after being at La Paz for a few days, Cesar invited the four of us from Florida up to his office for a meeting. His wall was adorned with pictures of his years as leader of the farm worker movement. I had by that time read his biography, so many of the pictures had a context for me. Photos of Cesar fasting with Sen. Bobby Kennedy, and other celebrities told how he had taken *la causa* into the hearts and minds of America. He had much to be proud of and I felt honored to be there with him. He told us stories about his years building the union. I learned to love the man, always touched by his humble ways.

Cesar told us a story about being on an airplane with United Autoworkers Union leader Walter Reuther. The UFW had won a few contracts and Reuther asked Cesar how many contract grievances they had filed in the last year. Cesar said he wanted to impress Reuther and told him the number. Reuther responded, "That's too many. You've got to have a relationship with the company." Cesar told us to go back to Florida and work in a cooperative way with Minute Maid. [8]

After two weeks at La Paz, each of us new staffers was sent to a different farm worker community to get some hands-on experience in seeing the union in action. I was sent to Coachella, California one of the strongholds of UFW activity. The UFW Second Vice President at the time was a rising star by the name of Eliseo Medina. I was put under his charge. Eliseo had shown great promise as a leader while working on the boycotts in the big cities back east, and now spent most of his time negotiating contracts. He was successful in large part because of the enactment of the Agriculture Labor Relations Act in California that made farm worker union elections legal and possible for the first time. Former Gov. Jerry Brown (D-CA.) had ushered this new law into existence, much to the chagrin of the agribusiness industry.

One day, Eliseo took me along with him as he went to negotiate a contract with a poultry company where the workers had recently won an election. I'd never experienced anything like it. I was moved by the moral arguments he made to the company negotiator about the plight of the farm workers, and I was also impressed at how he spoke forcefully to the negotiator, even arguing with him. Eliseo asked me to take notes of the meeting for him. I found that I could easily follow the discussion and still keep a near verbatim record of the meeting with a shorthand that I created on the spot. The next day Eliseo was surprised when I handed him a typed version of the meeting, a near complete record.

While in Coachella I was staying in the trailer of a Mexican worker who spoke no English. The night before I was to return to La Paz, he broke out a new bottle of tequila. We drank the whole thing, all the way down to the worm. I'd never had tequila before and didn't know what I was in for. By the end of the evening the most mystical thing happened. The man and I were speaking to each other like old friends. Each understood everything the other was saying. To this day, I am not sure what language we were speaking. But it worked!

In the Coachella farm worker office the next morning, waiting for my ride back to La Paz, I was of no use. I felt like death warmed over. I lay in a chair for hours and every time someone passed by he or she would laugh and say, "tequila?" I just nodded with a heavy head.

Before leaving La Paz to return to Florida, I had the chance to sit in on a session Cesar was running in the main meeting hall. There was butcher paper up all over the walls having been written on with markers. I soon learned that Cesar and the union were undertaking a major campaign to learn how to do internal planning called Management by Objectives (MBO). The union was no longer a movement. It was winning contracts and having to produce services to the membership. It was having to administer the Robert F.

Kennedy Medical Plan and the Martin Luther King Political Action Fund and the Juan De La Cruz Pension Fund. The union was becoming more business-like.

When I got back to Florida, I was transferred to the small town called Apopka, just north of Orlando on Highway 441. Here I was to work with a Mexican farm worker who had joined the staff. Together we were to run the local union hall that serviced a number of fruit picking crews between Kissimmee and Ocala. We lived in a two-bedroom apartment located in Apopka's black community. Our working days began before 6:00 a.m. and lasted until nearly 10:00 p.m. six days a week. Sunday was spent sleeping late, washing clothes, and having a real meal at home. Even though I was only getting paid $20 a week I never had any need for money. We qualified for food stamps, the union paid for our gas, and the old Plymouth Valiants were donated to the UFW by supporters.

One day, in 1979 a labor lawyer from Orlando walked into the Apopka union hall and introduced himself to me. His name was Joe Egan and he told me about two books I should read. One was called *The People's History of the United States* by Howard Zinn and the other was *Labor's Untold Story* by Richard Boyer and Herbert Morais. Each book documented, in stunning detail, the largely underreported struggle of the progressive movement in the United States. This also led me to read about a man who was to become one of my greatest heroes, Eugene V. Debs.[9] Debs grew up in Indiana and went from being a Republican to a five-time candidate for the presidency of the U.S. on the Socialist Party ticket. His last campaign, in 1920, was from behind bars at the federal prison in Atlanta, Georgia. Arrested for publicly speaking out against World War I, Debs served a sentence of nearly three years in jail.[10]

Many mornings, we were out in the orange groves to meet the workers as they arrived on the old school buses in which the company transported them. They would arrive before dawn and build a fire (nothing burns better and more reliably than citrus tree wood). This was the best time to have a meeting with the picking crew, usually made up of 20-30 men and women. Because we were constantly negotiating contracts, that was usually the topic of conversation. The workers were teaching me a lot about fruit picking and life in general. They climbed the ladder up to the top of the tree which was covered with thorns, and carried the fruit down in the big sack slung over their shoulders. Once full, the sack was emptied into a gigantic tub at the base of the tree. Many trips were required up and down the tree to fill a tub. If there was not a lot of fruit on the tree (and there often was not) and since they got paid by the piece, the less picked, the less money made. And if it rained, no work was done.

The price of fruit was set by a committee from the local union hall and Minute Maid representatives. This was a better system than the one in non-union situations where the fruit companies set the rate of pay and the workers had no say over it. But many of the union picking crews did not like others setting their pay rates for them. They had to pick the fruit and wanted to negotiate the piece rate with the company directly. This made sense to me because it gave the workers more power over their own lives. If they didn't like the price they got they had to take personal responsibility for it. Anytime the workers were not satisfied with the rate they could strike. But the company was putting pressure on the UFW to stop the strikes and Cesar was pushing the UFW to "develop a better relationship with the company."

So, over the next two years, while I worked with the UFW, how to set prices was the number one topic of conflict. The union staff would hold weekend-long meetings during which we would go through hours of Management by Objectives planning in order to try to settle the disputes over the piece rates and other issues. Then we'd go back through the groves all during the next week and try to sell the workers on the new plan. I began to wonder how we could say that the workers owned the union when the staff (made up largely of white middle class volunteers) was pushing the agenda.

One of my favorite workers was an old black man named Frank Lewis, who lived in downtown Orlando. We had only one picking crew from Orlando. Very few young black men would pick fruit anymore. Most of the workers in the groves were Mexican. But Frank had been picking fruit all his life and he was now in his late 60's. He also had emphysema and I cringed every time I heard him wheeze and cough his way up and down the ladder. He wanted and needed to retire, but his Social Security earnings had not been reported to the government by the Dr. Phillips Company, where he worked for over 20 years before the UFW got its contract with Minute Maid. This was a common practice in the industry and I heard the story over and over again. Frank was one of the kindest and gentlest men I ever met and we became very close as he often rode with me all over Florida to attend worker meetings. He lived alone and enjoyed the trips. Most of all he wanted to be part of making things better for those who were "coming up behind" him. Frank was a man of true non-violent spirit and always sought to offer unifying words in any conflict situation. He will never know how much he taught me, but I know he knew that I loved him like a father.

As it turned out, eventually, Frank was able to get a meager pension from the UFW, one of the first in Florida to get something from the union's pension fund. I have never forgotten though that Frank's life was cut short because he was black. My white friends fathers' would never have had to endure what Frank Lewis endured.

Years later, the Dr. Phillips Foundation was to make a much celebrated multi-million dollar grant to the arts community in Orlando to transform an old electricity-generating plant into an arts and cultural center. To this day, whenever I see that big building, I think about Frank Lewis and how the "progressive" Dr. Phillips Foundation stole his Social Security dollars and used them to make their tax deductible donation to charity.

When I've told this story over the years some people have wondered why the government did not step in to protect the farm workers from this theft of their Social Security earnings. In Florida, the Department of Labor (DOL) had the responsibility to ensure that employers were properly reporting such earnings to the government. What I was to learn, though, was that the agribusiness industry essentially controlled the Florida DOL. Thus, there was not a reliable enforcement body for legions of aggrieved workers to turn to.

Once, in 1979, while at a strike, near the citrus town of Frostproof in Highlands County, I heard Sylvester Evans, another old black man, tell the story of Ben Hill Griffin. Griffin "owned" Frostproof, Sylvester said, as we stood around the fire to warm ourselves. Sylvester had an entertaining way of telling stories, but this time he was angry as he carefully recounted how Ben Hill Griffin owned the shacks the farm workers lived in and owned the stores where they bought groceries. Griffin wouldn't pay much when they picked his fruit either. So basically, Sylvester said, they were working for nothing. Slavery was still alive, with just a new name and a new face.

In Gainesville, at the University of Florida, there is a big football stadium right on University Avenue called the Ben Hill Griffin Stadium. The Griffin name stands out at night, all lit up in big bold letters. (*The notorious Katherine Harris, who as Florida Secretary of State helped hand the 2000 election to George W. Bush, is the granddaughter of Ben Hill Griffin.*) And every time I see it, I think of Sylvester and all the others who really paid for the stadium renovation that got Griffin's name on it. I'm sure there are landmarks like this all over Florida and the nation. Makes you wonder where the justice is in America.

I got put on the UFW contract negotiations team when it came time to sit down with Coca-Cola over the Minute Maid deal. I guess the word came from California that I was a good note taker, because I was immediately given that job. State Director Roberson usually began the negotiations. In the room at a hotel, rented by the company, sat about 15 farm workers on the negotiations committee. The company flew in a couple of hot shot lawyers from Atlanta and then they had a few of their Florida people too. One thing they always talked about was how they were beginning to outpace the rest of the fruit growers in the state in wages paid out and they wondered when the UFW was going to go after some of the other companies like Ben Hill Griffin and Tropicana. I thought it was a good question.

The UFW had four offices across Florida where we served the Coca-Cola workers. So I saw a lot of farm worker communities. I witnessed some unbelievable labor camps where people working for non-union growers lived like animals and were treated even worse. The question of when the UFW was going to begin organizing the 100,000 or more unrepresented agricultural workers was an important one to answer.

Each year Cesar Chavez would come to Florida for a UFW convention. The staff would work for weeks to turn out the membership. We were also instructed to go out and find workers from other non-union citrus companies and get them there. Cesar would give a report on what was happening in California (which was usually a fight for their life and/or another boycott). He'd also give the workers the impression that next year the union was going to get going in Florida and would bring in folks from California to get Florida organized. Everyone would be excited.

One worker, Parker, would be standing off to the side and kicking up a lot of sand over this. Parker was one of the most loyal and dedicated union members. He lived in Avon Park and ran the medical plan for the union office as a volunteer. He'd pick fruit all day, and then be in the union hall every night to make sure the members got their medical bills paid. He had seen the young white staff volunteers come and go over the years and knew everything that had ever happened with the UFW in Florida. I spent my first year arguing with Parker, giving him the party line, and my second year on staff listening to and learning from him.

Parker said that Cesar was never coming to organize in Florida. He said the UFW was bogged down in California and would never get out. He wondered why we couldn't organize Florida ourselves. We had the farm worker leadership here and the supporters in the cities through the National Farm Worker Ministry. They had shown they could raise the money necessary to sustain the effort that would be required. Parker was not undermining Cesar. He was just raising important questions that no one wanted to hear.

My first arrest was in 1979 during a lemon strike in the groves near Fort Pierce, Florida on the east coast. We were having a weekend-long meeting to try to figure out how to end the strike. It had been going on for a week or two and the members were losing heart. Our director, Roberson, feared a breakdown. He was under pressure to end the strike from Cesar and from Coca-Cola. So, all day one Saturday, in a roomful of statewide worker leaders, we were going through sheets and sheets of Management by Objectives plans. We were getting nowhere fast and the air was coming out of the balloon. Finally, I couldn't take it anymore. Staff were not supposed to speak in these meetings unless called on. We were to keep our calculations to ourselves except in our staff meetings where we made our plans for the workers' future. But, against the wishes of our director I put my hand up and said, "I've got an idea. Instead of sitting here doing this, why don't we all go right now and knock on the doors of the workers who live here and are on strike. We've got leaders from all over the state and they will see they have support. Then, on Monday, we can get them all back out to the picket lines and the company will see they are stronger than ever. The company will have to give in. They want the lemons picked."

By this time everyone, even our director, was tired of the MBO's so they accepted the idea and we split up to start knocking on doors. The next day, Sunday, we did the same thing, and by that night we had reached most of the strikers. They had agreed to come out and give it one more chance. We had heard rumors the company was going to try to bring in some of their picking crews from other parts of the state to break the strike. So, the leaders went back to their communities to tell folks to honor the picket lines.

Fellow UFW organizer Carlos Garza, myself and two other staffers spent all Sunday night in a Denny's restaurant planning for the next day. We knew that the company would try to come into the groves from two different roads so we made plans to block-ade these roads with workers and staff. By dawn the next morning, with our plan in place, we were able to stop the company's attempt to sneak in almost a dozen buses full of fruit pickers from all over the state. Despite the UFW's warning to the workers that the strike was not over, Minute Maid told picking crews from other areas that the strike was settled. As we sat in the dirt road early that morning, one by one the workers from other areas refused to break the strike. Suddenly we found ourselves surrounded by

Indian River County Sheriff's deputies. Four of them picked me up and threw me into the back of a van like I was a sack of potatoes. Carlos Garza landed on top of me before I had a chance to recover. Then came several farm workers on top of him, including women. Eventually about 15 of us, including all the staff there that day, were arrested.

Word went out around the state that the company had tried to break the strike and had used force to arrest farm workers and staff. The next day, dozens of supporters from the cities, along with the media, showed up at the picket line. Within hours, the company settled the strike and the workers went back in to pick the lemons.

During the few hours we were in jail, farm workers and staff together, I got my first taste of the power of direct action. Not only had we non-violently escalated the situation, but we had created an energy that brought people as well as the media out in support. Under that scrutiny, the company was forced to cave in. I will always remember something that Cesar had told us the night we visited his office at La Paz. He said, "The company knows we are weak, we know we are weak. But it doesn't matter. What matters is what the public thinks. If you can get the public to take your side, the company will give in." From then on, I knew that I would never be afraid to use non-violent direct action as a way to bring the public into an issue. It would work for me over and over again.

# TAKING ON THE MAYOR

*"If there is no struggle, there is no progress. Those who profess to favor freedom, and deprecate agitation, are men who want crops without plowing up the ground, they want rain without thunder and lightning."*

– Frederick Douglas

I loved working for the Farm Workers Union. I learned how to organize and was inspired by the sacrifices of Cesar Chavez and the other leaders of the movement. I was deeply touched by people like Frank Lewis and Sylvester Evans. They showed me that poor people had more intelligence, spirit, and dignity than any rich person I'd ever met. The union gave me direction and challenges, and answered my prayers for a way to find myself. I've never had regrets about those two years with the UFW.

In the summer, there was not much to do at the union hall. Most of the workers went north to pick tomatoes in Ohio or apples in New York. The citrus season was over.

In 1979, on one of those slow, humid summer days a young man named John Hedrick walked into my UFW office.[11] John was just back in town after having been away at college, and was going around visiting the offices of progressive political organizations in the community. He was a solidly-built redheaded guy about 23 years old who was from Orlando. He had graduated, done some traveling, and, while on the road, had seen what cities all over the nation were doing to promote public mass transportation. John said that he felt Orlando was doing virtually nothing in this regard and wondered if I could help him pass out some leaflets at the public bus station downtown under the name of the Free People's Transit Organization (FPTO), a group he had just founded. Since I wasn't doing anything at the time, and I remembered what had happened the last time someone came knocking on my door asking me to pass out leaflets, I took him up on the offer.

It wasn't long before John offered me a job. His father was quite wealthy and had given him lots of oil stock money to go to graduate school. John wanted to organize with the money instead, and, offered me a job with the FPTO. When I accepted, the FPTO grew from one member to two.

The FPTO quickly made mass transportation an issue in the community. John and I were a great team. We began by packing the public hearings on transportation planning that no one from the public ever went to. John would get his church bus, visit the senior citizens' high rise building, and bring a busload of seniors to the meeting. I would get on the phone and call folks associated with other political groups in the community. As soon as the politicians and dull bureaucrats would begin the meeting, we'd jump up and demand the agenda be changed to discuss public mass transit. The senior citizens in the audience would stand and cheer. (All the politicians ever wanted to talk about was more and wider roads. Since the creation of Disney World, the developers had taken control of the county government and needed more roads built in order to make their land holdings in Central Florida even more profitable.) When we attended meetings, our actions were big news on TV and in the paper. One reason was that no one in the county ever organized like this before, and it was exciting. Secondly, John was the son of the local power structure, so he was able to get the attention of the local media. His father was part owner of the local *CBS-TV* affiliate.

At night, we'd go into his father's law office and run off thousands of leaflets on the big industrial copy machine and mail them, with law firm postage, to all the decision-makers in the community. During the day, we'd often go to the busiest intersections in the county with other volunteers and hold signs that read, *Tired of waiting at this light?; Price of gas out of sight?; We need mass transit, right?; The People's Transit Organization.*

We changed the name of the organization after a while, dropping the "Free" from the name when the politicians got hung up on the fact that we were advocating a free downtown shuttle as a way to showcase and encourage ridership. At the time the politicians laughed at the idea of a free shuttle, but today if you go to downtown Orlando that is what you will see taking the public from one end of downtown to the other. John had seen other cities doing this during his travels across the country.

It wasn't long before mass transit became a hot political issue, and local candidates for office, including the mayor, were getting their pictures taken down at the public bus station for their campaign brochures. We made the issue stick and soon enough the city of Orlando had doubled the number of buses on its routes.

By early 1980, I realized that John's money wouldn't last forever and I needed to find some other work. I heard about a job that was opening up with a new organization to be called the Council of Community-Based Organizations (CCBO). I applied for and got the job. People knew my work from the People's Transit Organization. The CCBO brought together social service providers and local black community neighborhood groups. The idea of the organization was to create better relations between service deliverers and those in need. My job was to make sure that poor people had input into the planning and delivery of social services by private organizations and government agencies.

The CCBO began holding its general membership meetings in the spring of 1980 at the state office building just on the west side of the interstate highway, in downtown Orlando. The relatively new state and federal office buildings, side by side, took up an enormous amount of land in the once large and proud black community called Callahan. Many of the old wooden homes were lost to these landmarks of "progress." I remember that one time when I left the state office building the security guard told me about a touching experience he had recently had. He told me that an old black man came to the state building every day and sat outside on a bench for hours staring at a huge old oak tree that adorned the office tower. The security guard finally got up the courage to ask the old man why he came there so often. Without hesitation the black man said to him, "This was my front porch. That was my tree."

The state Department of Labor grant to the CCBO was supposed to last for three years. But in fact it only lasted for one year, and after that I had to become a VISTA volunteer for a year, at a very meager stipend, assigned to the CCBO. The third year, 1982, I was hired by legal services as a paralegal and was assigned to the CCBO.

After a time in this job, I realized the government really didn't want its poverty programs to succeed. The bureaucracy tried to tie you up into knots doing needs surveys, filling out reports, covering your backside so as not to make any enemies in government, and then going back for more money each year, basically like a dog chasing its tail in a circle. I am convinced one reason we only got one year of funding from the state, instead of the original three promised, was because we were doing something. In fact, we were a royal pain in the ass.[12]

The needs survey was easy. It was supposed to take me several months to complete. I quickly polled our membership. They knew what the needs were. They worked with the poor every day. They were groups run by the poor. The needs were simple. They said, "We need jobs, housing, day care, health care and public transportation." Big surprise. We had our needs assessment. While the other CCBO groups around Florida were slogging about trying to finish their needs assessments, we moved onto implementation. We began to organize to get the needs met! Isn't that how you solve poverty?

There was a war on the poor underway at the time. Jimmy Carter was running for re-election against Ronald Reagan. Reagan was claiming that Carter was soft on communism and that our military was weak. So Carter, in his final two years in office, began cutting social programs and putting the money into the already-bloated Pentagon budget. Despite Carter's claim that the "nuclear arms race is a disgrace to the human race," he began to do even more to accelerate the arms race. The desire to remain in power will make most politicians change course in midstream.

At the CCBO, we immediately began to speak out against local, state and national cutbacks in job training funds. Jobs were one of our top priorities. There was little day care or health care for the poor. Housing was limited and of poor quality and the funds for that were getting harder to find. We had recently made some local progress on public transit, but not enough. So, at the monthly CCBO membership meetings I began to ask the membership how they intended to hold onto the little we were getting in social spending unless we publicly fought for it.

In the May, 1980, CCBO newsletter I wrote that a "People's Rally for Equity in Social Services" was planned because, "In this political year of budget cutbacks, the easiest areas to cut are the ones where the people are the quietest. This is, of course, social spending. Our community must be involved in the priority-making process. We must identify our friends who have similar problems and needs. We must work together to express these priorities." A month later, a meeting was held in Washington D.C. that created a National Network of CCBO's. Unfortunately, it was too little too late.

In fact, the powers that be had already decided years before that the gains of the 1960's and early 1970's were costing the wealthy too much.[13] The civil rights movement, women's movement, peace and environmental movements, the disability and gay rights movements had all been pushing a more democratic decision making process when it came to dividing the national pie. The 1980's was to be the time of retraction. Cut-back, give-back, take-back were all to become the watchwords for the decade. An attack on poor people's organizations ensued, and the programs that were about leveling the social playing field would be defunded. One of the first to be attacked was the Comprehensive Employment Training Act (CETA). That was where the money for my job at the CCBO came from.

In Washington D.C., the man who led the attack on CETA was none other than our own Florida Sen. Lawton Chiles, a Democrat who was the chair of the Senate Budget Committee. Sen. Chiles and others very effectively began a coordinated national campaign to "root out the waste, fraud and abuse" in CETA. Big stories with big headlines ran in papers all over the nation about some local neighborhood organization misusing $30,000 in CETA funds, while down the street at the Pentagon they were ripping the taxpayer off by hundreds of billions of dollars each year and getting more money from Congress for doing that! It was enough to make you sick.

My problem as an organizer was twofold. First, those who had jobs in the social service field, while they didn't like what was going on, were job scared and didn't want to get too "radical" for fear they would soon be unemployed too. Secondly, poor people didn't have confidence in the "reform-oriented organizations" like the CCBO because they understood that the clamp was coming down from the top and that the power structure had no intention of listening to groups like ours. People felt powerless.

In July 1980, riots erupted in downtown Miami and soon spilled over into Orlando. The Orlando police quickly set up a military line of operations in the heart of downtown just underneath the interstate highway overpass. This was the dividing line between the black community and the growing downtown tourist mecca that was in full blossom. The riots were met with police and fire hoses. The dejected people returned to their lives, things unchanged, except for the fact that new satellite police stations were set up in the black community. I called these "Community Policing Stations" forts on the Indian reservation.

In August 1980, I wrote in the CCBO newsletter the following: "The recent days' events in the streets of Orlando once again show how the unaddressed problems in the black community can be reborn in the eyes of the media and politicians at the slightest touch of violence. For years, people in the black community have been working to deal with the issues…but it doesn't seem like anyone hears the voices until the burning and hurting take place. The political and economic institutions must make a commitment to listen to the people and insist that the black community have an equal opportunity in this community. With equal opportunity must come an equal power to make decisions. The people in the community must be spoken with directly rather than going through white appointed leadership, as is now the case." These were strong words in Orlando— a total company town. Little changed after the riots.

One black leader in Orlando who impressed me during this time was a young man named Henry Betts. He led a federal agency that was working with the unions to place more black men and women into job apprenticeship programs. Henry was from rural Mississippi and had witnessed the early 1960's civil rights movement up close and personal. He was not worried about what white people in Orlando thought of him. He was full of fight. Henry liked the spirit of the CCBO and became our president in 1980. At one meeting, he asked us what we were going to do about the Callahan School that sat right in the heart of the downtown black community. I knew very little about it, but promised him that I would look into it and bring something to the next meeting.

Sitting on the corners of Parramore and Washington Streets, the old Callahan School building (formerly Jones High School) was the first permanent structure built in Central Florida for black students. Abandoned in the 1960's during desegregation, the city of Orlando bought the property from the School Board with the intent to demolish it and use the land for a fancy hotel and tennis courts. The land on which the school sat was originally donated by a local black man, Dr. Jones, and the community held BBQ's and bake sales in order to raise the funds to build the large school facility. In the white community, at least three of the old brick schools had been restored for use as cultural centers. Under Henry's leadership and my organizing, the CCBO developed a proposal to renovate the school and rename it the Callahan Humanities Center. It was our vision that a black history museum could be contained within it, a cultural center with studios for dance and drama and finally, and here was the kicker, that offices of community-based groups would be located inside. That meant the CCBO and other potential hell-raising groups would have a command center, a headquarters. The city was not at all interested.

Orlando Mayor Bill Frederick, one of the politicians who had put a picture of himself at the bus station on his campaign brochure during our People's Transit days, was our point of focus. The city council would follow him. The city, not wanting to appear to be obstructionist, told us that we'd have to prepare a proposal and come before the council for approval of our plans. So, we worked feverishly to get our proposal in for the January 26, 1981 city council meeting.

I remember this time so vividly because my partner, Becky Acuna, and I were about to have a baby. On December 13, 1980 Julian Vincent Gagnon was born. I was there for the birth, coaching her to breathe and she did very well. I was the first to hold the bloody little boy, and cried with joy. John Lennon had been killed just days before and we named our son after Lennon's son, Julian. I stayed home as the primary caretaker for the first six months and the best moments of my life were spent feeding and carrying on with Jules each morning. We called him Jules right away because of his propensity for drooling. Drools became Jules.

Back in Orlando, on January 26, 1981 the Orlando City Council voted unanimously to lease the Callahan School to the CCBO for $1 so we could have a chance to raise the more than one million dollars that would be necessary to restore the building. I didn't know how in hell we would ever do that, but boldly told the city that we had resources available to us. I worked hard with the local Callahan Neighborhood Association to turn out a good crowd for the meeting, and Mary Alice Drew from the neighborhood, a resident there for 61 years, told the mayor and council that, "Since the building was built by the community, the community should have it." Black City Commissioner Nap Ford agreed and stated that, "By approving this, you could turn the corner to improve black and white relations." Ford had attended the old Jones High School and had a personal stake in the decision. We all left that day feeling quite good about things, but there was just one problem: the roof of the Callahan school had a big hole in it and every time it rained I would lie in bed at night counting the dollars that were being added to the more than a million dollar renovation price tag. How the hell were we really going to do this, I wondered?

Everybody always talked about grants, but few ever tried to write any. Most foundations didn't fund bricks and mortar. The local historical preservation society in Orlando was not interested in funding a black community's renovation project. They had white people's buildings to restore. And the word was out within the power structure: don't help these radicals at the CCBO. Just let them fade away. We gave them the lease for a year; no one can claim the city isn't being helpful. Freeze them out!

However, I knew that the city and county governments got large community development block grants from the federal government. I had been to some of their meetings supporting black community groups trying to get sewer and water projects funded. So, I put an application into the city and county pipelines and went to work organizing support.[14]

I knew that we needed to make the Callahan school a household name in the community, and more importantly, we needed to make it a symbol for local black and white relations. City Commissioner Ford had already hinted at that. (I try not to miss too many hints from politicians.) I began organizing a major "Save the Callahan" campaign. I knew that we'd never come up with the million plus dollars, but I thought we had a chance to make the school so popular they'd have to save it.

We were set to go into the city planning board that was responsible for the community development dollars on April 21 of that year. On March 14, I organized a "Save the Callahan Rally" at the park that sat alongside the old worn-down school. Becky painted a big beautiful banner and we got a local flag company businessman to use his cherry picker van to hang the banner high onto the back of the auditorium of the rundown school. We hung the banner a week before the rally just for the effect. I got everyone I knew to help. Mary Alice Drew and the neighborhood association cooked for days making potato salad, sweet potato pies, and the best BBQ ever seen in the world. White and black friends volunteered to organize games for the local neighborhood kids and we set up a stage on a flat bed truck. City Commissioner Ford spoke and we had a band for entertainment. We counted over 1,000 people in the crowd and we made the evening news and the Sunday newspaper. We were on the record. Even Congressman Bill Nelson (now a Senator from Florida) came to work the crowd. I knew we were getting somewhere when the politicians turned out.

Throughout 1982, I worked hard to keep Callahan in the public eye and we got just over $200,000 committed to the Callahan building fund from the city and county community development pools. But, it was a long way from success. We needed to do something more to create the unstoppable momentum that would save the school. We continued to be visible by holding more large rallies in the park and held more BBQ's and car washes that raised just a couple hundred dollars each for the cause. But I wasn't looking for money so much as I was just trying to buy time and keep the issue in front of the community. Each rally we organized got us more media coverage.

In 1982, we were still struggling but we had a stroke of good luck. We met a black woman who was a high school art teacher. She had gone to Jones High School and wanted to help us save Callahan. She shared the vision for what we wanted to do inside the Humanities Center, the black history museum and the space for arts. Katie Wright was her name and I loved her and her big-hearted husband, John.

Katie soon had us out at the school on a Saturday morning taking down the plywood boards from the windows. We painted them with African symbols of life and hope and put them back up over the broken windows. The school sat on a busy street corner and now the Callahan had come alive. It still had a hole in the roof but now the public could see something was happening to the abandoned building. In our CCBO newsletter of January 1983 Katie wrote, "In 1983, we shall build a great trading place called the Callahan Humanities Center. People from all walks of life will acquire a new sense of self-confidence and many kinds of cultural talents will be tapped. Books will be written and published, poets will find audiences, films will be made and shown, plays will be written and performed, paintings will be painted and the arts of drumming and dancing will be shared."

Callahan wasn't the only thing I was working on at the CCBO. Ronald Reagan had been elected and dramatically escalated the cuts in social programs in order to support the Pentagon buildup. As we got more radical, the traditional social service providers who had originally belonged to the CCBO began drifting away.[15] They were afraid to speak up about the government cutbacks their organizations and constituencies were facing. They also got money from the local United Way. (Local weapons maker Martin Marietta, and Disney World, were the biggest contributors to the United Way.) I kept organizing events to educate and activate the public against these trends, but was seeing very little progress.

One day in early 1983, I came up with the idea of organizing a big cocktail party to benefit the Callahan effort. My idea was to send out invitations that would list prominent people as sponsors. But how could I get these prominent names? I went to City Commissioner Ford and asked him to get the mayor's signature on a letter that would go out to folks asking them to pay $25 to be listed, along with his name, on an invitation. The mayor was no friend of the project, but had to play along to keep black community leaders off his back. So, he reluctantly signed the letter along with Nap Ford. I had asked my friend John Hedrick to get a list of the 100 most powerful people in Orlando from his father, the wealthy local attorney and a part of the power structure. John's father gave me a mailing list and we mailed the letter from the mayor to these

100 biggies. About two dozen of them, surprisingly enough, sent in a donation and requested to be listed. When Nap Ford saw the final invitation with these names, along with many others of less prominent Orlando citizens, he was delighted. "Now we've won," he said. I made thousands of copies of the invitation with all these big shot names and distributed them all over the community. The cocktail party made very little money, but we now had publicly shown that some of Orlando's most influential people supported our project.

My VISTA year had come to an end and I applied for renewal. However, President Reagan had changed the VISTA guidelines and we were turned down because the CCBO had a history of "radical" activity. We were told by the government that no more VISTA positions would be awarded to groups who were not in the mainstream, like the hospital sewing circle or the gardening club. The folks at legal services had taken great pride in the fact that the CCBO was doing such good community work out of their office, so they hired me on as a paralegal and told me to keep doing what I was doing.

It had come to our attention that the City of Orlando was working on new downtown development plans that would be turning the entire Callahan neighborhood into a redevelopment zone. Of course, this would eventually displace the black community. The land had become as valuable as gold. With the expanding downtown business district, the once forgotten black neighborhood was now sitting on prized real estate. If we didn't do something soon there would be no neighborhood left to use the Callahan Humanities Center that we were working so hard to save. We had to expand our organizing.

I spent days in the county courthouse poring over land title records, finding out who owned all the land in the downtown black community. Mostly it was white slum lords. One of the biggest was K. Don Lewis, a member of the Downtown Development Board that was advising the City Council and the Redevelopment Agency. (Years later his daughter was to work with us in the peace movement.) Once I had an idea of who owned the land and what their plan was for the area, I put together a leaflet showing a bulldozer pushing over a house, and made thousands of copies. I visited every house, apartment and black-owned business in the Callahan/Holden black district and talked to every person I could about what was going on. I invited them to attend the big upcoming meeting at City Hall. It took me over two weeks, but it was one of the best organizing experiences I ever had. We packed city hall with black people, and, in the end the city was forced to build more low-income housing in the Callahan neighborhood. That helped to stabilize the situation, at least for another generation. Mayor Frederick was not happy with the packed city hall. He went out of his way to do his very best impression of a plantation master. He ordered the full house not to applaud after people from the neighborhood spoke. He called in the police and had them stand by the door in order to show that he was serious about throwing out anyone who defied him. I was sitting in the back of city hall alongside a black man who also worked as a paralegal at the legal services office. After each person spoke he and I clapped. The mayor scowled at us, but never called on the cops to remove us.

Each year, just for the hell of it, I entered the CCBO in the annual Disney Community Service Awards contest. Disney awarded $1,000 and $5,000 prizes to groups like the Girl Scouts, YMCA, Meals on Wheels, and mental health organizations—basic non-political groups. Applicant groups got one ticket to the awards banquet. One year I had gone to the banquet just to see what went on. The food was good and Disney had Cab Calloway come sing. This particular year, 1982, I asked another of our CCBO leaders to go. One afternoon, having forgotten all about the awards ceremony, I got a frantic call from the woman who had gone representing us. "We won, we won," she kept screaming into the phone. "We got the $5,000 award and another special award of $5,000. I gotta go." I was in a state of shock and couldn't figure out how in God's green Earth we could have won $10,000 from Disney! We were the town radicals.

We later found out what had happened. Dr. John Washington, a black political science professor at the University of Central Florida, was on the Disney award selection committee. He had recently been to our CCBO annual meeting and witnessed 50 black folks sitting alongside 50 white folks having dinner together and listening to Manning Marable, our keynote speaker.[16] He was impressed. He tried arguing for us to get one of those $1,000 awards but the others on the selection committee wouldn't go along with it. Apparently Dr. Washington got so worked up about it he had a heart attack and died right on the spot. What else could they do? They gave us the upper level $5,000 award and then threw in another $5,000 extra special gift in the name of the now-deceased Dr. John Washington. There, done, their conscience was clear.

The very public Disney award to the CCBO only increased pressure on the mayor and city council to settle the Callahan issue. The mayor decided to offer a deal: the city would save and renovate the Callahan school if the CCBO withdrew from the project. The city feared what would happen if the building became a radical organizing center, especially in this neighborhood which the developers had big plans for. The neighborhood association agreed to the deal, deciding that it was their one chance to save the school. The decision was painful and controversial, but under the circumstances it was a compromise that I accepted. Mary Alice Drew broke the news to me and thanked me for all I had done to help the neighborhood. We remained good friends.

We gave the Disney money to Katie Wright so she could begin to hold some of the black cultural programs in the Callahan park just to make sure that the mayor and the city council would follow through on their promise to renovate the school. Eventually they tore down half of the more than 35,000 square foot building, renovated the rest, and named it the Callahan Neighborhood Center. They put city recreation department staff inside to monitor the pool tables and ping pong balls. But, they also created some meeting rooms, a day care center, and a job training program. They put tables outside so the old men in the neighborhood could sit and play dominos. And, on the day the building was dedicated Katie, I, and other volunteers that helped us with the campaign all sat proudly and smiled when Callahan Neighborhood Association President Georgia Woodley publicly thanked the CCBO for helping to Save the

Callahan. The mayor, who was the master of ceremonies, almost bit his tongue off in anger. We applauded with pride.

A middle-aged black activist who helped us during our Callahan campaign pulled me aside one day for a word. His name was Tim Adams and he ran for mayor several times, trying to bring black community issues into the campaigns. I was near the end of my days working for the CCBO. Reagan was now cutting funding for the legal services corporation because they too had done too much good work representing the poor. Since I was low man on the totem pole at legal services, I was the first laid off. By now it was the spring of 1983. Tim told me that "we have been watching you for some time." He went on to describe how often, white folks came into the black community to "help us out" but all they did was "take." He said that the whites soon got a better-paying job and then were off and forgot all about the black folks. He told me, "you didn't do that. You did good work."

Tim Adams went on to tell me that he thought I should work where the real problem was: in the white community. He said the whites had the power, if they wished, to make life better for all people of color. It's the white folks who needed organizing, he concluded. I was struck by his sincerity and his honesty. I was also struck by his wisdom. I decided, right on the spot, to do just as he advised.

Often, during my 27 years of organizing, I have had to listen to a room full of white activists moan about the lack of "people of color" in the room. I've always tried to remember the Tim Adams' advice in those moments and suggest to folks that we should keep working in our own communities if we want to help people of color. If we could turn white people against the military-industrial complex, there would be more than enough money available to help the black community pull itself out of its multi-generational dependency on welfare and despair. It's the whites who control the society.

As the upper 2% revels in nearly 40% of all private wealth and social programs are gutted in the name of "reform", and tax cuts on the rich instead of expensive jet bombers raise the stakes of ordinary Americans, most Americans are lower-than-almost-anywhere-else-on-earth. The rich of America are lower-than-almost-anywhere-else-on-earth. There is a far greater gap between the wealthy and the rest of us than ever-before and the government is owned by the rich by the rich and for the rich... some remarks that things happening

(see below)

The best American People are beginning to realize it doesn't have to be like this...that if we'll forget our differences and work together we can make a better America that wants a better tomorrow.

# WORKING IN THE PEACE MOVEMENT

*"First they ignore you, then they laugh at you, then they fight you, then you win."*

—Mahatma Gandhi

On March 8, 1983, Ronald Reagan came to Orlando to deliver his famous "evil people" speech before the National Association of Evangelicals. He called the Soviet Union the root of all that was wrong in the world. Referring to the Soviets, Reagan said, "Yes, let us pray for the salvation of all of those who live in that totalitarian darkness— pray they will discover the joy of knowing God. But until they do, let us be aware that while they preach the supremacy of the state, declare its omnipotence over individual man, and predict its eventual domination of all peoples on the Earth, they are the focus of evil in the modern world."

For weeks before, while drawing unemployment insurance, I organized for a big protest at the Sheraton Twin Towers where Reagan was to speak. I got the unions, women's groups and the growing numbers of people moving into the peace movement involved. The demonstration was a big success and a picture of myself, wearing my Reagan mask made it into the *New York Times*. I was shown charging the crowd up with bullhorn in hand. *ABC News* TV correspondent Sam Donaldson walked through the assembly of protesters, but neglected to mention the event on the evening news.

I next approached the local Central Florida Nuclear Freeze Campaign and offered to be a free staff person. There was an international call out to organize local protests in October, 1983, to oppose Reagan's deployment of the nuclear-tipped cruise and Pershing II missiles in Europe. The Pershing was made in Orlando, at the local Martin Marietta Corporation facility, where my youngest sister was soldering the circuit boards for the missile. Even though the Freeze group only had a couple hundred bucks in its bank account, I talked the members into organizing a statewide demonstration in Orlando for October 22 in solidarity with the global actions. I set off around the state to talk to peace groups, encouraging them to bring buses to Orlando for the event.

While in Miami speaking to the local peace coalition, a man asked me what I was doing the next morning. "Do you have time to stick around and have breakfast with a friend of mine who could not come to the meeting tonight?" he asked. So the next morning, I met with an older man and his wife at a hotel across from the University of Miami. Little did I know they owned the hotel. During the meeting, the man asked me what I was going to do after the October 22 demonstration. I told him I didn't know. Fundraising from our growing local membership had been going so well that I was now getting $100 a week from the Orlando-based local Freeze group. In addition, I had a part-time job making sandwiches at a health food restaurant owned by one of our members. The next thing I knew, the man offered me $25,000 to start a statewide peace group.[17] The Florida Coalition for a Nuclear Weapons Freeze, which had been meeting as an ad hoc unstaffed networking group, took me on as its first full-time staff person.

The October 22 demonstration was in difficulty from the beginning. When we applied to the City of Orlando for a permit to march through the heart of downtown, they said we would have to pay $1,500 for "police protection." This was an arbitrary and outrageous slap at our constitutional rights. We secured ACLU attorney and Law school professor Bruce Rogow to handle our case. He immediately filed an injunction in Federal Court in Orlando, but we lost. Rogow then appealed that ruling to the Federal District Court in Atlanta, where we won. In the meantime, we had to come up with the $1,500 so we could get the permit while the case worked its way through the courts. I got on the phone and called a half-dozen people and asked them to make a special donation. Within an hour, we had the money in place.[18]

The demonstration was a smashing success. Over 800 folks from all over the state attended.[19] For Florida, this was a big deal. There was not a long history of peace organizing in Florida, a state heavily dominated by the military-industrial complex. As we started the march that day a torrential downpour began and my heart sank. But virtually no one left the march and it became a landmark event in the building of the Florida Coalition. For years people proudly told the story about how they had marched in Orlando through buckets of rain on October 22, 1983.

The lawsuit against the City of Orlando took several years to conclude. The City appealed the favorable federal district court ruling to the Supreme Court of the U.S. In the end, the Supreme Court ruled in our favor and protected the public's right to peacefully assemble. The City of Orlando had to change its unconstitutional "assembly and march ordinance." The Supreme Court found that by putting a price tag on demonstrations, the city was restricting the public's rights. The City had to pay our lawyer $40,000 in legal fees and reimburse us the $1,500.

On October 17, 1983, the Orange County Sheriff, a guy by the name of Lawson Lamar, sent his operatives to a briefing with Martin Marietta. They discussed the upcoming protest on October 22, and, in a report we later were able to obtain concluded that the "entire weekend would have to be tolerated." The internal police reports also stated that "Gagnon is now boasting of representation from about 75 groups to attend the rally....Contacts in the intelligence community have verified organized efforts to attend the rally from a state-wide perspective.....Nationally, intelligence contacts have revealed the advertisement of the October 22 rally by several recognized groups."

It took a while but we eventually confirmed that several spies from the Metropolitan Bureau of Investigation (MBI) had infiltrated our local freeze group over a period of a couple of years. We had long suspected some strange behavior by a certain person, but had no way of proving anything. Our suspicion was confirmed when one day I received a call from an unknown person who told me our group was infiltrated. With the help of an enterprising local newspaper reporter at the *Orlando Sentinel*, we were later able to determine that the phone call had come from the MBI's own attorney, who had been warning the MBI that its infiltration of our group was illegal. He was eventually fired, and the MBI tried to have his legal license taken away on the grounds that his call to us had violated attorney-client privilege. The MBI was unsuccessful in doing so and we were able to obtain a portion of the MBI's file that it had been collecting on our local group throughout 1983 and 1984.

On two other occasions we were able to ferret out more spies. In one case, the *Orlando Sentinel* reported, the police had asked a guy who was in jail for writing bad checks to spy on us in return for having his charges dropped. After coming to one meeting, he told the police he didn't want to cooperate with the scheme any longer. When asked why he had passed up the deal, the young man told the newspaper that, "They were nice people and their meetings were boring." Great, now the whole community knew that we'd put them to sleep if they came to one of our events!

The exposure of the spy cases in a cultural wasteland like Orlando was a big story and I got a reputation as a spy buster. The lid had come off this political backwater and any number of media outlets gave us excellent coverage. But it confirmed for me that working in Florida was not going to be easy as we tried to tackle the sacred cow of the Pentagon. Orange County Sheriff Lawson Lamar, a Vietnam veteran who worked as a military intelligence officer during the war, saw himself as an agent for the local aerospace corporations and was very unhappy to have been exposed while trying to use taxpayers' resources to keep tabs on our humble peace efforts.

The first MBI spy that we were able to expose once tried to sell me drugs. His cover story was that he was a pilot who flew vegetables in and out of the Caribbean, and before making a "run" one time, inquired if I'd like him to bring me back some "good stuff." He was not talking about bananas. It would have been perfect had they busted the lead protest organizer as a druggie. It was an important lesson to me how far the power structure would go to protect the war machine.

We got back at Lawson Lamar. When Ronald Reagan was running for reelection in 1984 the national group, Mobilization for Survival (Mobe), created a great poster of Reagan's scowling face with the words "We begin bombing in five minutes."[20] As it turned out, Lawson Lamar was running for reelection at the same time, and his campaign signs happened to be the same size as the Reagan posters we got from the Mobe. In the middle of the night, days before the election, Orlando Quaker and peace activist Steve Jordan and I drove throughout Orange County wheat pasting the Reagan poster over every Lawson Lamar campaign sign we could find. We were a bit nervous that we'd get caught, either during the adventure or after, but nothing ever came of it. I even called the local Republican campaign office the next day, disguising my voice as a typical redneck, wondering if they had seen the "terrible" thing someone had done to Lamar's signs. Yes they knew about it, they said. I always figured that Lamar had taken such a hit of bad publicity over the infiltration story that they figured if they went after us it would only serve to make martyrs of us. So this crime was best left alone.

# TRIP TO JAPAN: NEVER FORGET

*"The use of this barbarous weapon at Hiroshima and Nagasaki was of no material assistance in our war against Japan. . . . My own feeling was that in being the first to use it, we had adopted an ethical standard common to the barbarians of the Dark Ages. I was not taught to make wars in that fashion, and wars cannot be won by destroying women and children."*

—Admiral William D. Leahy, Chief of staff to President Harry Truman

A call came from New York. Would I like to go to Japan and represent Mobilization for Survival at the August, 1984 World Conference against Atomic & Hydrogen Bombs? "Yes," I said. "You have one week to get your passport and visa together—the Japanese will pay your expenses," I was told.

Normally, it takes longer than a week to get a passport and visa—but I made it.

On the plane out of Florida I found myself sitting next to Florida State Senator Curtis Peterson, from Lakeland. He was a conservative, but I talked most of the way to my Minnesota layover about Florida's participation in the federal government's *Nuclear War Crisis Relocation Plan*. Sen. Peterson said he thought Florida's plan wouldn't work—he said Florida couldn't even evacuate if a hurricane came. After a while, he didn't want to talk about it anymore, but his wife did. So, I leaned over old Curtis and proceeded to go through it all over again. Curtis just mumbled.

After about 17 hours on a few different planes I made it to Tokyo. I hadn't slept all the way—I was too excited. The Tokyo airport was surrounded by barbed wire fences and riot-decked police. This new airport was built an hour from Tokyo on farm land. Many farmers never warmed up to it and raided the airport now and again in an attempt to shut it down.

There were 128 international delegates at the world conference along with many Japanese representatives. The Tokyo conference lasted from August 1-3. Some key issues were: Japan's strong opposition to U.S. deployment of "Tomahawk" cruise missiles on Navy ships; the existence of 100 U.S. military installations in Japan; militarization of the Asian-Pacific region by the U.S.; nuclear waste dumping in the Pacific islands; and the urgent need for medical care for the 370,000 remaining Hibakusha (survivors of the U.S. nuclear bombs) throughout Japan.

After a long ride on the bullet train we arrived in Hiroshima and attended the national conference of one of the two main Japanese peace groups—Gensuikyo. In a big hall, 10,000 people gathered to reject the Tomahawk cruise missile and to criticize their Prime Minister Nakasone who said that he wanted to turn Japan into an "unsinkable aircraft carrier for the U.S." Visits to the Hibakusha hospital and memorial peace museum were unforgettable experiences. In the packed museum, a mother was showing her very young child photos of the cremation pits in Hiroshima where the bodies were dumped in great numbers. I was in tears. You could see that this national pilgrimage to the museum was a commitment by the Japanese people to never forget.

I was told the U.S. never helped with disaster aid after the bombings. The U.S. would not allow the Red Cross to enter Japan until radiological teams were sent in to study the damage and radiation effects. The U.S. radiological teams took many bodies and parts of bodies back to the U.S. for further study. (When I tried to write an op-ed for the *Orlando Sentinel* about this upon return from the trip, they refused to print it saying that I had no proof that my claims were true.)

On August 6, 1984, 45,000 people gathered at Peace Park (Ground Zero) in Hiroshima at 8:15 a.m., the exact time of the U.S. atomic bombing 39 years before. (When I returned home I read in American newspapers that Prime Minister Nakasone led those 45,000 people in Hiroshima. That was a lie. Nakasone was nowhere in sight. If he had been, the conference participants would have demonstrated against him.)

We took another train ride, this time to Nagasaki. We attended the national conference of Japan's second big peace group—Gensuikin. About 6,000 people gathered to hear speeches from their leadership and from the international guests.

On August 9, a commemoration of the Nagasaki bombing took place. Prime Minister Nakasone came to this one, but it was by invitation only, not open to the public. The world conference delegates issued a statement to the press condemning Nakasone as a hypocrite, and protesters were sent to hold banners outside the event.

The year before, Nakasone had visited the Hibakusha hospital and told the survivors that their medical problems were "all in their head." He vigorously opposed attempts to provide medical care for all the old people who suffer from illness related to the bombing. To acknowledge radiation sickness would be an admission that nuclear weapons had negative health effects that could last for many years, and no government wanted to admit this fact and then have to take responsibility for the resulting medical costs.[21]

I was invited to attend a memorial service to commemorate the Koreans who were killed at Hiroshima and Nagasaki. The Koreans were in Japan at the time of the atomic bombings as forced labor in the big Japanese military industries. Only in recent years have the 40,000 killed Koreans and 30,000 Korean Hibakusha been honored. I was asked to deliver a message at the service on behalf of Mobilization for Survival. I told them that peace activists were working hard all over the U.S. to try to bring about nuclear disarmament so this kind of catastrophe would never happen again. I told them that I would never forget the innocent Korean people who had perished when the atomic bomb was dropped.

After the concluding ceremonies in Nagasaki on August 9, I was invited to go to the city of Fukuoka (population 1 million) just north of Nagasaki. I was to be the guest of the local peace group (Gensuikyo) for two days. At first, I was a bit hesitant because of the language barrier. However, during the five-hour bus ride to Fukuoka with the group, I was made to feel like a part of their family. I made speeches to them on the bus that they could only partially understand, and I sang American peace songs. They in turn, shared their thoughts and community with me. And they kept plying me with lots of really good Japanese beer.

Fukuoka Gensuikyo has been in existence as a local peace group for 30 years. They opposed the Korean and Vietnam wars and had now taken up the fight against the deadly Tomahawk missile. In the 1960's they organized a human chain of 100,000 people around a U.S. Air Force base that occupied their city airport. They were successful in having it removed.

Yasunori Yoshihara, their full-time local organizer, and others in the group took me around Fukuoka to meet people active in the peace movement. Especially memorable was my visit to a union-built general hospital in the city for a meeting with the hospital administrators, who belonged to the peace group. We talked about how increased military spending in Japan was forcing cuts in social spending including medical care, just like in the U.S.

On August 11, Fukuoka Gensuikyo held a dinner reception for me. They showered me with beautiful presents and pleaded with me to share their fears of the Tomahawk missile with the American people. In a speech, a college professor urged me to tell America that the bombings of Hiroshima and Nagasaki were really done to show the USSR that America would use the weapon, as the U.S. and the Soviet Union wrestled for post World War II influence in the Asia-Pacific region.

By the end of the dinner that last night in Japan I was tossing in a sea of emotions—guilt, sorrow, pride, love, anger, fear—the works. I told them everything that I was feeling. I had never been around a kinder group of people.

# IN THE SHADOW OF THE TOMAHAWK

The trip to Japan had deeply touched me and I looked for ways to stay true to my promise to the folks in Fukuoka that I would take their message back home.

My task was made easier by the fact that the McDonnell Douglas Corporation was building the Tomahawk cruise missile at its Titusville facility, next door to Cape Canaveral in Florida. By this time the Florida Coalition for a Nuclear Weapons Freeze had changed its name to the Florida Coalition for Peace & Justice (FCPJ). I put out a call for members throughout the state to join me in committing civil disobedience at the front gate of the factory on August 9, 1985—the 40th anniversary of the atomic bombing of Nagasaki.

During that historic week, peace activists in over 15 Florida cities organized events to "Remember and Resist" the birth and mad escalation of the nuclear arms race in response to calls from national groups and from the Florida Coalition. Candlelight vigils, church bell ringing, community programs, street actions, and a tour by two Hibakusha, which I coordinated, were the key events organized throughout the state.

One goal that year was to create more dialogue across Florida about the real reason the bombs were dropped on Japan. Historian Gar Alperovitz's research on the subject showed that Japan had already lost the war by August, 1945. Alperovitz quotes Navy Admiral William Leahy, the senior military officer in the U.S. as well as chief of staff to Truman, as saying, "It is my opinion that the use of this barbarous weapon at Hiroshima and Nagasaki was of no material assistance in our war against Japan. The Japanese were already defeated and ready to surrender because of the effective sea blockade and the successful bombing with conventional weapons....My own feeling is that in being the first to use it, we had adopted an ethical standard common to the barbarians of the Dark Ages." [22]

The use of the atomic and hydrogen bombs signaled the start of the Cold War. The bombs were dropped as a military experiment and to show the Soviet Union that our post World War II foreign policy would be centered around the bomb. The nuclear arms race had begun.

We didn't get the 40 volunteers for civil disobedience that I had called for, but on August 9, 1985, in Titusville, thirteen of us from around Florida were arrested for trying to enter the McDonnell Douglas plant, where the Tomahawk cruise missile was made. We wanted to talk to aerospace officials about converting the plant to peaceful production. Over 200 people were present at the plant that day to stand in solidarity with those who were arrested. The two Hibakusha, who had been touring the state the previous week, were there with us and spoke at our rally before we were arrested.

On that 40th anniversary, we did "remember." We focused attention on the effects of nuclear war. Nearly every sane person agrees we cannot survive a nuclear war. But the bombs kept coming off the assembly lines. In spite of universal concern, we were developing the latest round of technological wonders. What could stop this madness? What else could we do?

In Florida, we showed that "active non-violent resistance" was a viable avenue for us to take. Ordinary citizens who were concerned about survival, had a right and a responsibility to take the actual step toward shutting down the weapons plants. We were witnessing the production of modern and mobile Auschwitz gas ovens before our very eyes. Should we just stand and watch?

# CATCH THE CRUISE

*"You can observe a lot just by watching."*

—Yogi Berra, Baseball Star

By 1986, the nuclear testing issue was hot in the peace movement and many activists would head out to the Nevada test site to protest the testing program. I was always looking for ways to make these same issues relevant in Florida.

We learned from the media that the Tomahawk cruise missile was going to be flight-tested over the Florida Panhandle. I remembered that Canada Greenpeace had organized a campaign to resist cruise missile testing in western Canada, and contacted them about a huge net they had used to try to "catch" the cruise. They sent me the 100 foot long net along with a "cruise catcher instructional video" that showed the net being hoisted by weather balloons. On the 50-foot high net were large letters spelling out the words "Stop Nuclear Testing."

When I got the net, I took it outside my Orlando office and stretched it out on the grass by the road to have a good look at it. A TV news reporter I knew drove by and stopped to ask what I was doing. I told him we were going to try to catch the cruise missile when it was tested over the panhandle. I explained about the video. He asked me if I'd give him the exclusive on the story, and I said I would if he made me a number of copies of the video. We had a deal. He ran the story first, and it created a media circus.

Next, I took the net, all rolled up, to a news conference in Fort Walton Beach, my old stomping grounds near Eglin AFB. The cruise would be launched from ships in the Gulf of Mexico, would fly over the Panhandle into southern Alabama, circle around and then crash land on the Eglin bombing range.[23] My plan was to say we'd catch the missile as it flew over the beach in Fort Walton.

The media loved the video which showed Greenpeace launching the net in the snows of Canada. Even though we never raised the net off the ground, the very TV image of the net being lofted with balloons somehow made people think that we were serious about the effort. Local Panhandle media ran the video footage on several TV news stations and the *New York Times* picked up the story. The media asked what I'd do with the cruise if we caught one and I responded that we'd split its belly open, clean out the insides, fill it with charcoal and have a fish fry on the beach. That statement made it into the press as well.

On October 19, 1986 the Florida Coalition organized a one day event in Fort Walton Beach called "First Strike! Gulf Coast Symposium on Preventing Nuclear War." Our guest speakers were Dr. Michio Kaku, professor of Physics at the City University of New York, and the Rev. George Zabelka, the Catholic chaplain assigned to the 509th bomber group that delivered the nuclear death blow in Hiroshima. We met at a hotel in Fort Walton and began with a news conference. This was my first interaction with Michio Kaku, who would later become one of the founding members of the Global Network Against Weapons & Nuclear Power in Space. At the news conference, I was awed by how Michio held the local reporters' rapt attention as he recounted his own story about relatives in Hiroshima at the time of the U.S. nuclear attack.

As Michio began to speak to the public at the conference, an old man from the local community approached him and yelled, "Give me liberty or give me death," while hurling eggs at him. Luckily Michio was not hit. I escorted the would-be assailant out of the event.

Rev. Zabelka told the crowd of one hundred that, "In 1945 my change of heart began. I saw real war...and I want to expose the lie of all war—the absolute contradiction to everything our religion has taught us."

Following the symposium, the assembled crowd moved outside for a four-mile march through the heart of Fort Walton's "Miracle Strip," past shops and restaurants and across the bridge over the Intra-Coastal waterway. We were led that day by Renee Williams of Fort Walton, whose husband was a colonel in the Air Force and assigned to Eglin. She was followed by a courtesy car carrying older activists who had less tolerance for the sweltering mid-day sun. It was topped with a mock cruise missile.

As we marched in one lane of traffic, a camouflaged convoy of troops passed us heading in the opposite direction. They were on maneuvers, practicing invasions on the local beach as part of a 12,000-strong "Operation Bold Eagle" exercise. Many of them waved and flashed peace signs to us as we passed so closely by each other in this military town where I had once lived. You don't often get that kind of interaction in a peace march.

Earlier that day one of our speakers Shafea M'Balih, from the American Friends Service Committee in Atlanta, told us, "We need to talk with the unconvinced...we must go in the places where we are afraid."

# CLIMBING THE GATES AT CANAVERAL

*"Disarmament can be accomplished, I believe, if enough people apply pressure."*

— Dr. Benjamin Spock, Pediatrician

Another way to make nuclear testing relevant in Florida was to look at the space center at Cape Canaveral Air Force Station. There, the military planned to launch the first flight test of the Trident II missile in January, 1987.[24] It was the perfect organizing tool to bring this debate to Floridians and beyond.

At that time, the Florida Coalition was a very loyal affiliate of Mobilization for Survival (Mobe.) The New York-based group was very interested in helping us organize a national protest at the space center and got Dr. Benjamin Spock, Odetta, and Peter Yarrow of Peter, Paul & Mary fame to commit to coming down for the action.[25] In addition, Mobe organized a peace train on Amtrak that began in Boston and stopped at the major cities along the east coast as it headed south, picking up bands of protesters who joined the action. At each stop, the local media covered the peace train picking up activists. This great moving protest brought several hundred folks to the Cape.

I also thought of doing a peace walk from Kings Bay, GA(where the Trident would be deployed, after flight testing) to the Cape. At the time, the Great Peace March was nearing the end of its long journey from the west coast to Washington D.C.[26] I asked Florida activists John and Martina Linnehan to coordinate the 200-mile Florida walk that became known as the "Peace Pilgrimage to Stop the Trident." The first thing John and Martina did was to join the Great Peace March for a while to learn how walks are organized, and to invite the marchers to join our Florida walk once they reached Washington.[27]

We planned to have the walk come south down Highway A1A and build support for a national rally at Cape Canaveral on January 17, 1987. We were calling the January 17 rally "Cancel the Countdown." Activists came in early from around the country to help us organize and we were able to open a temporary office near the Cape, thanks to support from local activist Smitty Hooper and her husband.

We tried to time the rally to coincide with the date the military had set for the launch of the Trident II from the Cape. As the pilgrimage came south, affinity groups were formed that began to plan back country occupations of the Space Center in hopes that they could enter the launch zone and thus delay the launch. Some affinity groups tried swimming across the Indian River onto the Cape. Others walked south along the beach. Still others tried sneaking through the palmetto scrub lands surrounding the launch facility. All had to pass through alligator and snake-infested waters and land. The media built up the drama with huge stories about protesters being apprehended by the military.

Helicopters, air boats and machine-gun-toting soldiers were searching night and day for the small affinity groups sneaking into the space center over the period of a week prior to the expected launch.[28]

Just a couple of days before the January 17 rally, we got a call from the Brevard County Sheriff's department telling us that they expected counter protesters to be present. They encouraged us to meet with them to discuss the situation. By that time, Mobe director Leslie Cagan had arrived in Florida to help with last minute planning.[29] Leslie joined us for the meeting with the police. They outlined their plan to create a police line down the center of the road keeping us on one side as we marched to the front gate of Cape Canaveral, and the counter protesters on the other. We agreed to the plan and left the meeting satisfied.

The pilgrimage arrived the day before the rally was to begin, and by this time scores of protesters were in jail for their attempts to sit on the launch pad. One black woman, named Willa Elam, actually climbed onto one of the space center launch towers and called security on the phone from the pad telling them to come get her. At first security thought it a joke but soon investigated and found out it was true. The media loved that one.

Over 5,000 people attended the powerful rally in an empty field at Port Canaveral. When it was over, the 5,000 followed Dr. Benjamin Spock, the famous baby doctor, as he led the march to the Air Force station gates. As we neared the gates, our Peace Keeper team halted the march because the police had not formed the line down the center of the road as we had agreed just days before in our meeting with them. We had been tricked. Rather, the police were all standing behind the military base gates, and standing in front of the gates were 100 counter protesters with signs on sticks, vowing not to allow us to climb the gates of the base as we had planned. In addition, many of them had been drinking beer while we held our rally, and were spoiling for a fight. The cops had created a potential disaster, just as their nasty little minds had intended. And the media were waiting at the gates, ready to film the entire bloodletting.

We sent our large team of peacekeepers ahead of the march and had them mingle with the counter protesters for a while.[30] Then, we slowly continued on with our march toward the fence line. By now, a loud military helicopter was hovering just over our heads as we moved toward the base, making it impossible for us to communicate with each other. The tension was high. It felt like we were in Vietnam or El Salvador during their bloody wars.

As we approached the fence, the counter protesters were overwhelmed by the thousands of peaceful and loving spirits in our march. A ladder was leaned against the gate and carpet remnants flung over the barbed wire, allowing Dr. Spock, and his wife, Mary Morgan, to be the first over the fence. In his memoir, called "Spock on Spock," the good doctor had a picture of himself climbing over the fence on the last page. Dr. Spock wrote, "Not many people see why civil disobedience is logical or right. For myself I will say that if I have used all legal means—voting, lobbying, letter writing, demonstrating—to influence my government and fellow citizens, and still believe that the government is on a criminal course, I'll participate again in nonviolent civil disobedience." In all, nearly 200 people were arrested at the Space Center that week trying to bring the Trident II nuclear missile to the public consciousness. I spent five days in jail myself for climbing over the fence that day. It was the most thrilling direct action I have ever participated in. [31]

Years later I learned how important the action was. I was at a grocery store in Orlando and a teenaged bag boy was pushing my groceries out to my car. As we approached the car, he saw my bumper stickers and said he'd like to have one. He mentioned the January 17, 1987 protest at the space center, and I told him I had coordinated the event. He said, "Oh I loved it. My father and I watched on TV as the people climbed over the fence. He was screaming at the TV calling them Communists. I loved it." It was in that moment that I realized that many more than 5,000 people were involved in that action. The power of non-violent public protest drew literally thousands into the action as they sat in their homes watching the production on TV. They became players in this public participatory drama. I would never again doubt for a moment the tremendous value of direct action.

# PERSHING MISSILE BASE MUTLANGEN, GERMANY

The Pershing II nuclear missile, made in Orlando, Florida was deployed in Germany creating greater tensions between the U.S. and the Soviet Union. In response the peace movement in Germany grew dramatically. One place of deployment was Mutlangen, a small community in southern Germany, south of Stuttgart. One day in early 1987, the peace group in Mutlangen invited us to send a representative to a conference they were organizing called "Trust Promotes Peace." I was pleased to represent the Florida Coalition.

In June I flew from Orlando into Luxembourg. From there I took a five-hour bus ride and an hour-long train trip to southern Germany. All around me were beautiful mountains that draw many tourists each year for hiking and other outdoor activities. During the trip, I saw countless U.S. military installations. Green army trucks, tanks, missile convoys, low-flying bombers and GI's were everywhere. The military acted like they owned the place. Most conquering armies do.

As I entered the Mutlangen Community Center, where the conference was held, I recognized a song filtering through the hallways of the building. A band of young high school kids was rehearsing. The kids sang "Don't go out tonight. It's bound to take your life. There's a bad moon on the rise."

Those lyrics from a Credence Clearwater Revival tune were very familiar to my generation. To me, they revealed with vivid irony the power and influence of the American military presence in West Germany. As the kids practiced this song, I wondered if they had been inspired to sing it by the Pershing II convoys that regularly passed just outside the community center.

On my first day in Mutlangen, I sat in the meeting room that overlooked the narrow street outside. Only 500 yards from the community center sat the Mutlangen Pershing Army Depot. Behind the heavy barbed-wired fences sat the Pershing II nuclear missiles. They had been assembled in my home town at Martin Marietta. I was given a photo of the missiles, raised and poised for launch at the nearby depot, from the previous Christmas Day. Imagine the horrible Christmas the people of Mutlangen had that year as word quickly swept the town that the U.S. Army was readying the Pershing for launch. Normally convoys carried the missiles out into the forests to practice putting them in firing position. This unusual practice made me realize what terrorists the U.S. military can be.

There were nine other Americans, three Soviets and 40 Germans at the Mutlangen conference. For one week in late June we sat and shared our stories as the Pershing convoys loudly rolled by the window—in one hour I counted 40 trucks.

Anne Stegmaier, a woman who organized peace walks all over West Germany, was in her late 30's when we met. She told us how her parents refused to discuss World War II when she was growing up. One day, she announced that she would not speak again until they told her about the war. Her silence lasted for two weeks before her mother finally revealed that she'd had an uncle who killed Jews.

Gisela Gohrum, a retired teacher, was one of the leaders of the conference. She was 20 when World War II ended. She experienced air raids, and barely escaped the Russians. Gisela said she was heavily indoctrinated by Nazi propaganda and after the war she became so fed up with politics that she tried to ignore it. Gisela traveled to the Soviet Union in order to get over her fear of its people.

Kate Kuhn and her family lived in a 200-year-old house formally built for Catholic priests. Kate encouraged Americans to protest at bases in the U.S. so families would be forced to discuss whether or not their children should join the military. As a school girl, Kate was terrorized by American pilots who would strafe her and her classmates as they walked to school. The kids hid in the trees. After the pilots landed, they would pass out gum to the post World War II occupied German kids.

Dr. Alexander Kokeew worked for the Soviet Peace Committee. He was a specialist on Germany and he told us how his fellow Soviet citizens feared that the Germans would invade them again. His job was to tell them that Germany would not or could not launch another invasion. "Our population is not always informed about the West. People

in the big cities are better informed than rural people. Many people don't read," he said. I liked Alexander a lot. You could feel that he was a direct and honest person. I couldn't accept for a moment that we were supposed to be enemies.

When it was my turn, I presented a slide show about our demonstration at Cape Canaveral on January 17. I told everyone that we were working hard to stop the militarization of our society. I told them we hadn't forgotten about the Pershing II.

One day, during the conference, I went to the front gate of the Pershing Army depot and started talking with the American GI's. Since I had been in the Air Force, it was easy for me to strike up a conversation with them. They usually refused to talk with the Germans, laughing at them and call them Communists and whores when they came to vigil at the base. One guard, a Mexican-American from Texas, told me he got a bonus of $18,000 to reenlist. He was bored with his job and was going to "party" when he got off duty. (It was clear to me he was only there because of the "poverty draft.") On this particular day, a convoy carrying three Pershing missiles was preparing to drive out to the countryside for maneuvers. Machine guns were everywhere.

A few days later, in the middle of the conference, we got word that a convoy was coming back onto the base. We all went outside and blockaded the street, forcing the convoy to stop. Immediately, GI's came pouring out of the trucks and lined up to guard the missiles. Little kids rode their bikes on the sidewalk, only feet from the nuclear warheads. Some people were in their yards clipping hedges. Protesters were dragged out of the way and, after a tense delay, the convoy made its way back to the base. These blockades happened all the time. Since the Pershings were deployed in Mutlangen a couple of thousand people had been arrested.

Most of the people in Germany didn't want the missiles in their country. Everywhere I went I heard talk about Soviet Premier Mikhail Gorbachev.[32] They were feeling positive about him but they were also cynical about chances for disarmament. They didn't trust the Americans.

On the last day of the conference, a rally was held at the U.S. Army depot to publicly report on the event. Over 200 people came. I was one of the first to arrive. I stood close to the gate and listened to the GI's. They closely counted the people as they arrived. The troops tried to act macho, but they were impressed with the crowd. When the singing of German peace songs began, they were further touched by the strong spirit of the people. I talked with a few of the soldiers. One of them tried to hold back his tears. I told him to remember we weren't against him. He nodded his understanding.

Dr. Alexander Kokeew and I planted a tree together on that last day—I brought soil from my garden at home. We shook hands. A friendship and a trust had developed between us. He had on his Florida Peace Pilgrimage T-shirt . He previously had asked me if he could have it. He looked like a good peace activist to me.

"HEY! <u>I'M</u> SUPPOSED TO BE THE MASTER OF SPACE!"

# WE'RE MOVING INTO SPACE

*"If you don't know where you are going, you will wind up somewhere else."*

—Yogi Berra

On September 29, 1988 I wrote in my diary, "Today the space shuttle flew again, following a long delay since the Challenger disaster on January 28, 1986. The media and the public are eating it up. No one is asking any serious questions. Now, on the 11 o'clock news, they are promoting the space station —the $100 billion effort being sold to us. The Russians are ahead of us, the media say. No one wonders whether the military takeover of the space program is a good idea. They just keep lying down like sheep. One sign I saw today on the news coverage of the launch was 'America is back on top.' The illusion of being on top is so typically American. Now I feel like I have a purpose, a mission. I want to help build in this country a citizens movement concerning space policy. I want to be sure that we don't move our global warfare system into space."

The first time I actually paid attention to the space issue was June 12, 1982. There were almost a million people demonstrating in New York City in favor of nuclear disarmament. I did not go to the event, but watched the rally on *C-SPAN*. Following the rally, *C-SPAN* switched over to a right-wing conference. The guest speaker was Lt. Gen. Daniel Graham, Ronald Reagan's head of the Strategic Defense Initiative (SDI), "Star Wars." During the question and answer period someone asked Graham if he was worried about the large demonstration in New York that very day. Graham, with great self assurance, said, "No, I think it is great. They are out there marching against ICBM's and we are moving into space. They don't have a clue. Let them keep doing what they are doing." At that moment, I began to pay close attention to the space program and I started talking to others in the Florida peace movement about the issue. I asked my fellow Floridians if we shouldn't become active around the plans to put weapons in space?

# No Chernobyls in the Sky!

# WHAT ARE WE DOING
# ABOUT NUKES IN SPACE?

*"Never doubt that a small group of thoughtful, committed citizens can change the world. Indeed, it's the only thing that ever has."*

—Margaret Mead

Sometime in 1986, I got a call from Brenda Meyerson in Miami who was a leader in the South Florida Peace Coalition. "Have you read *The Nation* this week?," she asked. I replied I had not. "There is going to be a plutonium launch at the space center. What is the Florida Coalition going to do about it?" I asked her to send me the article so I could look into it. The article was written by New York journalist Karl Grossman, author of several books on nuclear power. He described NASA's Galileo plutonium probe that was set for launch from the space center in the fall of 1989. I called Karl on the phone and introduced myself. We've been working together ever since.

I'll never forget the meeting on a hot summer day when the Florida Coalition decided to take on the Galileo plutonium issue. It was hard to get a good turnout for any meeting during the sticky Florida summers. Most people who could would leave the state. We had at most a half dozen people at the meeting. But those brave souls agreed we should take on NASA and oppose its nuclear launches.

We started a campaign to make NASA's launch of deadly plutonium from Cape Canaveral a controversial issue in Florida. We also hoped we could find a lawyer to help us take the issue to the federal courts in an attempt to block the launch. We hoped we could break the press censorship engulfing the Galileo story. In every case we surpassed our expectations.

The Galileo interplanetary space probe was supposed to be launched on the Challenger space shuttle's very next mission. But the Challenger blew up on launch on January 28, 1986, and the Galileo mission was delayed. It was Karl Grossman who first publicly reported that the Challenger was scheduled to carry a plutonium space probe. "What if the Challenger had blown up with plutonium onboard?" Karl often asked. "More than seven brave astronauts would have lost their lives."

Doubts about the safety of the Galileo space probe and its 49 pounds of plutonium-238 payload on the Atlantis shuttle were voiced by Karl Grossman in his *Nation* piece.[33] When most of his efforts to gain information about the Jupiter-bound space probe's proposed fuel system via the Freedom of Information Act (FOIA) were ignored, his concern grew even stronger. It took several years for him to get a response from NASA on his FOIA request. What was NASA trying to hide from the public? Was there more risk to the public than NASA was willing to admit?

On September 27, 1989 the Florida Coalition joined with the Christic Institute and the Foundation on Economic Trends to file an injunction in Federal Court in Washington D.C. to postpone the launch until the many questions about its safety could be satisfactorily answered. The lawsuit heightened media interest and we were overwhelmed with requests for interviews from radio talk shows, TV news, and publications around the world. In the end, the federal judge denied our legal challenge, but the international media coverage that resulted from the case made it worth filing.

Many protests were held at the space center prior to the eventual launch, drawing hundreds of people who spoke out against the use of nuclear power in space. A group of students from Rollins College in Winter Park, Florida were arrested for crossing onto NASA property to express their opposition to the launch. As the launch date drew near, media from all over the world gathered at the space center. There were launch delays and I knew the media would not have much to do, so each day for a week I would gather as many activists as I could find. We would hold a vigil at the Kennedy Space Center followed by a news conference. This helped tremendously to get our message out.

Meg Beresford, General Secretary of the British Campaign for Nuclear Disarmament wrote the Florida Coalition saying, "Reports are creeping into our papers about your case against Galileo. On behalf of CND, I would like to pass on our solidarity and support."

We heard from friends that our anti-plutonium in space protests were seen on TV in Tokyo, Australia and Africa. The West German Green Party took the issue to its parliament floor as did the New Democratic Party in Canada.

During the last week of the campaign, NASA, in its desperation to convince the public that plutonium was safe, challenged us to a public eating contest. They would eat a pound of plutonium if we would eat a pound of caffeine. The caffeine would kill us and the plutonium eater would walk away, they told the media. We politely refused the challenge.

We even made CBS Evening News anchor Dan Rather take notice. One evening, just before the Galileo launch, Rather came on for the nightly news and CBS flashed a plutonium generator on the screen behind him. Rather got out of his usual seat and pointed out that the generator was "indestructible" and thus would be safe in the event of a Challenger type accident. I knew we were making progress when the government needed Dan Rather to stand up to defend the nuclear launch.

We did not stop the launch of Galileo, but we did give birth to a global consciousness about the introduction of the bad nuclear seed into space. While this might not seem like much to brag about, in the end, over time, it will prove to be a historic step for humankind. There has long been a non-critical base of people who support all space-related activity. They marvel at the launches of rockets and they are impressed with the wondrous pictures that come back from spacecraft. But now there was born, around Galileo, the development of a new base of people who would begin to educate and organize around the world about protecting the heavens from the nuclearization and weaponization of space. Even these words, commonly used today, were then new to people. A new age was born.

We did not have much time to rest after the Galileo launch. NASA was preparing to launch another space probe, the Ulysses mission, with 25 pounds of plutonium, from the space center in October, 1990.

So, we went through the whole exercise again: the legal challenge in federal court in Washington; intense media work; frequent protests; and arrests at the space center. Meanwhile, as always, NASA continued to assure the public that things were safe. More activist contacts were developed around the U.S. and around the world that wanted to help us: Ulysses was eventually launched without a hitch. The game of nuclear Russian roulette was now well underway.

# JULIAN MAKES THE CALL

*"We have to do the best we can. This is our sacred human responsibility."*

—Albert Einstein

Today (October 21, 1988) I let my son, Julian, stay home from school. We rode our bikes to my office after lunch and I worked for about an hour and a half. Then we rode home. It felt real good to be with him. It was a beautiful sunny day.

When we got back I was listening to the local talk show on the radio and Jules (eight years old) was in his room cleaning up. He had the talk show on his radio, too. The show's host was going on about the new bumper sticker law they have that declares that so-called "obscene" stickers are against the law. A guy was stopped because he had a sticker that read "Russia Sucks." The host was explaining the situation and said he thought Russia sucked, too.

Jules got mad at that and told me he wanted to call in and say that Russia was a good country. So, I dialed the number for him. The producer told him they were not taking any more calls, which was a lie because they had two hours yet to go on the show. They just didn't want a kid on the air. I called back and stayed on the line long enough to get around the producer and then gave the phone to Jules. He told the host that he had heard him say bad things about Russia and didn't feel like he should have done so. Julian said that he liked Russia. The host, who is usually an asshole with everyone on the phone, apologized and said that he meant the Russian government, not the country.

Julian also asked the host if he had ever been to Russia, to which the host replied that he had not. At this point, the host was pretty impressed and asked Julian how old he was and whether he listened to talk shows frequently. Julian replied that he did.

When he hung up he was so excited that he ran around the house jumping up and down. He leaped into my arms and gave me a big hug. I was so proud of him. I saw that he had experienced a real sense of personal power. This was surely a moment in which Julian learned that determination could pay off. He also learned that it was important to challenge "authority" when you did not agree. To me it was also a lesson to use a good organizing opportunity when it presented itself.

# OPERATION JUST CAUSE
# AND PETE WILLIAMS

*"From Mexico to Argentina, Latin American governments today roundly
condemn the use of force by the United States against
General Manuel Antonio Noriega of Panama."*

—New York Times, Dec. 21, 1989, p. 24

*"I appreciate the support that we've received, strong support from the United States
Congress, and from our Latin American neighbors."*

—George Bush, Dec. 21, 1989, reported
in New York Times, Dec. 22, 1989, p. 16

On December 20, 1989, in the dead of night, George Bush (King George I) invaded the country of Panama ostensibly to go after one bad apple by the name of Manuel Noriega. It was called *Operation Just Cause,* but the cause was not just. Manuel Noriega had been on the CIA's payroll since the 1950's when he became an informant, paid over $200,000 a year by the U.S., to spy on his fellow classmates at a military academy. Over the years, this corrupt man had been a CIA operative during *at least* six U.S. presidential administrations, going back to the first years Nixon was in office.[34]

The invasion of Panama was done, in part, to re-establish U.S. control over the Canal Zone, but also to help justify the existence of the military-industrial complex. All signs

pointed to the collapse of the Soviet Union just two years later. We were about to lose our big enemy and had no good "enemy" prospects lined up. What was a war monger to do? Go bomb someone who could not retaliate of course. Another reason for the invasion was to field test new high tech weapons systems like the Stealth bomber. It was used to drop bombs that "liberated" the Panamanian people from our bad boy, Noriega.[35]

El Chorrillo, a poor neighborhood, was bombed, shelled with heavy artillery, strafed, and finally burned to the ground by U.S. troops. One resident, a young mother, told investigators after the invasion that "helicopters were firing all kinds of weapons because you could hear the bursts, and explosions were of different intensities...The lights in the neighborhood went out and houses began to burn. It was chaos. People tried to leave their burning homes but found themselves between two fires...tanks, and armored cars, and U.S. soldiers on foot advancing, firing. We could hardly believe it." Another resident reported that a group of U.S. soldiers came down his street and "entered each house. We saw the people—the residents—coming out, followed by soldiers, and then we saw the houses, one by one, go up in smoke. The U.S. soldiers were burning the houses."[36]

In order to hide the dead, the U.S. military dug mass graves and bulldozed bodies into them. Cremating bodies was another method used to destroy the evidence of the massacre. A report from the Panamanian National Human Rights Commission claimed that in Cocle province "hundreds of bodies were cremated" by U.S. troops using flame-throwers.

Some speculated that another reason for the invasion was that Noriega had not followed U.S. orders to assist in the illegal U.S. war on Nicaragua in 1986. This was punishment for his "betrayal" of his bosses in Washington.

For me, it was painful to watch the U.S. media grovel and promote the invasion as something patriotic, when in fact it was a sad and despicable moment in American history. The main Pentagon spokesman during the invasion was a guy named Pete Williams who, today, works as a reporter for *NBC-TV*. Now imagine that today you are watching your TV evening news wanting to believe that you are getting the best fair, balanced, honest reporting possible and then Pete Williams comes on the screen. My first reaction is to feel sick to my stomach. I remember that he was the Pentagon spokesman during *Operation Just Cause* and that he lied through his teeth about the reason for the invasion and insisted that we were not killing innocent civilians.

Pete Williams has no credibility. He is not a journalist. He is a Pentagon operative who has been placed inside the mainstream media to pose as a reporter. His job is to gain the confidence of the American people and to lie to us every chance he gets. And because very few people will remember all the way back to December, 1989, they will believe Pete Williams at *NBC*. But I won't. I will always remember that Pete Williams at *NBC* is really Pete Williams at the Pentagon. The same tall man with glasses—he lied to each of us about how the U.S. never killed innocent people in *Operation Just Cause*. It was an action to liberate the Panamanian people. Pete Williams said so......But I won't forget..........Pete Williams at NBC/Pentagon/NBCentagon......

# 1990: AN EXCITING AND HARD YEAR

The year 1990 was a busy one for me and the Florida Coalition. We organized a statewide "economic conversion" conference in Miami. The president of the International Association of Machinists and Aerospace Workers came to speak at our conference as did Congresswoman Carrie Meek (D-FL.). Now that the Cold War was over, momentum grew to reduce the bloated military budget, and to put converting the war machine to peaceful production on the nation's social/political agenda. With the dissolution of the Soviet Union, there was an important opening for the peace movement. Labor, led by the Machinists Union, was worried about jobs for military production workers and saw the peace movement as allies. All over the country groups were sprouting up counting on the coming "peace dividend" to finally move toward the day when human and environmental needs took precedence over war making.

In 1985, the military was absorbing 70% of the government's funding for research and development. Over 30% of all scientists were working for the war industry. Now was the time to act before these trends worsened.

Another big project in 1990 was the creation of the Florida Coalition's Youth Peace Camps. I had long heard from our elder activist base in South Florida that they were worried about how the peace movement would survive without the youth to replace the elders who were dying off. Florida had no indigenous base of peace activists; most of them were from the northeast, and had come south for the sun in retirement. "What is the Florida Coalition doing to get the young people involved?" they would ask. On my long drives back to Orlando, after my many speaking trips to South Florida, I would think over and over again about their heartfelt question.

I came up with the idea of the youth peace camps and took it to the Florida Coalition. We would rent a summer camp facility and then bring in volunteers to do the cooking, serve as camp counselors, lifeguards, nurses, and workshop leaders. The idea was met with great enthusiasm and we set to work. We raised enough funds from our membership and supportive groups to give scholarships to 40% of the campers, thus allowing us to bring kids from different economic, racial and ethnic backgrounds together for a week. Many of the kids had the first sustained contact with people different from themselves at the camps. Our first camp served 75 kids, ages 12-18. Although there were a few minor problems, the camps were well received. Our biggest problem was that the kids wanted to stay up all night talking and would fall asleep during the workshops. We held workshops on the environment, war and peace issues, the space program, vegetarianism, racism, the history of progressive movements as well as the traditional camp activities like swimming, canoeing, soccer and the like. Each year I would organize a basketball tournament at camp and I always put together a team mixing adults and kids. (My aging knees would eventually force me to stop playing basketball with the young folks.) Later camps grew to 100 students and during several summers we organized two camps. I am proud to say the Florida Coalition continues to organize the peace camps today, and just before I left the FCPJ, our original big donor gave $100,000 more to construct a building on the organizations land so that future camps could be held there each summer. I know the peace camps have benefited the young people over the years. Many of the campers have gone on to become activists throughout the country.

The other key area of work for us in 1990 was to organize against the impending Persian Gulf War. President George Bush was eager to develop a new enemy to replace the Soviet Union and to end all of this talk about the peace dividend and economic conversion. The military-industrial complex was frantic to come up with a new reason to maintain a $300 billion a year Pentagon budget before the American people found better things to do with their hard-earned tax dollars.

I went to work organizing a major local protest in Winter Park, Florida prior to the Bush initiation of war with Iraq. The City of Winter Park has a main street called "Park Avenue," it sees itself as the home of the Central Florida elite, and at first refused to give us a permit to march. I called their bluff and told them we would march anyway and that they would have to arrest hundreds of peaceful people. They eventually caved in after the story hit the newspapers.[37] We were able to draw over 500 people which was a great turnout for very conservative and war-friendly Central Florida. I learned during these times that people turn out to protest in large numbers before a war begins, but once it's started they lose heart and fall out. They became discouraged when we didn't stop the war and returned to their isolated lives, quietly depressed. It was not a good thing for them to do. The best antidote for "war depression" is to stay active and be around people who are of like mind and strong heart. It is also good for our children to see the adults they love actively working to stop war and environmental devastation. It gives the kids some margin of hope.

Despite intense political activity in 1990, we were not able to stop the Persian Gulf War. Bush's invasion led to endless war against Iraq. Hundreds of thousands of Iraqi kids would die over the next 10 years due to constant bombing over "no fly zones" and economic sanctions, supported by Republicans and Democrats alike.

Bush began his bombing of Iraq with 100 cruise missiles, costing $1 million each. At the McDonnell Douglas cruise missile plant in nearby Titusville they were working three shifts, round-the-clock to replace the missiles. Talk of economic conversion to peaceful production was gone in the flash of the attack. King George I had saved the day for the military-industrial complex. It was not to be denied.

# I'M NOT CHEERING

## Spring 1991, *Just Peace*, Florida Coalition Newsletter

*"Of course the people don't want war. But after all, it's the leaders of the country who determine the policy, and it's always a simple matter to drag the people along whether it's a democracy, a fascist dictatorship, a parliament, or a communist dictatorship. Voice or no voice, the people can always be brought to the bidding of the leaders. That is easy. All you have to do is tell them they are being attacked, and denounce the pacifists for lack of patriotism, and exposing the country to greater danger."*

—Nazi Herman Goering at the Nuremberg trials

Excuse me for not cheering. Sorry I won't wave a flag. The thought of 950 oil wells on fire—for some time to come—takes some of the fun out of the Gulf War Party. The thought of massive environmental damage from this war makes it hard to feel "proud to be an American." I'm prouder to be a pacifist.

I read that one Iraqi Republican Guard—those much-feared fighting men—explained that the difference between himself and other Iraqi troops was, "We get 30 dinars more and a patch on the arm. It means nothing."

Don't tell me that Bush, Cheney, Powell and Schwarzkopf didn't know that the Iraqi army was a paper tiger.

I couldn't cheer when I read the report that 100,000 Iraqi people had been killed, and they had stopped counting. What does it say about America's soul when we don't care how many people we kill in Iraq?

I am sick at heart to see the American media falling over themselves to wave the flag. They know, just like we do, that the war will make the U.S. military bolder. Our government won't wait too long before they "rescue" some other nation from "naked aggression."

I can't help but wonder if America will ever cheer for the poor, the hungry, the sick, the illiterate, the environment. How about a yellow ribbon for a real energy policy?

"The Persian Gulf conflict has propelled the U.S. into a new and astonishing era of warfare," said Ray Clines, former CIA Deputy Director and Iran-Contra figure.

Astonishing, I ask? Violence is our national product; our chief export; our logo; our symbol. It's in our fabric and our hearts. It's what we teach our school children. Beware world, our flag is unfurled.

Kuwait has been liberated. And so has the military-industrial complex. No more Vietnam syndrome. No more two-party system. No more peace dividend. Welcome to the New World Order.

# CLINTON COMES
# TO THE WHITE HOUSE

## Winter 1993, *Just Peace*, Florida Coalition Newsletter

*"Every child is an artist, the problem is how to remain an artist once he grows up."*

—Pablo Picasso

No matter what your feelings are about Bill Clinton (I never once voted for the man), I think we would all agree that little good will come of his administration unless there is a significant grassroots movement to press for change.

Those corporations with the power and their right-wing allies in our nation are now mobilizing to maintain as much of the status quo as possible. An example of this is the health insurance industry. They know the public wants health care now. They figure if they get out in front of the parade early enough they can influence the direction it goes. Thus their recent eagerness to call for some kind of national health care plan that will be a moneymaker for them and will keep the focus on privatization of health care.

As W. B. Park's wonderful cartoon *Transition* depicts, I've come to feel that our two-party system has become a large part of the problem. We are offered little choice in our elections. U.S. leaders used to joke that in the former Soviet Union you would either vote for Leonid Brezhnev or Leonid Brezhnev. It's not much different here in the U.S. We get corpo-

TRANSITION
by
W. B. Park

Okay, Bozos, let's get it over with

Hot dang – four more years!

Republican Lite

rate man #1 (Bush) or corporate man #2 (Clinton). Thus, we get little change. The "system" limits the debate, limits the solutions and limits the parameters for structural change.

The 1992 elections were frustrating for me. One night, before the New Hampshire primary I was watching *C-SPAN* on cable TV. Bill Clinton had just finished a talk with a small group of citizens and he was working the crowd. The camera stayed on him as a man asked him about the Middle East. Clinton responded that it was a terribly dangerous and unstable place (the very same words once used by U.S. politicians to frighten us about the Soviet Union). Clinton told the man that we needed a "NATO-like alliance" in the Middle East so that we could contain the menace.

Now as I look at the map of the Middle East I see permanent bases being established in Saudia Arabia and Kuwait. I cannot help but wonder if we are seeing the first signs of deployment of this new and costly military alliance, with Democrat and Republican Party cooperation making it happen.

I am now more eager than ever to see the emerging Green Party and the 21st Century Party take hold. We need freshness, more creativity, and dare I say, ideology, infused into our political process.

I hope that at the very least a Clinton Administration will give the public some sense of opening. And if the people think that there is a chance for something good to happen, they might help push things along. That could create an unstoppable dynamic. But for that to happen we will need the support of all progressive people.

So congratulations Mr. Clinton and Mr. Gore. Here are our demands:

- Cut military spending by at least 50% over the next five years
- Ensure that the military industrial complex converts to useful and environmentally safe products
- Extend the nuclear test ban beyond July, 1993
- Support a single-payer National Health Care Program
- Stop the embargo on Cuba—treat Cuba just as we do China
- End unemployment and homelessness
- Support human rights for our gay and lesbian citizens
- Support the return of President Aristide to Haiti—treat refugees humanely
- Support Native American treaty rights
- Stop the nuclearization and weaponization of space
- Develop a real energy program that promotes sustainable technologies
- Continue and expand economic aid to Russia
- Promote the teaching of conflict resolution in our nation's schools as an alternative to violence
- End participation in the global arms trade racket
- Lead the effort to remove violence from TV
- Replace the North American Free Trade Agreement with a North American Restoration Initiative

We shall remain vigilant. Please don't let us down!

# Blockaded Thinking
### by W. B. Park

① Mr. Congressman, a Cuban is here to see you.!

Wonderful! Please come in, and if you need a pen to write out your contribution to my next campaign...

② Let me assure you we are ignoring all peaceful overtures from Havana, and are slowly tightening the blockade, oops, hee hee, I mean embargo around their necks.

③ Think what it would mean if we permitted an independent, socialist (shudder!) country to survive in this, our Western Hemisphere – Other countries might realize they don't have to jump everytime we whistle – we might see genuine democracy take hold somewhere!

④ And aren't we having enough trouble conjuring up enemies as it is? What if we really have to cut military spending? Do you know what the stock market would do? Worst of all, our own people might begin to question, and think! Please take back to Miami my assurance that we will soon bring Cuba to its knees!

⑤ Sir, I'm not from Miami – I bring you greetings from a Co-op farm in western Cuba, and ask you to lift the blockade and let us live in peace.

Security!!

© 1994 W. B. Park

# A STRATEGY FOR THE FUTURE

## Winter 1995
## *Just Peace*, Florida Coalition Newsletter

*"We cannot control the direction of the wind, but maybe we can adjust our sails."*

—Fr. Emmerich Vogt

For several years I've been taking informal surveys about various things. In my travels across the nation I've found that about 50% of the public pay phones don't work. That comes as a surprise to me—especially as we enter the "information technology age."

Another of my survey findings is that most people won't write letters to Congress.[38] As an organizer you are taught to persuade people to take introductory steps into the political process. Writing letters is usually a good first step for new folks. But these days people say, "It won't do any good," or "They just throw them in the trash." In a moment of guilt, people might promise to write soon, but never get around to it. There is no inspiration.

I truly understand the hopelessness that leads people to opt out. Hell, I often feel it myself. In the meantime I'm supposed to be organizing people, so I continue to cast about, looking for answers.

My favorite band, *The Kinks*, sang, "Give the people what they want." Why not, I figure, find out what the people want to do and help them to do it?

In my research to find out what "we the people" want, I've come to realize that we want to stay home...close to the TV, so to speak. We are tired and drained, impatient but, at the same time, terribly tolerant. We want a clean environment and cheap gas. We want low taxes and a national health-care system. We want our cake and we want to eat it too. We are spoiled rotten. We are brats. The rest of the world hates us and we hate ourselves.

So how do we stop the right-wing roller at this point? First, let's look at a few facts.

We have the best Congress that corporate money can buy. It's no wonder the men and women sitting in it ignore our mail. The public understands this.

The richest 20% of the population own 48% of our nation's wealth. Those of us floundering in the bottom 20% of the heap own 3.6% of the wealth.[39] The corporate politicians know this. In other words, "we ain't got much they want."

In the November 1994 elections, only 21% of those eligible to vote, did so. Many of these are the top 20% who are now in the "protecting mode" as they accumulate more wealth.

Newt Gingrich is now quoting F.D.R., the man who saved capitalism by promoting social programs. But Gingrich is cutting social programs. Gingrich even suggested the idea that government buy laptop computers for poor people so they can plug into the "opportunity society."

So anyway, you get the picture. We're in a hell of a mess. What do we do? Write letters to Congress? Send a donation to some progressive group in Washington to hire a lobbyist? Give up?

I've got an idea. I think we should demand that the Washington D.C. based progressive groups (unions, women, gays & lesbians, peace, environmental, social justice, people of color, senior citizens, disabled) all get together and develop a 10-year national organizing plan.

We should demand they skeletonize their expensive Washington operations and pool those dollars as seed money to build a base that would, in time, begin to change America.

When I say "skeletonize" what I mean is this: Stop paying all those expensive rents on those lobby offices. Stop introducing legislation that will be compromised even before it's written. Stop paying lobbyists to fight the losing battle in Congress. Stop asking the "folks back home" to get letters into Congress. My research shows me that they're not writing.

I suggest that we take the money saved by my skeletonized D.C. plan (we would keep a small team of lobbyists in Washington—say two or three—just so we could keep one office open with a phone and a computer) and hire grassroots organizers by the thousands around the nation who would implement the national grassroots campaign. The campaign would be centered around the local reality that people face. We would seek to involve local people in issues that affect their lives from day to day. We'd organize campaigns around health care, education, fixing roads and bridges and cleaning up the local water system. We'd fight for more job training money. We'd call for conversion of the military-industrial complex. We would run folks for local offices, using the energies that would be unleashed when people see their allies moving together all over the nation.

Once each year state conventions would be held followed by regional conventions. At these events the collective demands of the people would be voiced. We want health care. We want clean water. We want phones that work!

I know what would happen next. The ground would shake. The sky would rumble. The Democrats would find a backbone, or a very strong third party would be formed. The politicians would begin to write legislation. Our two or three lobbyists in Washington would tell us so. A bill would be passed to fix the phones in America and the military budget would be cut to pay for it. Let's get started!

# WE MUST PUSH BACK HARD

## Fall 1995, *Just Peace*, Florida Coalition Newsletter

*"Service to others is the rent you pay for your room here on earth"*

—Muhammad Ali

I've had a difficult time of it in recent weeks. I've been watching too much TV—
*C-SPAN* in particular.

I got hooked on the Medicare debate in Congress. Watching the Republicans deny
public hearings on their huge (and revolutionary) bill was hard to take. I was so upset
after several days of this that I had to stay home from work one day. And what did I do?
I turned on *C-SPAN* just in time to witness the debate on Cuba and the horrendous
Helms-Burton bill that overwhelmingly passed the House. The bill will twist the arms
of sovereign nations that choose to trade with Cuba.[40]

During the same period I screamed into my pillow as the Gingrich-led Republicans
were opening up the last Alaskan wilderness to oil drilling and talking about privatizing
all the national parks. Can you imagine Disney in charge of Yellowstone? They'd kill
off all the animals, bring in robotic Yogi Bears and put a tram ride through the park. Oh
God, I think I'm starting to go crazy.

So I turned to the last card in my hand. President Clinton. He's got to veto all this
madness. I called the White House several times demanding that he act like a good
Democrat.

I don't mean to sound cynical, but I'm trying to cope.

The national political talk shows are all meeting with focus groups. They go back
and speak to them over and over again. Usually they are 95% white middle-class people
who, frankly, don't know what the hell is going on! All they know to say is cut the
budget deficit. Where should we cut, they are asked? Welfare, they say. They've been
well-trained by the monolithic drivel we hear from the corporate-controlled media.
When the focus groups are asked if middle-class programs should be cut (home mortgage deductions for example) they say no—of course not! But cut welfare, there is so
much fraud, waste, and abuse. It amazes me that these focus people never, ever bring up
the fraud, waste, and abuse in the Pentagon. But I shouldn't be surprised; they haven't
been programmed to say that.

I try to imagine what it would be like to be a poor, working class person of color
watching these focus groups. I can begin to see why many of them cheered the O.J.
verdict—they feel like they might have won something for once. So what are we to do?

When I came up with the idea for the Walk for the Earth (from the Florida Everglades to the capital in Tallahassee) it was at a meeting in Tallahassee where several of us were discussing the reality that we are getting killed on environmental issues in Tallahassee and Washington. The politicians are only listening to the developers. We need to do something to shake things up a bit. To me, the idea of a 700-mile walk represents something basic and fundamental. It's a way we can begin to take back some of our power and dignity. We can break away from the filter of the corporate media and go out and have direct contact with the people.

We can give the youth some needed experience and hope. We can reach people in communities who are struggling and say, "Yeah, we're here with you. We care!" We can say to the corporate-controlled political machine in Tallahassee and beyond that "maybe you are winning for now, but damn it all, we aren't going to give up."

Our world is sinking into rampant selfishness. Too many people have swallowed the line that we should hop into our red sports car or VW bus, ride off into the sunset, and forget about the world. Freedom!?

For us to get beyond this tough moment in history we must join hands and help each other along this rocky road.

We've also got to be bold at this time. It's important that we push back hard as the corporate politicians probe where they can take back social, economic and environmental gains in what is the biggest redistribution of wealth in our nation's history. We've got to push back hard as they attempt to rape the environment and make every single cent they can off it before they send our Mother Earth into toxic shock.

It's time for us to stop having any illusions about Clinton or the Democrats (what's left of them). We've got to know that it is we who must pull ourselves out of the fire. We've got hard work to do and hard years ahead.

Please come walk with us and help turn this silly system toward sanity. We can do it. We must do it!

# THE WALK, WATER AND
# AN END TO GROWTH

## *Just Peace*, Florida Coalition Newsletter

*"Nature will bear the closest inspection. She invites us to lay our eye level with her smallest leaf, and take an insect view of its plain."*

—Henry David Thoreau

I drove the 700-plus mile Walk for the Earth route four times before our official beginning in late February, 1996. I had plenty of time to think about the enormous undertaking and what it was "all about."[41] During these long drives I mapped the walk route and scouted for places for the campers to sleep. I met with local groups along the way and got them to commit to join the walk when it passed through their community. Many of the groups took on the task of organizing meals for the walkers. I made contact with the local media to publicize the walk and the local issues we'd be illuminating. Quite often, there was a community forum to set up.

I knew that we were going to walk through communities of color where poor people were struggling, often alone, over local environmental issues. I knew we were going to try to help return a sense of power to people in our state who feel powerless in the face of corporate political dominance. What I didn't know was that water contamination would be the issue that everyone talked about, up and down the state.

The Everglades are being diced up—big sugar, citrus groves, vegetable production and urban sprawl are impacting South Florida's primary water source. We met with black people in Belle Glade and listened to their stories about water contamination from sugar cane production.

In Polk County, where miles and miles of phosphate mining has impacted poor communities, water contamination has reached epidemic proportions. While in this region, we met with black people whose communities were contaminated by the phosphate industry. There are no environmental groups speaking out for the people. Even the Audubon Society is taking money from the phosphate industry while poor people die from cancer.

While walking through the citrus belt of Central Florida, walkers met with Hispanic farm workers who talked over and over again about pesticide poisoning. We learned that drinking water is being contaminated by these chemicals.

Urbanization (whether in Miami, Orlando, Tampa, or Jacksonville) is creating massive amounts of pollution (from more and wider roads and millions of cars) that is getting into our underground water aquifer.

# The Animals Speak Out

## by W.B. Park

Good evening. We're here to try to convince you that unless you folks wake up, our whole eco system is going to crash. Agri-business and lawn sprinklers are draining our aquifers and swamps. DDT, dioxin, and a soup of other toxins are seeping into our drinking water and eating away our ozone protection. Mining and ranching interests slash and burn our jungles. Paper and lumber companies level whole forests in days. Developers concrete what's left. As a result, our source of oxygen is disappearing. Our topsoil is eroding. Whole species are in danger. The food chain has holes. Cancer, respiratory diseases, miscarriages, dropping sperm counts... I mean, how bad does it have to get before you people start trying to help?

Hello? Is anybody out there listening?

We held a protest in the Ocala National Forest where the Navy has had a bombing range since World War II. Once out in the middle of nowhere, the range is now being surrounded by urbanization.

Up in north Florida, in Perry, deadly dioxins are being dumped into the Fenholloway River by the Buckeye paper mill. The river carries the toxins from the plant right into the Gulf of Mexico where aquatic life is now dying as a result. We held a rally in front of the paper mill while standing in the pouring rain.

At each stop, local authorities talk about dilution. They admit that pollutants are reaching the aquifer, but insist that they are diluted when they enter the enormous underground water systems. But this is a lie because pollutants are entering the aquifer up and down the state in such vast amounts that they must certainly be having cumulative adverse impacts.

What we learned from the local people we met on the walk is that they want someone to stand up with them. They want someone to tell it like it is. They can't drink the water. They can't eat the fish. The birds are dying.

Our walk was led by Bobbie C. Billie, the spiritual leader of the Independent Traditional Seminole Nation. His family, still legally at war with the U.S. government, is the one holdout family within the Seminole people who never submitted to the reservation system. Bobbie was the only person who was able to walk every single step of the 700-mile walk. On the weekends, members of his family would join us for the walk. One high school teacher from Miami brought a busload of her students to begin the walk in the Everglades and ended up bringing them back virtually every other weekend as well.

At the end of the Walk for the Earth, about 600 people turned out from all over the state to march the last three miles to the State Capitol with us. Two days later, about 50-60 of us went into the capitol to lobby. Some of us held a day-long vigil inside the capitol rotunda, while others visited their representatives. One of our signs read, "The corporations control the government." Corporate lobbyists, running around with their cell phones, were not amused. But many capitol staffers came by and discreetly whispered, "You're right." The native people from South America who joined us played their magical flutes inside the rotunda, and people were drawn to us like snakes responding to charmers. It was an exciting and empowering day.

When you speak the truth in the heart of power, sparks literally fly. The Walk for the Earth: A Journey for Future Generations was a success. We saw that with our own eyes. We heard it from the public with our own ears. And now we must speak about it with our own voices.

If there is to be a future for our children then we must move now to protect what little natural life is left in Florida. We must stand before the government and the corporations and say "enough!" We must call for a moratorium on growth and development in Florida. If we don't, who will?

# CASSINI: A LOOK BACK
# AND A LOOK AHEAD

*"We are cups, constantly and quietly being filled. The trick is, knowing
how to tip ourselves over and let the beautiful stuff out."*

—Ray Bradbury

## Winter 1997, *Just Peace,* Florida Coalition Newsletter

The Cancel Cassini Campaign began three years ago when the Florida Coalition
first learned about the plans to launch 72 pounds of plutonium-238 from the space
center in 1997. During those years we slowly and steadily built an organizing core of
activists around the U.S. and in Europe who understood the issues of space nuclearization
and weaponization.[42] By the time the national media began to focus on the controversial nuclear space mission, just a few weeks before the launch, they were surprised to
see an alive global movement in motion.

It was always our strategy to go out and build a real grassroots effort to cancel
Cassini. We didn't try to go through the large and sometimes cumbersome national
groups first. We knew that if we educated and activated ordinary people, the big groups
would follow. An example of this was the Sierra Club's late but welcome resolution
opposing Cassini; however, it only came after their grassroots members had made it
happen.

In 1989 and 1990 when NASA launched the Galileo and Ulysses plutonium mis-
sions, respectively, not one member of Congress came forth to help us. This time, we
had over 20 members of the House of Representatives onboard and one U.S. senator,
John Kerry (D-MA). Many city and county governments (in California, Massachusetts,
North Carolina, Washington state, and Florida) passed resolutions opposing Cassini.
Even the Massachusetts House of Representatives called on President Clinton to cancel
Cassini.

We heard from sources inside the White House that they had received more calls
and letters on Cassini than on any other issue in U.S. history.[43]

This was made possible by the incredible support we got from all over the world.
One of my favorite stories is about the folks in Tasmania, Australia, who sent us word
that they had organized 1,000 faxes to Bill Clinton.

Our friends in Germany and England were especially active and helped spread the
issue to activists in other European countries. Thousands of postcards were sent from
the United Kingdom to the White House on behalf of our campaign.

The action was furious. Demonstrations were held in New York (300 people), Washington D.C. (200), San Francisco (500), Vermont (400), and Germany (200). Many, many smaller actions were held in cities and towns all over the U.S. and around the world. And, on October 4, over 1,000 people marched to the front gate of the Cape Canaveral Air Force Station, led by 87-year-old Peg McIntire from St. Augustine and the Grandmothers for Peace delegation.

On that day 27 people, including Peg, were arrested as they attempted to non-violently enter the base in an effort to sit on the Cassini launch pad. Others had been previously arrested at the White House in September, at NASA headquarters in Washington D.C., in Vermont and in London as they protested the plutonium launch.

Some individuals made extraordinary personal efforts. One man walked 1,000 miles from Baltimore to Cape Canaveral, talking to people about Cassini all along the way. A West Palm Beach lifeguard swam 13 miles in the Atlantic Ocean to bring attention to the cause and got great media coverage. As usual, New York journalist Karl Grossman was engaged non-stop, doing everything he could to support the campaign. Karl wrote countless articles, created videos, and did endless media interviews as we neared the time of the launch. Dr. Michio Kaku and Dr. Helen Caldicott made speaking trips to Florida to lend their support. Helen met with the editorial board at the *Florida Today* (space coast) newspaper.

A man by the name of Alan Kohn volunteered to help us. Alan had been the Emergency Preparedness Officer at NASA during the Galileo and Ulysses plutonium missions. By the time Cassini was to be launched Alan had retired and felt free to speak out. He told the *New York Times,* just prior to the launch, that NASA had no plan to contain and clean-up after a launch pad accident that released plutonium into the environment. He said the operating plan he had worked with during the two previous nuclear launches was a joke and was only intended to serve as reassurance to the public. Alan told us that a long-time family friend, working in the White House, had informed him that more people contacted Washington about Cassini than any other issue in U.S. history.

The phone in the Florida Coalition office rang non-stop in the three months prior to the plutonium launch. People were asking for space organizing packets so they could help spread the word. I particularly remember one woman who called from Detroit. She described herself as a single mother who worked as a waitress in a restaurant. She had read about Cassini in the newspaper and wanted to help.

Media calls were frequent and often a bit hostile as many reporters, who knew nothing about space issues, were given the story by their editors with an early evening deadline. They wanted to just defer to NASA's public relations department and print the party line, but our public opposition forced them to expand their articles just a bit. NASA and the Department of Energy public relations specialists always told the media there was no way the 72 pounds of deadly plutonium-238 on the space craft could ever be released. The Titanic was unsinkable as well!

But we had one thing on our side: The documents, including articles from space industry and U.S. Space Command publications. Karl Grossman taught us this. Show the media the documents, he would say. We gathered the materials by subscribing to

*Aviation Week & Space Technology* magazine and *Space News*. Our friends in Colorado Springs picked up the now famous Space Command *Vision for 2020* during the annual Space Foundation arms bazaar held in their community. By acknowledging that a pluto-nium release could be carried by the winds for a 60-mile radius, NASA's own environ-mental impact statement was damaging. These pieces, all put together, revealed the picture of U.S. plans for military control and nuclearization of space. All we had to do was get the overworked mainstream media reporters to read these documents before their deadlines! No easy task.

By the time Cassini was successfully launched, we had won a victory of sorts. With the segment on *CBS's 60 Minutes* as the icing on the cake, we knew that we had achieved, even surpassed, our goal. We had made people seriously consider and debate the nukes in space issue. For instance, in an *Orlando Sentinel* call-in poll just days before the launch, 71% of the 1,257 respondents said "No" to the Cassini launch. And those were folks from the Central Florida "space community" speaking!

In 1992 I brought the idea of creating an international network of groups opposing the nuclearization and weaponization of space to the Florida Coalition, to journalist Karl Grossman and to our friends in Colorado Springs, CO, (home of the U.S. Space Command). Together we organized a founding meeting of the Global Network Against Weapons & Nuclear Power in Space in Washington D.C.[44] At this meeting we shared the bits of information about plans for space control and domination that we each had access to. We decided that it would be important that we meet each year to keep the communication lines open, and to support one another by spreading our annual meet-ings around to the different communities that played a key role in the space warfare infrastructure. Between 1992–1998 I coordinated the work of the Global Network as well as the Florida Coalition for Peace & Justice.

In 1998, I left the Florida Coalition in order to give my undivided attention to the Global Network. It was clear that the space issue needed full-time coordination if we were to stand any chance of stopping Star Wars.

# AN INSIDE LOOK AT SPACE CONGRESS

*"In the counsels of Government, we must guard against the acquisition of unwarranted influence, whether sought or unsought, by the Military Industrial Complex. The potential for the disastrous rise of misplaced power exists, and will persist. We must never let the weight of this combination endanger our liberties or democratic processes."*

—President Dwight Eisenhower

I spent $50 to attend the *36th Space Congress: Countdown to the Millennium* being held at Cape Canaveral, Florida from April 28-29, 1999. The meeting was sponsored by NASA, Boeing, Lockheed-Martin, the Air Force and other such luminaries.

I chose to attend the event because on two of the days they were focusing on what I see as the two key directions of the space program—military space and Mars.

A three-hour plenary session called "Military Space for a New Century" was chaired by Brig. Gen. Randall Starbuck, Commander of the 45th Space Wing at nearby Patrick AFB (which is also in charge of Cape Canaveral Air Force Station). Several times during the session, Starbuck reminded the 300-400 people in attendance that on April 30 they should stick their heads outside to see the exciting Titan IV rocket launch the Air Force was planning. Little did Starbuck know at the time that the troubled Titan IV would fail to place the military satellite (Milstar) into the proper orbit, rendering the mission a total failure. Three Titan mishaps in a row ensued (only $3 billion wasted).

Starbuck and two other Air Force officers unveiled their new Vision for 2025 (no copies were available), that calls for more of the same. The "full exploitation of space" using the resources of the military, aerospace corporations, national labs and academia was the bottom line. Starbuck reminded the eager attendees that at the time only 9% of the total Air Force budget went for militarization of space, but they hoped to push the number to 20% in the near future.

Funding was one barrier to their drive for total "domination for the war fighter." Another obstacle, according to Col. Tom Clark, was that certain "policies and treaties" were in the way. He concluded that "some treaties may need to be renegotiated. We should not ignore the potential for combat in space." During the questions & answer period Col. Clark, responding to my written question about testing and deployment of Anti-Satellite (ASAT) weapons, stated that deployment would be ready around 2008, but this issue was "politically sensitive." Col. Clark went on to say that ultimately the U.S. would "need an event to drive the public to support ASAT deployment. But it will happen. We are now talking, planning, doing research and development. Someone will attack one of our systems."

Col. Clark's last sentence was stated with such certainty that I had the cold feeling that somehow he knew the who, how and when of this future attack that would enable the U.S. to finally push beyond the "policies and treaties" to full deployment of ASAT's.

In the meantime, Col. Clark assured the crowd that we have the "defensive" Ballistic Missile Defense" (BMD) system (just approved by Congress). It is "obvious that dual use is clear" he said, referring to the fact that weapons in space could be fired either defensively or offensively.

In other areas of "space control evolution" the war fighters, as they constantly call themselves, reminded us that the U.S. now has 26 ground-based space surveillance stations. These "down link" facilities, spread all over the planet, receive the data from satellites in split-second "real time" and send it directly to U.S. Space Command HQ in Colorado. Recognizing that in a full-blown war these sites would themselves be targets, the Air Force now intends to reduce the size of these stations with new generations of computer technology and our tax dollars.

Gen. Starbuck concluded the military space plenary by responding to a question about the future of the Air Force in space. Some in Congress have called for the creation of a separate "space force." Starbuck said the Air Force was opposed to the idea. The Air Force, he said, views space as seamless; air and space must go together, not be divided. He countered by saying they should become the "Aerospace Force."

# MARS OR BUST

The other area of major focus at Space Congress was the mission to Mars.

NASA currently has a couple of spacecraft on the way to Mars. The Mars Global Surveyor mission began mapping the planet's surface in March, 1999.

One of the most eye-opening speeches was delivered by James Ball, Director of the Kennedy Space Center Visitor Complex (tourist trap). Ball reported that each year three million people, most of whom are children, visit the complex. His mission at the tourist facility was, he said, to "prepare the way for us to go to Mars by increasing the public's enthusiasm for the mission." The complex is undergoing renovation in order that the Mars mission receive the highest promotion possible.

When you consider the amount of money it would take to put "manned colonies" on Mars you can see why NASA and the aerospace industry are working so hard to convince the public of the efficacy of Mars colonization. (They refused several times to answer questions regarding anticipated costs).

But besides the money there is one other big problem: propulsion! Mars is far away. To get there they need a particularly powerful propulsion system.[45]

In a plenary entitled Beyond Shuttle: Continued Access to Space, I asked for a report on the status of the nuclear rocket to Mars. Russ Turner, an executive with the United Space Alliance responded that the nuclear rocket was "a bigger political question than a technical question. I predict there will be political problems." Obviously he was referring to our long opposition to nuclear power in space. But just to make things clear, another panelist, Rick Stephens, Vice-President of Boeing Reusable Space Systems added, "The last one was Cassini and a lot of you lived through that one." All in all there were 3-4 direct references to our work against Cassini during my two days at the event.

But in a workshop called Space Systems—Mars and Beyond, attended by well over 100 people, the issue of nuclear rockets to Mars would not die. Michael Houts, from the Marshall Space Flight Center in Huntsville, Alabama made it clear that the "key to future manned Mars missions" was the nuclear rocket. The audience was in near consensus that NASA needed to work harder to get the visitors at the space center visitor complex to support the mission to Mars as quickly as possible. That meant "remove the barriers of money and politics" right away!

In the second plenary, I was actually able to get two of my written questions answered. My second one was "How can we ensure that the bad seed of war, greed and environmental degradation not be taken with us as we move into space?" Now I must admit that I never thought this question would be read to the assembled audience. But David Gump, President of Luna Corp. read it to the entire crowd, and I smiled with glee as I listened to the chorus of groans from around the big meeting room. (The audience was filled with military space personnel, NASA employees and aerospace corporation executives.)

Anyway, Mr. Gump responded to my question by saying, "First, about the environmental degradation: You can't hurt the moon and asteroids because they are already dead." Luna Corp. is planning to put a nuclear-powered rover on the moon to search for water and minerals. Then Gump concluded, "Greed? I'm in favor of greed." The audience laughed. Gump didn't have anything to say about the war part of the question.

# REPORT ON TRIP TO VIEQUES

*"Only those who will risk going too far can possibly find out how far one can go."*

—T. S. Eliot

On November 4-8, 1999 I traveled with three other Floridians to Puerto Rico at the invitation of Victor Rodriguez , a leader of the Global Network (GN) affiliate called Comité Contra las Experimentaciones Ambientales. The three other persons were Joe McIntire, and Don & Matt Lockard all from St Augustine. The Comité Contra las Experimentaciones Ambientales is the organization that led the protests against NASA in 1998-99 that forced cancellation of the Coqui II rocket launches in the town of Vega Baja. The Coqui II were a series of atmospheric experiments by NASA. The rockets released chemicals into different layers of the atmosphere in order to test their effects on communications and radar signals. Protests forced NASA to close down the operation after eight tests even though 11 had been scheduled.

Upon arrival in Puerto Rico our four-person delegation met with several key Puerto Rican activists to discuss the content of a news conference at which we would be speaking the following day. The news conference, held at a beautiful cultural center in San Juan, featured representatives from the Comité Contra Las Experimentaciones Ambientales, el Proyecto Caribeño de Justicia y Paz, Misión Industrial de Puerto Rico, the Florida Coalition for Peace and Justice (FCPJ), and the GN. The content of the news conference covered the existence of nuclear weapons in Puerto Rico (despite denials by the U.S. Navy) and the plans to put weapons in space by the U.S. Space Command. The largest paper in Puerto Rico, "El Mundo," covered the event and ran a good story with a color picture the next day. The top-ranked TV station in Puerto Rico, *TPR*, also featured the news conference and ran the story two days in a row.

The next day our delegation, plus a large group from the Congreso Nacional Hostosiano, took the one-hour ferry ride from Fajardo to Vieques. Hundreds of people were on the ferry, some going to a baseball game on the island, others just visiting, but many going for protests against the Navy bombing range on the beautiful island. I sat next to New York City Councilwoman Olga Mendez who was part of a 75-person New York political delegation going to Vieques. Also on the ferry was an old man named Carmelo who was born on the island and remained one of the leaders in the struggle to stop the 50-year naval bombing of Vieques. He told me how he trained wasps to attack Marines when they invaded Vieques on maneuvers, and how he dispersed poison ivy dust, which gets into the troops' clothes and drives them crazy.The Navy controls about three-quarters of Vieques. The people live near the center of the small, elongated island, with the military bombing ranges on either side of them. From the port in Vieques, we took a 30-foot fishing boat with two 200 horsepower engines on the 20-minute rough ride to the protest camps inside the military zone, occupied by the protesters. Along the short journey, we passed 3-4 other fully-loaded boats heading back to the port, with Puerto Rican flags flying and people waving to us.

My first reaction when we landed on the beach was awe at the sheer beauty of the water and the rock cliffs and mountains. My second reaction was disgust at the evidence of bomb parts in the water and on the land. But the most remarkable thing was to see the Puerto Rican flags flying from every direction: Up on top of one hill, where there was a camp of resisters; down the beach at another camp; on a faraway mountain top, another. People were taking over the island. The Navy must have been going crazy!

I was to stay in the new "school" recently built by the Congreso Nacional. The chickee-style shelter with a tin roof was just next door to the small chapel, also newly erected. Immediately after we arrived, people began installing the solar electric system they carried over from San Juan. Within a couple of hours three compact fluorescent light bulbs were working.

I learned the U.S. had declared it would send in 350 Spanish-speaking federal marshals in December to arrest those occupying Vieques in opposition to Navy bombing. On the ferry New York City Councilwoman Mendez told me she would return to do civil disobedience (CD) if this happened, even though she had never believed in CD as a political tactic.

Just down the beach, a camp had been set up by a group of teachers from the village on Vieques. (The tiny village is surrounded on both sides by bombing ranges.) They were cooking fish and offered me food and drink. They told the story about Angel Rodriguez Cristóbal who had been hanged just 20 years before in a Tallahassee, Florida jail after having been arrested for non-violent CD on Vieques. Twenty-one people had been arrested on that occasion, among them a Catholic bishop.

I also learned that 67% of Puerto Rican people receive food stamps. At the same time, K-Mart, Sears and J.C. Penney stores sold more products in Puerto Rico than in 30 other states. Puerto Ricans were dependent on both the U.S. and our corporate masters. The "colonization" process has had a staggering effect on the people and the environment of the "commonwealth." Nevertheless, the spirit of independence remained strong. The resistance on Vieques is but one example. On Vieques, I was asked to do a presentation at the school about the GN's work on space. With Joe McIntire ably translating, I spoke about U.S. plans for control and domination in space and showed the 20 people present the U.S. Space Command's *Vision for 2020* brochure[46] and the industry poster of a space-based laser weapon firing at targets on the Earth, with the U.S. flag flying overhead. I talked about the connections between space and Vieques, saying that the U.S. intended to make the whole earth and space above a colony, like we have done to Puerto Rico. I later learned that this workshop was the first such event in the school on Vieques. It was an honor to have helped open the school.

The next day was unforgettable. Victor took our delegation on a long hike, up the mountaintop to one camp and then down the beach to another. We visited the camp of a

National Congress senator from the Puerto Rican Independence Party who had been on Vieques for the past six months. As we walked about, we saw the enormous evidence of years of destruction on the island. Bombs — exploded and unexploded—were everywhere. Wetlands were drained and bombed. Trucks, tanks, and planes used as targets, were scattered everywhere. One tank was being used to hold up a tarp for shelter at one hilltop camp. As we looked out over the beautiful ocean beyond Vieques we saw a U.S. navy nuclear submarine in the near distance.

When it was time to leave the island our fishing boat anchor got caught on a bomb on the ocean floor. Our captain very carefully worked the anchor free and you could see the fear on the faces of the passengers. We saw bombs sticking up out of the water near the shore and we saw tiny islands just off Vieques that had been blasted to bits. In fact, the years of Navy bombardment had destroyed the endangered coral reefs all around Vieques.

On the mainland, our friends Victor and Juan Rosario showed us around old San Juan that, except for the cars and the fresh paint on the buildings, reminded me of Havana, Cuba. One huge fountain with several statues of people and nature was a striking symbol of Puerto Rican nationalism. The statue and fountain had been commissioned to celebrate Columbus' discovery of the new world 500 years before. The artist had revealed that the centerpiece of the statue, a woman on a rock with arms raised to the sky and holding two eagle feathers, meant that she was taking the feathers off the U.S. eagle. Signs of that pesky spirit of independence once again. Our friends in Puerto Rico urged activists from all over the world to join them on Vieques as soon as possible to help block any attempts to remove them from the island:[47] They said, "it was very easy to get there and once there all you need is a sleeping bag and some food and water to share. You will be made to feel most welcome on this otherwise tropical paradise. Be sure to bring your bathing suit!"

# JOURNEY TO NORTHWEST & ALASKA

On November 6, 2001 I concluded a two-week speaking tour of Oregon, Washington and Alaska.

Michael Carrigan at Oregon Peaceworks ably coordinated my visit to Portland, Florence, Eugene, Hood River, Corvalis, and Salem in that state. I spoke directly to over 450 people in Oregon and did two one-hour radio interviews in Portland. In Eugene, I did a third one-hour radio interview as well. I was able to speak to students at Portland State University, Oregon State University, the University of Oregon and Linn-Benton Community College.

From there I headed for Olympia, Washington, where I was hosted by our dear friend, Holly Gwinn Graham (who wrote the song, "We're Planning a War in Space.") She and I did a two-hour show on Evergreen State University's public radio station, where we talked about Star Wars, and she sang a couple of peace songs. That evening I spoke to a group in town that Holly had organized.

Next I visited Seattle where I spoke at a meeting of people brought together by members of the Northwest Disarmament Coalition. There I met with local leaders Mary Hanson and Geov Parrish as well to discuss the need to broaden organizing of "missile defense" to include Theatre Missile Defense (TMD), the space-based laser and the need to defund Star Wars research and development.

The next stage of the trip was to Alaska with stops in Anchorage, Fairbanks, and Kodiak Island.

In Anchorage, I was hosted by Alaska PIRG, where Steve Cleary and Stephen Conn kept me busy for the next 48 hours with two TV interviews, four radio interviews, two debates with a GOP candidate for governor (who drives an $80,000 military humvee with a license plate that reads WAR), and an evening presentation at the local library. In addition, Steve Cleary and I had a great meeting with two members of the *Anchorage Daily News* editorial board.

In Fairbanks, which is the city nearest to the proposed National Missile Defense (NMD) deployment site at Fort Greely, Stacey Fritz and Lynn DiFilippo (No Nukes North) arranged for me to do two more TV interviews and three radio interviews. A long report appeared in the local paper after I spoke to the 90 folks who turned out at the University of Alaska. It was fascinating to watch the people arrive at the university auditorium for my talk. Never had I seen people so enchanted with each other. The sparks were flying into the air. People exchanged greetings as if they had not seen another person in a very long time. I figured the long, harsh, Alaskan winters made people more friendly and excited about getting out of their homes to visit with others.

My last stop was beautiful Kodiak Island, the place where the Pentagon will be doing Star Wars experiments in coming years. Stacy Studebaker and Carolyn Heitman took me on a four-hour drive to the far end of the island to see the Kodiak Rocket Launch Facility that was "sold" to the people of the island as a "civilian" launch facility. Now the truth has emerged and the Ballistic Missile Defense Organization (BMDO) will be launching 20 missiles from this location in the next 4-5 years. During the drive, we saw countless numbers of bald eagles along the pristine river banks where salmon run during spawning season. Launching toxic rockets, from what local residents call "Space Pork Kodiak,"[48] will seriously jeopardize the environment and the local fishing industry. Several fisherman were among the 60 residents who turned out for my talk. The mayor and a councilman also came. The local newspaper ran a long advance interview with me, and the Kodiak Rocket Launch Information Group purchased ads in the local paper that featured a cartoon of a Kodiak bear nailing a "Fallout Shelter" sign to its cave as a rocket crashes in the background.

This trip to the northwest, far from the Global Network's home office in Florida, was an important link for our movement to keep space for peace. Once again, it is incredibly encouraging to see people in far off places like Kodiak Island working to stop the nuclearization and weaponization of space. It is also encouraging for them to know of the growing activity around the world, such as our recent October 13 day of protest that included events in 19 countries and at over 115 locations (including actions in Oregon, Washington, and Alaska.)

# TRIP TO NEW AND OLD ENGLAND

*"To climb steep hills requires slow pace at first."*

- William Shakespeare

This trip, from September 23 to October 8, 2002 took me to Massachusetts, Connecticut, Rhode Island, Maine, Wisconsin and the United Kingdom (UK).

On September 23 I arrived in Western Massachusetts and was hosted on this leg by AFSC staffer Jo Comerford. During this trip (Great Barrington and Pittsfield) I spoke at the Quaker Friends Meeting House and at Berkshire Community College. Jo also arranged three radio interviews, two of which were on stations that beam their signal throughout the state and Vermont. While I was at the AFSC office I noticed that Jo and others were faxing a big stack of letters to Sen. John Kerry (D-MA) opposing the impending war in Iraq. I asked Jo how their effort was faring. She told me that Sen. Kerry would not meet with folks from the peace movement, and they feared he would support the war. (In the end Kerry did support Bush's invasion of Iraq.)

From there I went on to speak at Trinity College in Hartford, CT in an event organized by Political Science Professor Brigitte Schulz.

On September 25 I was back in the care of another AFSC worker, Anna Galand. She had scheduled talks for me in Falmouth, MA. and Providence, R.I. that day. The two talks (Falmouth Public Library and Brown University) were separated by a one-hour live phone interview on statewide Wisconsin public radio. While I did the radio interview (promoting an upcoming space conference) over 900 people were gathering on the steps of the state capital in Providence to protest Bush's plans for war in Iraq.

The next day I drove to Portland, Maine where I joined a very diverse demonstration in the heart of downtown at 5:00 p.m. to protest the impending war. The gathering turned into a spontaneous and thrilling march through the streets of the busy downtown, with a surprised but cooperative police escort. Traffic was halted all around and people on the sidewalks and in office buildings and local shops gave us a remarkably warm reception. Following the march, I met for dinner with Sally Breen and Karen Wainberg of Peace Action Maine to discuss the impending move of the Global Network office to Maine.

I next headed to Milwaukee, WI. to speak at a daylong regional conference called "Keep Space Safe" held at Marquette University. I was hosted by Arnold Kaufman who had previously been to GN space conferences in Cleveland and Berkeley, and had worked to help Milwaukee Peace Action organize a similar one in that important Midwestern city. The Milwaukee conference concluded with a pledge by the participants to work on Sen. Russ Feingold (D-WI) to get him to introduce a version of the Kucinich "Outer Space Protection Act" in the Senate, where a sponsor has yet to surface.

When I arrived at the Milwaukee airport the next morning to fly home, the local Sunday newspaper carried a full page advertisement (with hundreds of signatures) calling for NO U.S. WAR AGAINST IRAQ. Once again I was seeing the evidence of lively and growing public sentiment opposing war. Polls were showing intense national and international opposition to war. Peace activists everywhere maintained that there were no weapons of mass destruction in Iraq, that the weapons inspections over many years had indeed worked by dismantling the Iraqi arsenal.[49]

After returning home for two days rest I flew to England to join the Yorkshire Campaign for Nuclear Disarmament (CND) for several activities during the October 4-11 Keep Space for Peace Week.[50]

My host, Dave Webb, a leader in Yorkshire CND and the GN's webmaster, took Stacey Fritz (No Nukes North in Alaska) and me to Harrogate to do a presentation to the Menwith Hill Forum. We were joined on the panel by Dave Knight, former chair of National CND and currently chair of the GN's Advisory Committee.

Menwith Hill is a U.S. satellite spy base now being upgraded with new technology to participate in the Star Wars program. The UK peace movement has made ending their country's participation in the U.S. Star Wars program a top priority.

Earlier that day I had been the guest of the Peace & Emergency Planning Department of the City of Leeds and accompanied their staff to two city-sponsored functions that marked the 50th anniversary of British nuclear tests in Australia. The U.K. atomic veterans, like their counterparts in the U.S. who were used as guinea pigs, have never been acknowledged or compensated by the British government. Several widows placed wreaths at a marker to honor their husbands whose lives were cut short by cancers caused by their proximity to the 1952 above ground nuclear tests. Leeds city staffers also organized two radio interviews for me that day on regional Yorkshire commercial radio stations.

On October 4, Dave Webb and I took the train to Sheffield where we joined a noon-time march at the university to protest the recent signing of a 15 million pound deal with Boeing Corporation to involve the institution of higher learning in "aerospace" technology development. A group of students and local activists marched to the vice-chancellor's office to present a letter opposing the high-tech deal, knowing that inevitably Sheffield University will be drawn into Star Wars work, as Boeing is now the top space weapons contractor. I was interviewed over cell phone by the regional Yorkshire newspaper just as we prepared the march. Later I spoke to those assembled at the vice-chancellor's office. I told them about University of Santa Clara (CA.) students and their recent hunger strike to draw attention to huge Lockheed-Martin "donations" to pull their campus into the space weapons gambit.

Later that day, many of us joined the Women in Black anti-war vigil at the Sheffield Town Hall as the streets swelled with people heading home after work. My favorite banner at the vigil read, "Abolish war and replace it with something nice." Once again the response was positive, as many Brits were aware of the 400,000 people who had marched days before in London calling on Tony Blair to get off George W. Bush's lap. Polls in the U.K. show over 70% of the citizenry are opposed to the war.

During this same time, Blair's Labor Party had just concluded its national party conference, and despite the presence of Bill Clinton, giving Blair his "total" support, 42% of Labor delegates voted for a resolution calling on Blair to back away from war. (Many others were sympathetic to the peace resolution, but didn't want to offend Blair, I was told.)

On October 5-6 Stacey Fritz and I attended the main event of our U.K. trip, the "International Conference on Missile Defense, Globalization and the Militarization of Space," organized by Yorkshire CND. Among the speakers was an Inuit leader from Greenland, where the U.S. has the Thule radar facility, which also must be upgraded to help direct Star Wars. Actually, Kuupik Kleist is one of two elected leaders from Greenland who serve in the Danish parliament. Denmark essentially controls Greenland. Kuupik spoke about how the Inuit people were removed from their native lands years ago so the U.S. could build the large base in the north of their country. His leftwing political party opposes upgrading the Thule installation and wants it closed.[51]

Among the speakers at the two-day conference were elected officials representing the Green Party, Labor and the Liberal-Democrats. The Lib-Dems (as they call them in the U.K.) politician told this joke: "Who gave George W. Bush the right to be the policeman of the world?" Answer: "His brother!"

On October 7 Dave Webb, Dave Knight, Stacey and I drove to Fylingdales in the Yorkshire moors, a U.S.-constructed space radar facility that sits in the middle of their beautiful national park, surrounded by fields of heather. There we met with local leaders of the Fylingdales Action Network who have been protesting plans to upgrade the installation for participation in Star Wars. We were welcomed by the head of security, a nice man named Jimmy, who gleefully told us he regularly checks the GN's website and recognized Stacey from it. (She later gave him a No Nukes North T-shirt which he gladly accepted.)

We asked if we could meet with the "Wing Commander," the Royal Air Force (RAF) official in charge of the facility.[52] After a 10-minute wait, the commander came out to the front gate to talk with us. The RAF maintains that Fylingdales is not an American facility even though the U.S. built it, will pay to upgrade it, and lists it as a U.S. Space Command facility. It's done this way to maintain the illusion of British authority rather than subservience to the U.S. Pentagon.

The group of us questioned the commander, while two reporters from local newspapers snapped photos and took shorthand of the lively discussion. I asked the commander about health effects from the massive facility, knowing that a similar PAVE PAWS radar on Cape Cod, MA has become controversial for emitting dangerous radiation waves that reportedly causes cancers. The RAF officer, a son of the British elite, stated that the emissions were within acceptable levels, set by a government board, who are all, he reluctantly admitted, appointed by the same politicians that now support Star Wars.

After the visit to Fylingdales, we had tea and biscuits at the 100-year-old stone house of one of the local peace activists, who lives nearby. Following that, a "quick nip around" to the seaside town of Whitby for fish, chips and mushy peas, and then the four of us headed back to Leeds.

The next morning we took a nerve-racking train trip to the Manchester airport. Trains all over the system were being cancelled as Maggie Thatcher's "privatization" of the once-proud British rail system has come back to haunt the country. The rail system, now controlled by several private corporations, is an example of what happens when the basic public services of a nation are dismantled and sold to the highest bidder. Education and health care in the U.K. are now under attack, as well.

The visit to England was inspiring, and once again I'm filled with great hope as I see the resistance to war on Earth and in space growing worldwide. Britain's long history of peasant struggle against feudalism, a slow, but steady progress, reminds me that each of us represents a stone in the honored battle of David versus Goliath. While the challenge at times can feel daunting, I know I carry the spirit of those who came before me in my heart and take courage from their sacrifices and their joy. I will keep on and know that all our efforts, added together, are changing the world, one Jimmy, the gate guard, at a time!

# COLUMBIA SHUTTLE ACCIDENT

*"To see what is in front of one's nose requires a constant struggle."*

—George Orwell

On January 31, 2003 I flew to Phoenix, Arizona where I was hosted by Celeste Howard who arranged my first speaking tour ever in Arizona. The day after I spoke to local peace & justice folks, I was preparing to leave for Tucson when I heard that the Columbia shuttle had burned up on reentry to Earth and spread its debris over large portions of the states of Texas and Louisiana.

The media calls immediately began pouring into our office back in Florida. Mary Beth Sullivan directed them to me while she worked with Karl Grossman on drafting a Global Network (GN) news release. On the two-hour ride to Tucson with Celeste, I did some media interviews on her cell phone. The *Arab News* gave us extensive coverage on the shuttle accident. Once it was posted on their web site, it was picked up by other media outlets including the *St. Petersburg Times.* Our main points to the media where that the aerospace industry was cutting back on safety measures for shuttle flights as they increased profits by laying-off workers. We also made the case that space technology can and does fail. This, we warned, should give us pause as we consider launching nuclear power into space. We asked people to imagine the environmental disaster if the Columbia, shown on TV spreading its debris over Texas and Louisiana, had nuclear devices on-board.

In Tucson, Jack Cohen Joppa, publisher of the *Nuclear Resister,*[53] coordinated my talk to a filled room at a local church. He also cooked wonderful meals during my visit. Tucson is the home of Raytheon, where the hit-to-kill mechanism for the "national missile defense" system is being built. Jack gave Celeste and me a driving tour of the local air base that is the "graveyard" for generations of U.S. military planes. Literally miles of these planes bear witness to the wasted tax dollars and growing poverty in our world as a result of these misplaced priorities.

My next stop was Albuquerque, N.M. to hold two days of protests at the *20th Annual Symposium on Space Nuclear Power and Propulsion* hosted by the University of New Mexico (UNM) Nuclear Engineering Department. The night before the vigils began, local hosts Bob Anderson and Jeanne Pahls organized a well-attended community event where Bob and I spoke about the plans to move the arms race into space. Just days before, Bob had provided documented evidence to the UNM student newspaper, *Daily Lobo,* that the school's Nuclear Engineering Department had been working on space nuclear reactors for over 20 years under contract to the Pentagon. This was an important disclosure. It broke through the cloud of denials whereby all parties had maintained that nuclear reactors for space-based weapons were not a reality.

By this time, the media calls about the shuttle accident were pouring in. Bob and I stood out in front of the space symposium protesting and simultaneously doing radio and newspaper interviews. A few times I had to go into the hotel lobby to find a quiet space to do a long interview on *KPFA* (Berkeley), the nationally syndicated *Peter Werbe Show*; a Montreal radio station; *WBAI* (New York); or others. On February 3, GN board members Karl Grossman, Dr. Michio Kaku and I appeared on *Democracy Now* with Amy Goodman for an hour-long interview. This opened the door to many more media calls.

Karl Grossman told me that he too had done interviews non-stop for days, after the Columbia accident. It was clear to us that the national/international media were beginning to recognize the Global Network as a valuable resource on the space issue. It was encouraging that our message of stopping the nuclearization and weaponization of space was getting out into the public consciousness. To underscore this point, our web site, which typically averages 150 hits a day, had over 1,000 hits in a 24-hour period following the Columbia tragedy.

One evening, while in Albuquerque, Bob Anderson and I watched the late night news and witnessed men dressed in hazardous-material suits (including oxygen tanks on their backs and gas masks) using Geiger counters to wand residents in Texas who had come in contact with Columbia debris. Placed in the context of the warnings coming from local authorities in the region who claimed they were told by NASA that there were radioactive sources on-board the Columbia, we were devastated at the possibilities. We later learned from a reporter, who was told by the Environmental Protection Agency, that there was radioactive Americium[54] on-board. What was the Americium being used for? How much of it was there? NASA refused to comment. We speculate that the toxic Americium was powering a small reactor that was used to perform one of several military experiments during the space mission.

NASA had intended to hold a "Town Hall Meeting" about "Project Prometheus" at the Albuquerque symposium. Project Prometheus is the name of the nuclear rocket powered by reactors under development at NASA's Cleveland, Ohio and Huntsville, Alabama centers as well as at the UNM and University of Florida Nuclear Engineering Departments. Prometheus is part of George W. Bush's $3 billion "Nuclear Systems Initiative" that will dramatically expand research and development of space nuclear launches. When we first heard of the Town Meeting, we requested entry and were told it was only open to those attending the symposium. The night before the event, Bob and I prepared a news release with the headline "Town Denied Entry Into NASA Nuclear Town Hall Meeting" and faxed it around to the local media. In the release, we listed the key questions that we intended to ask and stated that local residents were indeed going to enter the "closed" event. The next morning the local media began calling the space symposium organizers about how they were going to respond to our plans, and by midday, they had cancelled the town hall meeting, citing the Columbia accident as the reason. Hardly!

In the end, the Columbia disaster made the point that space technology can and does fail. When you mix nuclear payloads into the equation you are asking for trouble. There is nothing like personal experience. People all over the planet can now see with their minds' eye the long path of debris covering several states in the southwestern part of the U.S. NASA, the Department of Energy and the Pentagon would be wise not to go forward with their dangerous agenda to move nuclear power and war into the heavens. The public is beginning to catch onto their plan.

After a one-day trip back to Florida, just enough time to wash clothes, Mary Beth and I headed to Portland, Maine for a one-week working vacation in that snowy wonderland. We were hosted by Sally Breen, a leader of Peace Action Maine, and her husband Keith Williams. Our plane had to land in New York City because of bad weather so we, and three other Mainers from the flight, rented a car and made the seven-hour drive to Portland.[55]

While in the La Guardia airport in New York, we ran into Mel Martinez, who was the Secretary of Housing and Urban Development under George W. Bush.[56] I coached Little League baseball with Mel when our kids were young. His family left Cuba after the revolution, his father had money, and he was obviously determined to make "good" in the USA. I told him I was disappointed that he had chosen to join the Bush administration. His reply: "You have to do what you have to do." Here was a guy who wanted to be accepted by the political elite. So he did what was expected of him.

On February 8, I had the privilege to speak to 250 people assembled for the Peace Action Maine annual supper. This event was very special for us as Mary Beth and I planned to move to southern Maine in the coming months of 2003. We were able to meet many of the key activists in the state.[57]

During the week of house hunting in Maine, I stayed busy with local radio interviews and a speaking gig at the University of Southern Maine. I also did an hour-long interview from Maine on the nationally-syndicated right-wing *Michael Medved Show*. Expecting to be torn to shreds, I actually held my own. After hearing of my years as an organizer in the peace and social justice movements, Medved asked if I'd ever had a real job. My answer that I had been in the military during the Vietnam War, where I became a peace activist, stopped him short.

# TRIAL FOR OBEDIENCE TO THE FUTURE

*"Our scientific power has outrun our spiritual power. We have guided missiles and misguided men."*

—Martin Luther King, Jr.

On March 30, 2003, I flew to Denver, Colorado to attend the trial of three Dominican Sisters, Ardeth Platte, Carol Gilbert and Jackie Hudson, who were ultimately found guilty of sabotage and injury to government property for their October, 2002 *Sacred Earth and Space Plowshares* citizens' weapons inspection of a Minuteman nuclear missile silo in Colorado. The judge would not allow them to talk about international law and the Nuremberg defense, their reasons for the action. The nuns clearly proved that their action was a symbolic one that was intended to open hearts, minds, and doors. Two military officers admitted that the action had not, in the end, interfered with the "defense of the nation," but the military and the court made a big deal about the amount of "damage" the sisters had done to the outer fence that surrounds the underground missile silo. They had cut a 30 foot section out of the long fence so that the world could see that the U.S. has weapons of mass destruction.

The evening before the trial began I spoke, along with Elizabeth McAllister (wife of the late Catholic anti-war activist Phil Berrigan) and Bill Sulzman (from Citizens for Peace in Space in Colorado Spring), at a well-attended Festival of Hope held at a local church. I recalled how Ardeth had spoken at our Global Network annual conference the previous May in Berkeley, California and she had told us that we in the U.S. have become excellent killers, "We can kill fast and we can kill slow," she said. The Minuteman would qualify as the fast version and the steady, nagging hunger of the Iraqi people is the slow version.

In the courtroom, the military and the prosecution sprang a few last-minute surprises that were objected to by defense attorneys. But the judge, a recent Bush appointee, was not in the mood for justice. After spending nearly the whole week at the trial, I had to leave at mid-day on Friday just when the sisters began their closing arguments. They spoke of their years of work for social justice, and how seeing the poor and working class robbed of social services, led to their decision to tell the truth, that President Dwight Eisenhower's warning about the takeover of our democracy by the military-industrial complex had come to pass. In the end, one juror held out for a few hours but withered under the steady barrage of expectations from the legal system. The sentence will be handed down in July. The three sisters face 30 years for the dastardly crime of trying to sound the alarm that the gates of hell have been sprung open. I left with the hope that their action would shake many of us up, and make us half as courageous as they have been.[58]

On April 7, 2003 I traveled to Los Angeles for a week-long speaking tour in Southern California organized by GN members Cris Gutierrez and Randy Ziglar who live in Santa Monica. My first day began with a live interview on the *KPFK Morning Show* talking about how space was directing the war in Iraq and about plans for future control and domination of the Earth via space technology. This widely-heard Pacifica radio program gave me a chance to promote my tour itinerary, and at each subsequent stop I heard from folks who had come as a result of hearing the radio interview. That same day I joined another activist on a panel at Santa Monica High School for a teach-in on the war that was attended by about 120 students. Their impassioned testimony had recently helped convince their city government to pass a resolution opposing the war. That evening, I spoke to a good-size audience at a local church in Santa Monica. Two radio stations, including a black station from South Central Los Angeles, covered the event.

Randy does not like cars and has not had one for many years. A retired beach lifeguard, he prides himself on his public transit habits and his urban gardening. He is also an excellent cook, and with each visit (this is now my third to their home), I've had a chance to taste his wonderful creations (like the egg foo yung burrito). Cris works as a public education consultant and keeps busy with a whirlwind schedule that includes much anti-war protesting.

Randy rented a car so we could get to several outlying talks in Northridge, Santa Barbara, and La Verne (in San Bernardino County). The traffic was intense as we drove to each of the talks and underscored the need for more public transportation, especially in such a heavily-populated region.

On the last day we attended a vigil in Claremont. About 60 anti-war protestors shared the four corners of a busy intersection with 20 pro-war folks. One 13-year-old boy, holding a large "We support our troops" sign, stood next to me for a while. I asked him how he felt about the fact that we had bombed innocent civilians in Iraq. He answered that, "It's their problem; they had a bad president." I then asked him if another country, for instance Canada, didn't like our president, did it have the right to bomb the USA? "That's a DUMB question. Canada is part of the United States!," he replied. I urged him to ask his teacher about Canada when he returned to school.

My host for the last talk I did in La Verne, Marjorie Mikels, is an attorney who ran for Congress in the last national election. She ran as a Democrat when no one else would take on Rep. David Dreier, (Republican chair of the powerful House rules committee). Marjorie got 37% of the vote in the election and said that neither the state nor the national Democratic party gave her any help. San Bernardino County reminded me a lot of Florida. Agribusiness, weapons corporations and military installations are the predominant economic forces, and conservatives control local politics. Folks wondered what they could do to impact the thinking of the local citizenry. I told them two key things: first, everyone in the room should run for some office in the next national election cycle—from local to national offices—and they should run a coordinated campaign, each talking about the same four or five key issues. In other words, they should use the elections as an opportunity to do outreach and public education.[59] The second thing I suggested was a "Price of War" campaign in the community, focusing local attention on the enormous damage military spending is doing to our economy at every level. We must, I told them, show the local impacts of Bush's endless war on the world, and there will certainly be plenty of them.

It was a good trip at a difficult time. Our country was destroying Iraq and ruining the lives of the Iraqi people in much the same way as Saddam had done. It was shattering to hear the stories of looting of hospitals and the famous historical museum that was ransacked of its 7,000-year-old artifacts, while U.S. troops sat on their tanks nearby watching the whole show. Bush talks about rebuilding Iraq, but it seems clear that Iraqis will live a the chaotic existence for a long time, giving Bush and the oil barons an excuse to control and dominate their lives.

# GLOBAL NETWORK
# AUSTRALIA CONFERENCE

This trip began when I flew to California on May 9, 2003 to speak at the Women's International League for Peace & Freedom (WILPF) western regional meeting, held at a beautiful oceanside retreat center in Monterey. Sheila Baker and Ellie Bluestein made the visit possible. There were women in attendance from several western states, and I was able to speak to the entire group in a plenary session as well as to conduct a workshop. The weekend gathering, was uplifting and filled with useful content. It was great to see several old friends there with whom I've worked over the years. WILPF has been very supportive of the space issue in the past and will work to promote the October 4-11 *Keep Space for Peace Week* this year. While there, I heard that the theme of Garrison Keelers' *Prairie Home Companion* show on National Public Radio that week was that the U.S. has only one political party. It's a subject that comes up everywhere I go these days.

On May 13, I flew to Melbourne, Australia and was thrilled when Dr. Michio Kaku and I ran into each other right before boarding the plane in Los Angeles. He was going to Melbourne to be the keynote speaker at the Global Network (GN) 11th annual membership conference on space organizing. It turned out that he was the hit of the show as well. (More on that in a bit.) Things began on May 16 when new GN board convener Dave Webb, from CND in England, and I did a half hour live radio talk show on a community radio station in Melbourne that feeds the entire state of Victoria. The hosts were pleased when notes were passed to them during the show with questions from callers, something that rarely happens, they said. Clearly, the use of space to direct the recent Iraq war has made people more interested in the subject of U.S. control and domination via space technology.

Later that day, in downtown Melbourne, a protest was held in front of the Optus

corporation headquarters opposing the launching of Australia's first-ever military satellite. It's reported that the satellite will cost Australian taxpayers over $500 million even though the government cut back the national health service due to "lack of funds." Protestors held banners, I was dressed up as Prime Minister John Howard with my arm around Star Wars storm troopers, while others leafleted along the busy street in front of the corporation. Optus, among other things, is a cell phone provider, and Australians are talking about organizing a boycott of Optus products. On behalf of the Australians and the international delegates who had come for the conference, Dave Webb delivered a letter to the head of the corporation. Leaflets that were handed out concluded with the statement: KEEP SPACE FOR PROPHETS NOT FOR PROFITS. A large but generally respectful police force was there to ensure activists did not enter the corporate building. They wouldn't even let me, dressed as the Prime Minister, into the corporate HQ.

The GN conference was held at the famous Trades Hall in downtown Melbourne. The hall was built in 1874, and has been the site of virtually every significant progressive movement activity since then. The stately stone building, built by the workers themselves, housed the 1917 anti-conscription campaign that opposed World War I. Inside are many memorials to the passage of the eight-hour work day. (Eight hours of work, eight hours of leisure, eight hours of rest.) Thanks to Jacob Grech, the manager of the Trades Hall, and a GN advisory committee member who coordinated our conference, we had full use of the historic site for the entire weekend.

On Friday afternoon, I was asked to speak to a group of trade unionists who were being trained at Trades Hall. They wanted me to speak about my experiences working for the United Farm Workers Union and Cesar Chavez. In addition, they wanted to learn more about space issues. Several of the union activists and their leaders attended our weekend conference. Later that evening Dr. Michio Kaku gave a stirring keynote to begin the conference. Michio talked about the new right-wing foreign policy architecture that he called "New Rome." He said the containment strategy, in place for the last fifty years, is now obsolete because of U.S. moves toward a policy of preemption, which will bridge "New Rome" and space. Michio reminded the assembled that "now is the time to educate the peace movement about the new strategy and its use of space technology." In response to several questions about getting young people involved in activism, Michio said that, "Young people understand what is going on and many feel hopeless. We have to articulate an alternative vision for the future that will provide them direction and hope." Michio had to leave on Saturday afternoon to fly to Europe, but conference attendees talked about his message for the rest of the weekend. By the end of the event, most people were using the expression "New Rome" as a short cut to describe U.S. military and foreign policy.

Activists from 11 countries, including England, Fiji, Philippines, Japan, India, U.S., Romania, as well as the Palestinian representative to Australia attended the conference. Over 17 Australian peace groups from all over the country sent delegates to the event. Senator Lyn Allison (Australian Democrats) also addressed the conference saying that the Optus military satellite would give Australia the ability to spy on nations as far away as India. She predicted that the future would bring more military spending and more government secrecy to Australia. Senator Allison declared her support for the goals of the conference and, then, quite unlike most politicians, stayed most of the day, and took notes as others spoke on various space-related topics. Several Australian speakers, including Jacob Grech and GN board member Dr. Hannah Middleton, reminded us how important the U.S. Pine Gap spy base in Australia was to future plans for fighting war in space. Like similar facilities in other parts of the world, Pine Gap will be upgraded to help direct war from, in, and through space. We were lucky to have Ema Tagicakibau with us. She was representing the Pacific Concerns Resource Center located in Fiji. She spoke of the Pacific islanders who are still suffering from the legacy of atomic testing, and now face the reality of "missile defense" testing in the Marshall Islands. The Western Pacific is more militarized then ever due to the expanding forward deployment of U.S. forces in an effort to encircle China.

On Sunday, we met for the annual GN business meeting and spent much of the time brainstorming future space organizing. One theme that struck a chord was to make greater use of the moon as a universal symbol of peace in the heavens. Yet several folks felt we must drag the moon back down to Earth, to show how war and insanity on our planet is facilitated by space military technology. Another important suggestion was that we must all talk more about how the space command will be the military arm of corporate globalization. Australian activists explored how they could get their people's attention during the October 4-11 *Keep Space for Peace Week*. Most felt it was best to focus on their own nation's new role in militarizing space, while highlighting issues like the development of space facilities (one example being Pine Gap). Finally, we decided to hold the May, 2004 GN international space conference in Maine after receiving word from Peace Action Maine, Maine Vets for Peace, and WILPF (Brunswick branch) that they would join as co-sponsors of the event. The presence of Bath Iron Works, builder of Aegis destroyers with the new Theatre Missile Defense interceptors onboard, and the need for more links with peace groups in the Northeast, made Maine the perfect choice. So many thanks to all our kind Australian hosts who often feel so isolated out there in the middle of the Pacific. We were proud to be with all of you. And, as you say in Australia....no worries!

# DETAINED IN AIRPORT BY COPS

*"They that can give up essential liberty to purchase a little
temporary safety deserve neither liberty or safety."*

——Benjamin Franklin

On July 28, 2003, I was returning home after two days of speaking in Louisville, Kentucky. While in the Louisville airport, having just received my boarding pass, I got a call on my cell phone from a reporter with the *Columbus Post-Dispatch* (Ohio). I often do interviews like this at airports while waiting to board my plane. The reporter wanted my comments about the Global Network's position on NASA's "Project Prometheus,"— the nuclear rocket to Mars. The interview lasted 10 minutes at the most and in it I outlined these three key points:

1) The escalation of launches carrying nuclear power into space dramatically increases the chance of an accident.

2) The Department of Energy (DoE) has a long and sad track record of contamination of workers and local communities while building nuclear bombs. Can we expect anything else as they now ramp up the labs to produce more plutonium for nuclear space missions?

3) NASA has announced that from now on all space missions will be "dual use," meaning that each NASA mission will include both military and civilian objectives. Thus, the development of nuclear reactor technology for space missions will also become a military technology.

Immediately after finishing the interview, I bought a newspaper and headed for the airport security screening line and my boarding gate. Just as I entered the line, two policemen asked if I was Bruce Gagnon. They, then, directed me to follow them to the other end of the airport and would only say that I had been overhead making dangerous statements. Amazingly, they knew my name and had a copy of my boarding pass. All of this within a few minutes after checking in at the airport. As we walked to their office, I racked my brain to understand what I might have said and to whom!

Once inside the police inner-sanctum, I was questioned by three officers who wanted my name, my ID, my reason for being in Louisville, where I had spoken, to whom I had spoken. They informed me that I had been overheard talking about bombs and contamination. They searched my bag and one officer found my copy of the U.S. constitution. He asked if I always carry it with me. I told him "Yes, you never know when you might need it."

It took me a moment to realize that someone must have overheard my statements to the reporter about the nuclear rocket. I explained the interview to them. Luckily, I remembered the name of the reporter. One of the officers then called information, got the number for the Columbus newspaper, and called the reporter. The reporter verified that I had just spoken to him about bombs and contamination and suggested they let me go. But they were not done. They ran a national ID check on me to make sure I was not on some terrorist "wanted list."

Finally, they let me go and I headed for my gate. I still made my flight, but as I was boarding, one of the cops stood by the door at the gate to make sure I got on the plane.

The remarkable thing to me is how paranoid people have become since 9-11. I told the police I thought potential terrorists were not likely to stand in the middle of an airport and talk on the phone about bombs and contamination.

My Louisville airport experience underscored to me the dangers we face of losing our civil liberties. While we all are concerned about terrorist attacks, I am frankly much more concerned about the loss of our civil liberties in the name of protecting us from terrorism. The constitution is a very fragile document. It is something we should all carry with us and fight to hold on to.

My trip to Louisville was sponsored by the local Fellowship of Reconciliation chapter. On Sunday July 27 (my birthday), I spoke at the Central Presbyterian Church about the militarization of space, and then, on Monday, a different group heard me talk about the "Price of Endless War" at a local restaurant. Veteran activist Jean Edwards was the leading organizer of the trip and I stayed in the home of retired Presbyterian minister, David Bos.

Just the week before, David Bos had arranged for me to fly to Daytona Beach, Florida to deliver two workshops at the annual conference of the National Association of Ecumenical & Interreligious Staff. This was an important opportunity to present our message to religious leaders from throughout the nation. One person who attended one of my workshops, and added much to it, was former Congressman Bob Edgar, now the General Secretary of the National Council of Churches. Not only did he understand the issue, he also took a strong stand against the notion of the weaponization of space.

We don't get to interact with religious communities as often as I would like. Many church leaders fear introducing "controversial" peace issues before their congregations. They fear the church will split apart, they will lose income, or even their jobs. This is a time when we need the religious community to be more proactive and talk about the moral and ethical implications of U.S. foreign and military policy.

# ARKANSAS AND CLINTON'S DARK PAST

I made an organizing trip to Arkansas on behalf of the Global Network in September of 2003. The trip was coordinated by my old friend Mark Swaney and Dr. Dick Bennett (retired English professor), both of Fayetteville.

I met Mark back in the early 1980's when I worked for the Florida Coalition for Peace & Justice, which at that time was headquartered in Orlando. Mark was working as an engineer at Martin Marietta where they were building the Pershing II missile. I was organizing protests regularly outside the production facility. Our signs often read *Good People, Bad Product.* Mark contacted me when he decided that he wanted to quit his job because he didn't want to work for the military industrial complex any longer. I suggested we organize a news conference to announce his leaving. We don't often get the chance to have a weapons industry worker talk publicly about his conscience. Mark agreed and the event was quite successful. Soon thereafter, Mark moved his family to Arkansas. We've kept in touch over the years.

While in Arkansas, Mark started working with a small group of people who were investigating, then broke the story, of secret government cocaine and weapons trafficking at the Mena airport. Involved were both Bill Clinton, the governor, and George H. W. Bush, the president. Quite a number of books written on the subject name Mark as a major investigative source of information.[60] Today, Mark is a key leader in Arkansas's Green Party.

While in Fayetteville, I was kept busy with three talks, the last at the University of Arkansas. At this event, I invited two wonderful folk musicians to play a couple of songs. I had heard them the night before at an Omni Peace Center coffee house. One really moving song told the story of the escalation of the arms race, from stones to the nuclear bombing of Hiroshima and now Star Wars.

The next day, Mark drove me to Little Rock where I was to speak. All the way I quizzed him about the Mena drug smuggling story. He recalled that when Bush the first was in office the Democrats were all over the story, calling him for bits of evidence his Arkansas team had dug up. But when Clinton was elected the Democrats suddenly were no longer interested in the story because they knew that as governor of the state he allowed the CIA to use Mena as a base of operations. Instead, the Republicans began calling Mark wanting information on how Clinton was involved in the scandal. Such is politics in the good ole USA!

My talk in Little Rock was organized by Nancy Dockter and held at the University of Arkansas/Little Rock. Midway through my speech, three young African-American men came in and sat down. During the question and answer period they took a very active part in the discussion. One young man said he felt like the U.S. was a terrorist nation and that black people were essentially being used as cannon fodder in Iraq. It is not often my talks are attended by African-Americans, and afterwards I went up to thank them for coming. They told me, "We talk about these things every day." It was a clear reminder to me that even though we think the greater public is not listening to the debate on war/peace/military spending issues, in fact they are. In this case, the war was touching these young men's lives very closely and they were extremely interested.

I spent the night in Little Rock at the home of Jean Gordon, who told me she hosted the first-ever political event for Bill Clinton. Since she had a huge living room, she was asked to open her home for Clinton's first campaign event when he ran for Arkansas Attorney General. Clinton showed up, holding his mother's hand, and a career was born. Jean also hosted the founding meeting of the grassroots group ACORN,[61] with nearly 300 people meeting in that living room.

Another thing of interest in Arkansas was talk about Gen. Wesley Clark's bid for the presidency. (He had been NATO Supreme Allied Commander for the Kosovo war.) Some peace activists I met in Arkansas were talking about supporting his campaign. I guess once you have one president from your state, the temptation is to go for another.

I can't get the pictures of the bombing of Yugoslavia out of my mind. NATO hit hospitals and TV stations, used depleted uranium, and contaminated major rivers in that part of Europe. The U.S. denied satellite reconnaissance information to the European partners in the war, which led Europe to begin to develop its own military space capability. Never again, the EU said, will they allow the U.S. to hold all the cards. Gen. Clark, nice as he might be as a person, was smack dab in the middle of all that. Since Clark announced he will run for president, my e-mail traffic has picked up with folks sending me letters saying they are happy he is running. Word was starting to circulate about how Clark took positions for and against the current war with Iraq.

Some peace folks are so eager to "win" this 2004 election, that they will even support military officials, hoping to be led out of this dark tunnel we are in today. Remember what Eugene V. Debs said long ago about leaders: "I don't want you to follow me or anyone else. If you are looking for a Moses to lead you out of the capitalist wilderness you will stay right where you are. I would not lead you into this promised land if I could, because if I could lead you in, someone else would lead you out."[62]

# NASA HIRES PR FIRM TO HELP BLUNT OPPOSITION TO NUCLEAR ROCKET

*"The secret to creativity is knowing how to hide your sources."*

—Albert Einstein

**December 12, 2003**  Fearing another public relations defeat like it had during the 1997 Cassini campaign, NASA hired a public relations outfit to gather information from potential critics of its latest space nuclear project. Project Prometheus, the nuclear rocket being developed under the Bush Nuclear Systems Initiative, will spend $3 billion during the next five years to expand the launching of nuclear power into space.

I actually began organizing the Cancel Cassini Campaign in 1994 by writing articles, speaking to groups around the world, and expanding the numbers of interested contacts. By the time the 1997 launch came around and the media began paying attention to the issue, there was a tremendous grassroots movement in place to oppose the plutonium launch. Even the TV program *60 Minutes* covered the issue, just a week before the lift-off.

This time NASA wanted to be prepared. While Project Prometheus was in the development stage, NASA retained *The Keystone Center*, based in Colorado, to gather information about potential critics so they could effectively combat any expected opposition.

The Keystone Center called the Global Network office in the fall of 2003 wanting to send one of its representatives to our office in Maine to "interview" me about our concerns. It was clear from the conversation that the real intention of the visit was to find out what strategies we intended to employ to block the launch of the nuclear rocket. I wanted no part in helping NASA — they have lots of money and easy access to the corporate-dominated media. Neither was I about to help *The Keystone Center*, which is being paid quite well with taxpayer dollars, I'm sure. I told them I was not interested in being "interviewed," and left it at that.

Months later I received a second interview request. In a letter the *Keystone Center* said that wanted to "converse with you about NASA's Project Prometheus Nuclear Systems Program......We are undertaking a round of meetings and structured interviews with some 25 people, many of whom are long-standing skeptics or critics of NASA. Our sole focus is to understand what public involvement strategies, above and beyond the National Environmental Policy Act (NEPA), might be appropriate for NASA as they begin to develop Project Prometheus."

So basically *The Keystone Center* was being paid big bucks by NASA to find out what "critics" are saying and/or planning around Project Prometheus so they can then advise NASA on the best way to sell the project to the public and blunt the critics. And they had the audacity to ask me to help them!

I know this should be taken as a supreme compliment. NASA was (still is) worried about the work of the Global Network. They feared the public response to Bush's plan to dramatically expand the launching of nuclear power into space. And so they should! But to ask us to help them create a plan to circumvent our very opposition is the height of arrogance.

What made it fun though was that a reporter from the *New York Times* also called. The Times was doing a story on Project Prometheus and wanted to know if we were going to organize to oppose it. I told him we were already organizing and he wanted to know why he had not seen anything in the media. I told him the reason was because the corporate media usually isn't very interested in what we have to say. He said that he doubted that NASA was very worried about our opposition, and I said, "Hey let me read you this letter I just got from *The Keystone Center*." After hearing the content the reporter asked me to fax him the letter, which I gladly did.

The *New York Times* called because Bush is expected very soon to make a big announcement about going back to the moon and Mars.[63] The nuclear rocket will be a key component of this plan.

Pyramids to the Heavens, Inc.

It just goes to show our work is being watched by the government and the corporate media. They know what we are doing, and as much as they like to make us think they ignore us, they don't. They watch all of us like hawks because they are worried to death the public might catch on to what we have to say. If anything should tell us to keeping doing what we are doing, this is it.

So, put this one into your mental file cabinet—NASA's Project Prometheus, the nuclear rocket. Keep it close to your heart because it is going to be another hot issue down the road. How do I know that? Well, *The Keystone Center* told me so.

# NEW ENGLAND TRAVELS

I just returned (January 19, 2004) from a trip to Hartford and New Haven, Connecticut where I spoke at meetings organized by the Green Party. The meeting in New Haven was at the home of local activist Charlie Pillsbury, who ran for Congress in the previous national election against the liberal Democrat Rosa DeLauro. He lost, but felt it important to run since DeLauro was going along with growing militarism and not fighting hard enough as cutbacks were made in social programs. The same story about local dissatisfaction with the Democratic Party is heard everywhere you go in America these days.

(During the next couple of months I traveled throughout the New England region, New Mexico, and New York to promote the Global Network's 12th annual international conference that will be held on April 23-25, 2004 in Portland, Maine. The event will be called **Resisting Empire: Understanding the Role of Space in U.S. Global Domination.** Already we had confirmed Dr. Helen Caldicott as the keynote speaker.)

In mid-January, during a big northeast cold snap, I drove three hours north to Blue Hill, Maine to speak to a meeting of the Island Peace & Justice group. Fellow Veterans for Peace member Dud Hendrick made the arrangements. The island, in the midst of freezing temperatures and howling winds, was breathtaking. Some have asked how I am doing in Maine since our move here last spring from Florida. Let me assure all of you that I LOVE IT HERE. The people in Maine have been so very welcoming and the natural wonders of the state are something to behold. My biggest challenge so far is learning to drive in the snow. SLOW DOWN, BRUCE!

I also started a cable TV show called *This Issue.* It will be an interview format. I plan to do two shows a month and they will air on three different cable TV stations (Portland, Bath, and Brunswick.) As I've traveled, I've been the guest on many local cable TV shows. I always wanted to do one where I could interview lots of great folks who are doing good work, but I never lived in a place that had a commitment to public access like they do here in Maine. Through the program, I hope to show the connections between the various issues of peace, military spending, globalization, human needs, the environment, and so on. Plus, it is a lot of fun, energizing, and a nice break from the constant barrage of bad news.

Speaking of bad news, this past week George W. Bush made his space exploration announcement. He intends to have the U.S. return to the moon and then go on to Mars. What he didn't explain is that by establishing military bases on the moon, the U.S. can take control of helium 3 to be used for fusion power, a resource which could become as profitable in the future as the "gold rush and the oil boom," according to a *New York Times* op-ed on space.

Knowing that Bush's announcement would be a good media opportunity, I wrote a news release with the help of Dr. Michio Kaku, and sent it out to our media list.[64] The release outlined our concerns that the Bush proposal would violate the U.N.'s 1979 Moon Treaty that says no country may put military bases on the moon or make ownership claims on the lunar surface. As a result, during a two day period, I was doing nonstop interviews as were several of our allies in other groups who work on the space issue. Here is a list of those who called our office:

- CBS Radio News
- Democracy Now radio show
- WBAI Radio, New York City
- Reuters
- KPFK Radio, Los Angeles
- WZBC Radio, Boston
- Meria Heller Show (webcast)
- Globe & Mail newspaper, Canada
- KIRO Radio, Seattle
- Times Record newspaper, Brunswick, Maine
- The Power Hour (webcast)
- St Louis Post Dispatch
- WSKY Radio, Gainesville, FL
- WERU Radio, Bangor, Maine
- Between the Lines radio show (on 35 stations)
- KPFA radio, Berkeley, CA (morning & afternoon shows)
- WBEZ Radio, Chicago
- Peter Werbe Show (nationally-syndicated radio)

Our new video, *Arsenal of Hypocrisy: The Space Program & the Military Industrial Complex,*[65] had only been out for a couple of weeks and was selling like hotcakes. Already we'd gone through our first order of 100 of them and had to place a second order with our producer, Randy Atkins, in Gainesville, Florida. The video was recently accepted into the *New York International Independent Film and Video Festival*. I also received a call from a filmmaker in Hollywood who viewed it with other people in the industry and gave us very good reviews.

Our work during this period reflects our two primary strategies: work hard to reach people by speaking to them directly; and utilize mass communications where possible. When mainstream media is not available to us, create our own and promote it widely.

# NEW MEXICO: LAND OF NUKES, GERONIMO AND COCHISE

This report covers the period of February 7-15, 2004. It began with an inspiring protest march through downtown Portland, Maine on Saturday, February 7 in support of people from Latin America and Somalia who have been targeted for harassment by the U.S. Border Patrol under *Homeland Security*. Raids throughout immigrant businesses in Portland in recent weeks put the fear of deportation into the hearts of many people – even those who have legal status. The march through the snow was attended by about 250 people, including the mayor and many other elected officials.

That same day I spoke to a gathering of the Maine Green Party who wanted to hear more about the work of the Global Network during a candidate forum they sponsored.

The Maine Democratic Presidential Caucus was held the next day Sunday, February 8. I had to vote absentee because I was on my way to Albuquerque, N.M.  My absentee vote for Dennis Kucinich was just one among many that gave him 16% of the vote in the state. My partner, Mary Beth Sullivan, was asked to give the pro-Kucinich speech to over 500 folks who attended our town caucus. I was sad to have missed her stump speech, but I heard that she knocked some people off the fence into the Kucinich camp. She got a rousing reception, and afterward several people called on her to run for political office.

I went to Albuquerque to hold protests at the *Space Nuclear Power Symposium* organized annually by the University of New Mexico's (UNM) Nuclear Engineering Department.

I didn't arrive in Albuquerque until late Sunday night (after three plane rides) and I missed a showing of our video, *Arsenal of Hypocrisy,* that evening at the Peace & Justice Center.

On Monday, February 9 we organized two protests at the space symposium at the Albuquerque Hilton hotel. During the middle part of the day we vigiled outside the hotel; then we returned at 7:00 pm to be there while a Boeing-sponsored awards banquet was held. We had made it known that we wanted to speak to the gathered proponents of weapons and nuclear power in space, but no formal invitation came our way. So 20 of us, including many students from the UNM Greens, marched into the hotel with our signs, down the long hallway, past the corporate displays, and the 1967 space nuclear reactor, before we were stopped just outside the door of the big banquet room. Since we couldn't go in we began chanting "No nukes in space" and "No weapons in space." The door swung open, now and then, when someone had to go to the toilet. It was delightful to see the shock on the faces of the participants as they ran headlong into our signs and chants! We were certain our voices echoed inside the banquet room. Score one for direct action!

The police were slow to arrive, so after 15 minutes we decided to leave. We again marched through the hotel and out the lobby door. Spanish-speaking TV came to film us, and luckily we had a Spanish-speaking student who could deliver our message to the public. During the next two days we were on the front cover of the UNM student paper with photos and articles about our protest. While in New Mexico I also did four radio interviews, and the *Albuquerque Tribune* invited Bob Anderson to write an op-ed explaining our concerns. The paper invited me to write an op-ed talking about what motivates me to return to Albuquerque each year to organize protests at the space nukes convention.

My next stop was Taos, located in northern New Mexico and surrounded by beautiful mountains. The evening talk gave me a chance to see the lovely moon nestled in the night sky just above the snow capped mountain peaks. The next morning I returned to the same spot to speak to 55 students at an alternative high school. I was very pleased that they had so many questions for me that the teachers had to extend my time by 15 minutes.

On February 12, I made my way back to Albuquerque where I met Bob Anderson, who drove me three hours further south to Silver City for a talk to local citizens. In order to get there we had to go through the Gila National Forest, over the mountain pass into Silver City, the home of the wild west gangster, Billy the Kid. But before Kid's time, this was Indian country—the home of the great Apache leaders Geronimo and Cochise. My heart ached when I thought about the fact that Geronimo's skull today sits inside the Yale University "Tomb," the club house of the powerful and secret *Skull & Bones Society* that both George W. Bush and Sen. John Kerry belong. Sen. Prescott Bush,[66] the grandfather of our current president, led a grave-robbing party years ago that stole Geronimo's skull as a prize for their clubhouse. *Skull & Bones* is where select elites, irrespective of party affiliation, are taught how to manage and control the U.S. empire.[67]

Silver City is a mining town. As we approached we passed huge mountain-like piles of tailings from the strip mining of copper that has gouged enormous holes in the Earth and polluted the water supply. Many famous labor struggles took place in Silver City as workers ran up against the greed of the giant mining corporations.

The turnout for my Silver City talk was much higher than expected for such a small community; besides, we had competition that evening—a theatre production of "The Unsinkable Molly Brown." The response to our new video was excellent, and I answered questions until my voice began to give out. By this time it was 9:00 p.m. and Bob and I still had the drive back to Albuquerque ahead of us. My plane home was leaving early the next morning. We headed north, but had to take the long way around to avoid the mountain pass, as a snowstorm was in our path. Halfway back to Albuquerque we hit the blinding storm and witnessed one car upside down on the highway and several more in a ditch. We later learned that two people perished in highway accidents that night. We were lucky and made it home by 2:00 a.m. After a quick check of my e-mails, I was in bed, only to be wakened by Bob at 5:30 a.m. for the trip to the airport.

Once home, I had one day to rest before Mary Beth and I headed south to Cambridge, Massachusetts to hear Noam Chomsky talk at MIT about the militarization of space and science. We got there 1 ½ hours before the talk began, and set up our literature table. Students and community people arrived early in order to get seats. The auditorium eventually filled to capacity. I would guess well over one thousand people were there. During the question period I introduced myself and the GN and began to announce the upcoming GN conference in Portland, Maine, but many in the audience roared "Ask a question!" Noam held up his hand, stopped the noise, and urged them to listen to me, saying that the Global Network did important work on the issue. The audience then applauded. I invited folks to come to our table in the lobby, which many did. Afterwards, I thanked Noam for saving me from certain lynching by the crowd.

All during these recent trips I was reading the autobiography of Emma Goldman. It was striking to see the similarities between her time and ours. In the period 1919-1920 during the famous raids by Attorney General Palmer (with assistance of his young aide J. Edgar Hoover) over 16,000 people were arrested in America. More than 250, including Emma, were deported. Under President Woodrow Wilson, who was a Democrat, many were sentenced to long years in jail for speaking out against World War I and the draft. All I could think about were Code Orange, Homeland Security, the Iraq war, and the Patriot Act. Learn from history.

# CONNECTING 9-11 AND
# THE PEACE MOVEMENT

*"When people are engaged in something they are not proud of, they do not welcome witnesses. In fact, they come to believe the witness causes the trouble."*

—John Steinbeck

On March 25, 2004 I flew to San Francisco to speak at the *International Citizens Inquiry into 9-11* conference organized by old friend Carol Brouillet and others in the Bay Area. The event coincided with the 9-11 Commission hearings being held in Washington. It was held at the historic and beautiful Herbst Theater just across the street from City Hall. About 500 people from all across the U.S. and Canada attended.

I was asked to speak about the "big picture." My topic was *The Blueprint for World Domination*.[68] I began with the story of my own conversion, while in the Air Force during the Vietnam War, and how Daniel Ellsberg's release of the *Pentagon Papers* finished me off. All my remaining illusions were shattered, I said, as I read the government's secret history of how the CIA invented a pretext to enter the Vietnam war and how it manipulated Congress, the media, and the public along the way.

Then I talked about the *Project for a New American Century (PNAC)*. This is a group led by Dick Cheney, Donald Rumsfeld, Jeb Bush, Paul Wolfowitz, Richard Armitage, John Bolton, Elliott Abrams, James Woolsey, William Bennett, and William Kristol, and others. Long before the 2000 election, this group was planning to steer U.S. foreign policy toward greater empire building.[69]

In a report called *Rebuilding America's Defenses: Strategy, Forces and Resources for a New Century* PNAC asked, "Does the U.S. have the resolve to shape a new century favorable to American principles and interests?"[70] What are the principles and interests to which PNAC refers? I argued that they include corporate "control and domination" of the world; the advancement of conditions that create a greater market for the number one industrial export of the U.S. today—namely weapons; and control of the oil and natural gas fields not only in the Middle East but throughout Central Asia, Africa, and Latin America. All of this would require a massive investment in the Pentagon. The PNAC report concluded that this "needed" military transformation was "likely to be a long one, absent some catastrophic and catalyzing event—like a new Pearl Harbor." After 9-11, PNAC's "military transformation" took off with the U.S. invasion of Afghanistan and Iraq. Today, we pay the price.

Another speaker at the event was Ellen Mariani, whose husband was a passenger on one of the planes that crashed into the South Tower of the World Trade Center. Ellen refused the millions of dollars offered her by the government if she would just leave the case alone. She is suing the Bush administration for negligence. She told the audience that she does not trust the 9-11 commission to uncover the truth. She, like many others, has no answer as to why military planes were not scrambled when the four airliners went off course and were clearly hijacked. Federal Aviation Authority guidelines **require** this be done.

On my way to the airport early Saturday morning, I picked up a copy of the *San Francisco Chronicle* to read its coverage of the event. The report noted that former San Francisco mayor Willie Brown had previously acknowledged that on September 10, 2001 he had been planning to fly to New York on 9-11 for a mayors' conference but had "received a call the day before from someone in security at San Francisco International Airport advising him that Americans should be careful about air travel" on September 11. Brown cancelled his plans to fly on that fateful day. This is just one of many stories about high-level persons receiving warnings not to fly on 9-11.

In Boston, I was met by Mary Beth. We spent the night with her brother in the city before heading west to Amherst, Massachusetts. In Amherst, I was to address the annual meeting of a local community group. Before the meeting, I spoke to a large gathering of people who were involved in a statewide March to Abolish Poverty that was making its way through Amherst on that very day. I asked the assembled what the number one industrial export of the U.S. was today? "Weapons," they answered. I told them America was like an alcoholic, addicted to war, violence and military spending. How could we afford social programs to lift up the poor when our priorities are promoting war around the world? What had become of our collective soul, I asked?

Later, inside the Unitarian Church, I told the community group that we could never stop war until we became willing to take on the issue of military production right in our own communities. I added that a positive, non-violent program was needed to create healthy debate about the implications of military spending if we ever hoped to make any progress to stop war. It's one thing to travel across the country to demonstrate at some other community's military base, I said, but when we begin to regularly create debate and positive non-violent conflict in our own communities, then we can begin to move the hearts and minds of our fellow citizens.

Following my talk at the church, I was approached by 85-year-old peace and justice legend, Frances Crowe, who lives and works in western Massachusetts. Frances said she was planning to come to the GN annual international conference in Portland in April 2004. She told me that, to kick-off the conference, she planned to commit civil disobedience when we protest at Bath Iron Works because it would help create debate in the community.[71]

On Tuesday, March 30, I participated in an hour-long telephone debate with two NASA representatives (one astronaut and a public relations person) on the national radio show called *Native America Calling* that is beamed to radio stations in Indian country all over America. During the show, I made our case against the nuclearization and weaponization of space and then sat back and listened as callers from reservations in New Mexico, Idaho, Wisconsin, Wyoming and other states called in to criticize NASA and its growing relationship with the Pentagon. The callers talked about the need to heal the earth, and to use our hard-earned tax dollars for clean-up of this beautiful planet before we head off to "colonize" the dead and dusty planet of Mars.

At moments like that hope fills my heart because I am reminded of the good sense of the people. The people want peace, justice, cooperation, love and hope. Clean air, clean water, and jobs they can be proud of. Give the people what they want!

# —THE BOYS IN THE BAND—

# BLUEPRINT FOR WORLD DOMINATION[72]

There is nothing like personal experience to inform a person. During my time in the Air Force during the Vietnam War, while stationed at Travis AFB in California, I was exposed to the peace movement for the first time. I had come from a career military family and had been the Vice-chair of the Okaloosa County, Florida Young Republican Club at 16, while working on the Nixon campaign. My first roommate at Travis AFB turned out to be a leading GI-resistance movement organizer in the barracks, and at night there were meetings of anti-war GI's and Black Panthers from the cities talking about racism. I was to get the education of my life.

When the *Pentagon Papers* came out, thanks to the courage of Daniel Ellsberg, all my patriotic illusions were shattered. Here was the U.S. government's own account of how it had fabricated the pretext to drag our nation into the Vietnam war and how it was literally sold to the public by manipulating the media and Congress. My life was never the same after that and I've been a professional organizer since 1978, first trained by the United Farmworkers Union and then leading peace and justice organizations ever since. In 1992, a group of us created the Global Network Against Weapons & Nuclear Power in Space in order to try to prevent the next round of the arms race from moving into the heavens. Today, I live in Maine and travel all over the U.S. and around the world talking about how space technology now allows the U.S. to militarily control the entire planet. With space satellites in place, the U.S. can see everything on the Earth, hear everything on the Earth, and ultimately target anyone or anyplace on the Earth below.

The day after 9-11, I went to my World Atlas to look up the Central Asian countries I admittedly knew very little about. What I found is common knowledge these days. They have some of the largest deposits of oil and natural gas in the world. Uzbekistan has the world's largest goldmine.

My *Pentagon Papers* experience taught me to always ask the next question. Who? What? Why? When? How? For me, 9-11 unleashed a slew of new questions about U.S. foreign and military policy.

Five days after 9-11, I boarded a very empty airplane in Gainesville, Florida to fly to Cleveland in order to speak about space to a Rotary Club in a Republican neighborhood. While reading the *Gainesville Sun* on the plane, an AP story jumped out at me. The piece quoted an "unidentified" Pentagon spokesman as saying, "We've been planning this war for the last three years." Of course, the Pentagon spokesman was referring to the bombing and invasion of Afghanistan. Memories of reading the *Pentagon Papers* flashed through my mind.

A few years ago I was sitting in my office in Gainesville watching *CNN* when the program was interrupted for an announcement that a private plane carrying the golfer Payne Stewart had taken off from Florida and had lost contact with ground control.

*CNN* reported that the military had immediately scrambled two jets. This, we were told, is routine when planes lose contact with the control tower. We were told the military pilots had seen Stewart and his pilot slumped over the cockpit controls. It was theorized that their on-board oxygen had malfunctioned, and they were dead. The military jets were to escort the plane to its final crash site and only shoot it down if it posed any threat to a population center. *CNN* stayed with the story and tracked the plane's descent until it crashed somewhere in the empty countryside of a southern state.

On 9-11, for some reason that defies logic and standard operating procedure, four big American airliners, filled with people, lost contact with the control tower and dramatically changed course. No fighter planes were scrambled until history had been made.

We know that the Chairman of the Pentagon's Joint Chiefs of Staff, Gen. Richard Myers was meeting with then Sen. Max Cleland on Capitol Hill the morning of 9-11. While planes crashed into the World Trade Center towers, Gen. Myers and Sen. Cleland went right on with their meeting. It was not until after the tragic episode was over that Gen. Myers and NORAD commander, Gen. Ralph Eberhart made the decision to scramble jets. This clearly suggests that the two generals knowingly violated mandatory procedures that call for direct military intervention when such an instance of hijacking occurs. Why did the military not take action that fateful day? Who ordered those in charge to stand down? Surely, on-duty commanders would not have made such a monumental decision on their own. The Pentagon does not have to seek permission to scramble jets during hijackings, it is required to do so.

On March 23, 2004 I was listening to *National Public Radio* coverage of the 9-11 Commission hearings in Washington. Secretary of War Donald Rumsfeld was being questioned. The one woman on the panel, Jamie Gorelick, asked Rumsfeld why Pentagon jets were not scrambled to intercept the hijacked planes? Rather than answer the question, he droned on about some other nonsense. No one attempted to follow-up. I was not totally surprised. Not long after, I heard a Washington insider say that the 9-11 commission hearings were theater. He said all the questions had already been asked in private sessions. The public sessions were just show-time.

In 2000, a report was written by the now well-known right-wing think tank, the *Project for a New American Century*. This is an organization which Cheney, Rumsfeld, Jeb Bush, Wolfowitz, Armitage, Bolton, Abrams, Woolsey, Libby, and William Kristol, among others, belong to. The report, called *Rebuilding America's Defenses: Strategy, Forces and Resources for a New Century* asked, "Does the U.S. have the resolve to shape a new century favorable to American principles and interests?"

What are the principles and interests that PNAC refers to? Could they be corporate "control and domination" of the world? Could they be the advancement of conditions that create more of a market for the number one industrial export of the U.S. today – namely weapons? Could it be control of the oil and natural gas fields not only in the Middle East but also throughout Central Asia, Africa, and Latin America?

PNAC says this: "The U.S. is the world's only superpower, combining preeminent military power, global technological leadership, and the world's largest economy... America's grand strategy should aim to preserve and extend this advantageous position as far into the future as possible."

But to undertake such a grand and sweeping strategy would be an enormously expensive and highly controversial undertaking– not only at home but all over the world. And PNAC knows that. So, the report says that accomplishing this transformation of the world was "likely to be a long one, absent some catastrophic and catalyzing event – like a new Pearl Harbor."

We now hear from Bush administration insiders, like former Treasury secretary Paul O'Neil and Richard Clark, the former counter terrorism chief under Clinton and Bush, that the Bush team was preparing for war with Iraq from its first days in office. Once "selected" by the Supreme Court, George W. Bush began to implement the PNAC strategy by withdrawing from the 1972 ABM treaty that outlawed testing and deployment of "missile defense," dramatically increasing military spending, and planning for military transformation. In fact, the first trip that Donald Rumsfeld took as Secretary of War was to Berlin for a NATO Defense ministers meeting. He took along Henry Kissinger, Sen. John McCain, and Sen. Joseph Lieberman. Lieberman stood beside Rumsfeld and told the NATO military leaders that, "We have bipartisan support for 'missile defense' in the U.S. so your countries had better get on-board or get left behind."

Then came 9-11, and the gloves came off. In his State of the Union speech in 2002 Bush declared that, "Our war on terror is well-begun, but it is only begun." By June of that same year he signaled his support for pre-emptive war saying that the U.S. was "ready for preemptive action when necessary to defend our liberty and to defend our lives."

Everything, thanks to 9-11, was now in place. It is hard to imagine that by using conventional democratic means — such as holding national debates that involved the taxpayers, Congressional hearings and voting — an administration could have successfully committed so much money and so many lives to such a radical new foreign and military policy. But the debate never took place. The democratic process was ignored. It was all done ipso-facto by claiming to be a response to 9-11.

I am reminded of another Bush administration and another invasion. Following the demise of the former Soviet Union there was much debate in the U.S. about the "peace dividend." People were saying we would not have to keep these incredible high levels of military spending any longer, we could stop spending billions a year on NATO. We could take care of things back at home. But all that was lost in a minute as George H. W. Bush terrorized Panama, killing several thousand innocent civilians in the El Chorrillo neighborhood as U.S. troops burned it to the ground. Panama's Manuel Noriega was apprehended in "Operation Just Cause" and talk of a peace dividend was put to rest.

And, there is much more to come. Because of computerization, mechanization, and robotics we now have superfluous populations around the world. Rather than share the great wealth and the diminishing resources (like oil and water), the corporate power structure intends to impose a new $21^{st}$ century form of feudalism that will insure maximum corporate profits and minimum social progress for the people. In order to "control and dominate" the growing legions of "have-nots," predicted by the Pentagon in the U.S. Space Command document called *Vision for 2020*,[73] new high-tech space technologies will be utilized and a fast moving military will be forward deployed to new, smaller, "lily pad" bases in global hot spots. The U.S. now rents or owns more than 700 bases in about 130 countries, in addition to the hundreds of bases in North America.

Key regions like Africa, Central Asia, South America, and the Middle East that have scarce natural resources, though not yet under corporate control, will see a string of new U.S. bases established, all presumably to fight the war on terrorism. Deputy Secretary of War and PNAC member Paul Wolfowitz[74] told the *New York Times* in 2002 that the function of the new outposts "may be more political than actually military." The new bases, he insisted, would "send a message to everybody, including strategically-important countries like Uzbekistan, that we have a capacity to come back in and will come back in...."

China and Russia will be militarily surrounded and contained. In order to pay for this perpetual war, cut-backs in human needs spending (social security, health services, education, etc.) will be necessary in all the "industrial" or "first world" societies as the allies are brought in at some level or another to help pay for and implement this new global vision.

The Democrats argue around the edges of the policy, but essentially agree with a U.S. corporate empire—the New Rome. They only disagree on the way the policy is implemented—they'd rather see a "friendly sheriff" than the macho tinhorn cowboy style presented by Bush and his posse. The two parties play good cop—bad cop with each other.

Hundreds of billions of dollars will be spent on Star Wars research and development, and both parties will support this spending. The space-based laser, what the Pentagon calls the Death Star, is now being developed, and will be powered with nuclear reactors. Bush will say let's deploy right away and the Democrats will say let's test a bit more before we deploy. Both are hostage to the weapons corporations, who generously donate to the political campaigns of compliant politicians. Gen. Richard Myers, the chairman of the Joint Chiefs of Staff, was previously the commander of the U.S. Space Command, which has been put in charge of giving the U.S. "full spectrum dominance" of the earth and space battlefield. His promotion to head the Joint Chiefs shows the ascendancy of Star Wars within the military hierarchy.

Permanent bases, 14 of them, are now being established in Iraq, where U.S. troops will be deployed for years to come—remembering George W.'s words that "The American people had better be patient; it's going to be a long, long war."

The U.S. is a violent society that is addicted to war and military spending. And like any addict we must have our regular fix to keep us going. We must always have an enemy, and if need be, an enemy can be created. And most importantly, we must remain in denial about our addiction. We cannot look ourselves in the mirror for fear of what we might find standing there. But there are people who are clamoring for treatment.

They want to acknowledge the reality of our disease. And these voices will not go away.

I can assure you that for a year or more after 9-11, every place I spoke, someone in the audience would ask me what really happened on 9-11. The entire story of 9-11 might not ever be fully known, but people have begun to develop their own thoughts on what happened and why. Legions of people around the world are highly suspicious of "official explanations," and the demand for the truth will only grow. The 9-11 families are leaders in the citizen movement that seeks real answers to serious questions. Events like this Citizens Inquiry are the real democracy these days.

People often ask me what we can do about the corporate-controlled media. I tell them we have to become the media. And when we have a corporate-controlled Congress and a 9-11 Commission that is replaying the Warren Commission[75] theme, we, the people, have to become the body that explores the issue and asks the tough questions.

Could it be that one important purpose of the notorious Patriot Act is to help create the climate of fear and intimidation in the U.S. that will make the public reluctant to become involved in events like we see this weekend here in San Francisco? Is the message to the public, stay away, don't get involved, keep your nose to the grindstone?

My congratulations to the organizers of this historic event. I have high regard for the citizen activists who have come in search of the truth. Don't let anyone tell you that you are joining the "conspiracy theorists." The only conspiracy is deception and silence. The only conspiracy is one that creates the lack of courage to participate in real democracy.

# SPACE PRIVATIZATION: ROAD TO CONFLICT?

The news (June 21, 2004) brought us the story of "space pioneers" launching privately-funded craft into the heavens. A special prize was offered to the first private aerospace corporation that can successfully take a pilot and a "space tourist" into orbit.

Is this "privatization" of space a good thing? Is there any reason to be concerned about the trend? Are there any serious questions that should be raised at this historic moment?

Three major issues come immediately to mind concerning space privatization: Space as an environment, space law, and profit in space.

We've all probably heard about the growing problem of space junk. Over 100,000 bits of debris are now tracked on the radar screens at NORAD in Colorado as they orbit the earth at 18,000 m.p.h. Several space shuttles have been nicked by bits of debris, resulting in cracked windshields. The International Space Station (ISS) was recently moved to a higher orbit because space junk was coming dangerously close. Some space writers have predicted that the ISS will one day be destroyed by debris.

The chances of accidents grows with the launch of each privately-funded craft. Very soon we will reach the point of no return. Space pollution will be so great that an orbiting minefield will have been created, hindering access to space. The time has certainly come for a global discussion about how we treat the sensitive environment called space.

When the United Nations concluded the 1979 *Moon Treaty,* the U.S. refused, and still does, to sign it. One key reason is that the treaty outlaws military bases on the moon, but also forbids any nation, corporation, or individual to make land "claims" on this planetary body. The 1967 U.N. *Outer Space Treaty* takes similar positions in regard to all of the planetary bodies. The U.N., realizing that we needed to prevent potential conflict over "ownership" of the planetary bodies, mandated that the heavens were the province of all humankind.

In addition to building space hotels and the like, the privateers want to claim ownership of the planets. They hope to mine the sky. Gold has been discovered on asteroids, helium-3 on the moon, and magnesium, cobalt and uranium on Mars. It was recently reported that the Halliburton Corporation is now working with NASA to develop new drilling capabilities to mine Mars.

One organization that seeks to rewrite space law is *United Societies in Space* (USIS). It states, "USIS provides legal and policy support for those who intend to go to space. USIS encourages private property rights and investment. Space is the Free Market Frontier."[76]

Taxpayers, especially in the U.S. where NASA has been funded with taxpayer dollars since its inception, have paid billions of dollars for space technology research and development (R & D). As the aerospace industry moves toward forcing the privatization of space what they are really saying is that the technological base is now at the point where the government can get out of the way and let private industry begin to make profit and control space. Thus, the idea that space is a "free market frontier."

Of course, this means that after the American taxpayer provided all the R & D, private industry now intends to capitalize on the knowledge and gorge itself on profits. One Republican congressman from Southern California, an ally of the aerospace industry, has introduced legislation in Congress to make all space profits "tax free." In this vision, we taxpayers won't see any return on our "collective investment."

So, let's just imagine for a moment that this private sector vision for space comes true - profitable mining on the moon and Mars. Who would keep competitors from sneaking in and creating conflict over the new 21st century gold rush? Who will be the space police?

The Congressional study published in 1989, *Military Space Forces: The Next 50 Years,*[77] gives us some inkling of the answer. The forward of the book was signed by many politicians including former Sen. John Glenn (D-OH) and Sen. Bill Nelson (D-FL). The author reported to Congress on the importance of military bases on the moon and suggested that with bases there the U.S. could control the pathway, or the "gravity well," between the Earth and the moon. The author told Congress that, "Armed forces might lie in wait at that location to hijack rival shipments on return."

Plans are now underway to make space the next "conflict zone" where corporations intend to control resources and maximize profit. The so-called private "space pioneers" are the first step in this new direction. And ultimately the taxpayers will be asked to pay the enormous cost incurred by creating a military space infrastructure that would control the "shipping lanes" on and off planet Earth.

After Columbus returned to Spain with the news that he had discovered the "new world," Queen Isabella began the 100-year process of creating the Spanish Armada to protect the country's new "interests and investments" around the world. So began the global war system. Soon all the European powers were building their navies and in conflict with one another over control of the "new world."

Privatization does not mean that the taxpayer won't be paying any more. Privatization really means that profits will be privatized. Privatization also means that existing international space legal structures will be destroyed in order to bend the law toward private profit. Serious moral and ethical questions must be debated before another new "frontier" of conflict is created.

# BOSTON: HOME OF REVOLUTION AND FREE SPEECH ZONES

*"The most pathetic person in the world is someone who has sight but has no vision."*

—Helen Keller

During the period of July 22-25, 2004 I drove to Boston to attend two events that were organized to coincide with the Democratic National Convention (DNC).

On July 22 and 23, I attended the annual convention of Veterans for Peace (VFP), an organization to which I proudly belong. I led a workshop entitled *Nuclear Hypocrisy: Preemption & Empire Building* along with longtime American Friends Service Committee staffer Joseph Gerson who works in nearby Cambridge. The convention, with 220 advance registrations, swelled to over 400 attendees as veterans from WW II, Korea, Vietnam, and the Iraq wars came from all over the nation. I attended a series of great workshops over the course of the two days I was there. One of the most moving was *Iraq Vets Sound Off*. Six men and women who have recently returned from service in the Iraq war theatre impressed us with their heartfelt stories of personal transformation as a result of being witnesses to the insanity of the war.

One of the most moving for me was Jimmy Massey, a Marine Staff Sergeant, who was recently discharged after nearly 12 years of service. He told us the incredible story of being part of a squad that repeatedly killed innocent civilians. According to Massey, "We were pretty much rolling death." He began by describing how he witnessed the planning for the war at least six months before the actual U.S. invasion of Iraq. Marine commanders told him that the Ramallah oil fields were the "prized jewel."

Early on in the invasion, as his Marine unit entered Iraq, they came upon empty Iraqi military bases with weapons lying on the road. "We shot it [the empty base] up with everything we had and we were laughing

and having a good time. The Iraqis let us in the country; we didn't take it."

Upon entering Baghdad, his unit came upon an unarmed pro-Saddam demonstration and killed several of the demonstrators. "I knew we caused the insurgency to be pissed off because they had witnessed us executing innocent civilians." Massey told us how the U.S. embedded reporter, Ron Harris, from the *St. Louis Post-Dispatch* wrote that there was a "ferocious battle" between his unit and the Iraqi military, but it never happened. The reporter was writing what the Marines wanted him to write.

Showing the signs of severe depression for which he now takes medication, Massey told how his mental state began to decline one day when an Iraqi man asked him in near perfect English, "Why did you kill my brother?" After that, Massey tried to put himself in situations where he would be killed because, "I didn't want to carry the burden anymore." He soon became belligerent toward his military superiors, telling them how he really felt about the war. Quickly enough they asked for his resignation for fear he would infect the unit he led. "We are committing genocide," Massey told us as he shared how the U.S. military is firing depleted uranium shells into buildings, ensuring that the toxic debris would leave a wave of contamination in the country for years to come.

When I arrived in Boston, the local papers were talking about the city's denial of protest groups' requests to have a rally outside the Fleet Center, where the Democratic National Convention would take place. Instead of a rally permit, the city proposed a "designated free-speech zone" be created nearby. One journalist described the designated space as follows: *The zone is large enough only for 1,000 persons to safely congregate and is bounded by two chain link fences separated by concrete highway barriers. The outermost fence is covered with black mesh that is designed to repel liquids. Much of the area is under an abandoned elevated train line. The zone is covered by another black net which is topped by razor wire. There will be no sanitary facilities in the zone, and tables and chairs will not be permitted. There is no way for the demonstrators to pass written materials to the convention delegates.*

One of the workers building the "free-speech" area was quoted in the *Boston Globe* calling it an "internment camp." By the time the word got out about the controversial space in the city, most activists decided to boycott the designated zone and demonstrate elsewhere.

The obvious irony is that Boston is popularly known for its *Freedom Trial*. It's called *The Cradle of Liberty*. In Boston's famous Faneuil Hall protest meetings were held under the leadership of Sam Adams and others opposed the British Empire's Sugar Tax of 1764 and Stamp Act of 1765 that ignited the revolution. Anti-slavery advocates held numerous rallies in Faneuil Hall in the 1840-1850s. They featured the likes of William Lloyd Garrison and Frederick Douglass. Preservation of the Union and women's suffrage events were also held inside the hall. The grounds around Faneuil Hall are now overflowing with tourists, but the revolutionary spirit on most days has been reduced to just another consumer product.

In keeping with the revolutionary history of the place, the Veterans for Peace held an evening rally in Faneuil Hall on July 23. The words "Liberty and Union Now and

Forever" are permanently emblazoned on the stage under a huge painting of early revolutionary leaders. Among the speakers this evening were young organizers of a new group, Iraq Veterans Against the War,[78] and parents of soldiers in Iraq who formed Military Families Speak Out.[79] VFP members in the audience raised the rafters as they stood to support these courageous Americans. Howard Zinn and Daniel Ellsberg also spoke at the event. Ellsberg, famous for releasing the *Pentagon Papers* to the *New York Times* during the Vietnam War, told the packed hall that "We don't expect and demand courage from people in government. We need more of it, and we need it now!"

On July 24 and 25, I moved to the Boston Social Forum, being held at nearby University of Massachusetts Boston. Several thousand people had come from all over the country to participate in over 500 workshops and panel discussions on almost every progressive issue imaginable. I had been invited to participate in a panel entitled *The Dangers of Nuclear War & The Imperative of Abolition*. In addition, I held two workshops during the forum on space weapons issues. The place was packed with organizers tabling, and I can't remember when I saw such a diversity of people and issues all in one place.

At the forum, I attended one session on community organizing being facilitated by a group of low-income women fighting to stop cutbacks in social spending. They spoke about how corporate profiteering destroys networks of people as jobs move out of communities to other parts of the world. Movement building becomes extremely difficult when you have a transitory society where every "man" is on his own — a dog eat dog culture. The women talked about how creating our own cultures, and celebrating our diversity and spirituality, have to be relied upon to ground people so they can begin to become politically active again.

The women also spoke about the need for our organizing strategies to be multidimensional. Many times people ask, "What is the one thing we can do?" In order to ultimately defeat the overwhelming power and control of corporate America, we must do many things at once that in the end overwhelm the system causing its breakdown and thus opening the door to fundamental structural change.

It was a great four days of witnessing the coming together of tremendous people from around the country and around the world. One really special moment came when I ran into Dolores Huerta, whom I first met in 1978 when she was Vice-President of the United Farm Workers Union. She administered my entrance interview when I applied to join the staff of the UFW. I spent time with her on several occasions while with the UFW, including as a note taker in contract negotiations between the union and the Coca Cola corporation as she led the talks over contract extensions for fruit pickers with the Minute Maid company, owned by Coke. She told me she had left the UFW four years earlier to create a foundation dedicated to local community organizing.

# SERMONS IN THE GYMNASIUM

On July 28, 2004, I flew to Los Angeles to begin several days of speaking events. The initial invitation came from Jeff Dietrich at the Los Angeles Catholic Worker community.[80] Global Network members Randy Ziglar and Cris Gutierrez organized several other events in the region for me while I was there.

Before I left Maine, I did three radio interviews to promote the trip. One was on Pacifica station *KPFK* in Los Angeles, another was at a college station in Orange County, and one was in the Santa Barbara area. Immediately after arriving in Los Angeles, six of us viewed a new documentary video being produced by GN advisory board member MacGregor Eddy about Vandenberg Air Force Base (AFB) where George W. Bush intends to deploy "missile defense" interceptors prior to the upcoming national election. The video, called *A Space 4 Peace,* was put together by a budding filmmaker, Dan Reilly, and features GN board members Loring Wirbel and Helen Caldicott and former Clinton Pentagon official, Phillip Coyle.[81]

Over the next two days, I spoke to groups in Anaheim, at the Catholic Worker House, and to a packed "salon" in a beautiful, magical house in Los Angeles organized by Jonathan Parfrey of Physicians for Social Responsibility. The house, made of used beams from sailing ships, had the grounds and atmosphere of a Tolkien movie.

On July 31, Cris Gutierrez and I headed north to Santa Barbara where we had a breakfast meeting with local organizers to discuss upcoming 2004 events, including the GN's Keep Space for Peace Week, and a September rally outside Vandenberg AFB featuring Dr. Helen Caldicott.

From there, Cris and I drove another hour north for a midday rally at the front gates of Vandenberg AFB. About 30 people assembled, surrounded by military police on horses, in off road vehicles, on foot with video cameras filming our every move, and in a military helicopter circling overhead. I spoke at a short rally about the importance of getting people out for the September action. I told the assembled crowd I thought the real purpose of the over abundance of military personnel at the gate was not out of fear of us protestors. They were actually putting on a show for those driving along the busy highway outside the base. The message to the public was — STAY AWAY FROM THESE PROTESTS. THEY ARE DANGEROUS AND YOU MIGHT GET IN TROUBLE. The "militarization of protest" is about creating fear of association with peacemakers. From Vandenberg, Cris and I made a speedy return back to Santa Monica because I was scheduled to speak at an event organized by the Green Party that evening.

After coming back home for a couple of days, I headed out to Minnesota on August 7. Here, I was wonderfully hosted by Leslie Reindl & Marie Braun who work with the group called WAMM (Women Against Military Madness). Leslie has a cable TV show and immediately took me to the studio to tape a one-hour interview. As soon as I finished that, Chris Spotted Eagle, who hosts a local Native American radio show called *Indian Uprising*, came in to interview me for his show. Leslie, and her husband Wilhelm, then proceeded to videotape the radio interview and said they'd put it on their cable show as well. The interview with Chris Spotted Eagle was quite lovely. We spent a lot of time talking about the need for a spiritual reconnection with the Earth as a key element to changing the politics of the U.S. I told him about a book I had read many years ago, called *Lame Deer Seeker of Visions*. Chris said he had taken the cover photo for the book. It was a wonderful sharing with a sweet and gentle man.

That evening, Leslie and Marie organized a potluck supper and talk for me at a local church that was quite well attended. Several leaders from the local Veterans for Peace chapter, the largest in the country, were there. They had hosted me in Minnesota on two previous trips; it was great to see them again.

On Sunday, August 8, I had the surprise of my life. Marie attends the St. Joan of Arc Catholic Church in Minneapolis and had arranged for me to deliver the homily at the 9:00 a.m. and 11:00 a.m. services. Some 800 people attended the service in the church sanctuary, set inside a gymnasium. It's a slow time in the summer, Marie said, normally there are about 1,000 at each of the two services. This was the most beautiful and progressive service that I had ever witnessed. An excellent band played *Imagine* by John Lennon and other great music. They read from my article in the latest *Space Alert* newsletter. I was deeply moved by the reception to my homily. I talked about the fabric of America being one of violence and war beginning with the genocide of Native Americans, the introduction of slavery, the taking of vast lands from Mexico, and then expansion and wars ever since. I asked them what it said about America's soul when our number one industrial export was weapons. And, I concluded with the statement that we will never end war until we deal with the jobs issue. We must convert the weapons industry if we ever hope to end our national addiction to war and violence. Following the two services I was surprised to see about 100 people come to hear me speak at the church's Adult Education class.

In Minneapolis, they understand about weapons production. Alliant Tech (where Depleted Uranium munitions are made) and Lockheed Martin are located in the community. When I arrived at the local airport, Lockheed Martin had a huge sign at the entrance to baggage claim that read *We Know Who We Work For*. I bet they do!

My last stop on the trip was in Rhode Island where the Quakers were holding their annual Northeastern Yearly Meeting at Bryant College. I was hosted by Frances Crowe and Marguerite Hasbrouck and showed our new *Arsenal of Hypocrisy* video twice during workshop sessions.

At virtually each event I was asked, "What will John Kerry do about Star Wars?" I answered by saying that Kerry has long supported research & development spending for Star Wars and still pledges to continue to do so. While Bush wants to rush "missile defense" deployments, Kerry and the majority of the Democratic Party are in no hurry to deploy — considering that the testing phase has not even concluded or shown terrific success. But in the end, I responded, Kerry and the Democrats are in full agreement with the Republicans on the expansion of the U.S. military and economic empire. The main point of contention is implementation of the plan. George W. Bush, the tin-horn dictator on a horse, wants to go it alone, while Kerry and the Democrats think we have to give the "allies" a piece of the action. Thus the Democrats contend they will do a "better job" of Homeland Security, the war on terrorism, and military transformation because they will have the "support" of the allies. There is no real difference of opinion between the parties on the U.S. "controlling and dominating" space or the U.S. having 14 new bases in Iraq so that we can control the region's oil.

# VIGIL AND FAST AT NAVY BASE

*"Take the first step in faith. You don't have to see
the whole staircase, just take the first step."*

—Dr. Martin Luther King Jr.

In the summer of 2004, Mary Beth and I were feeling a great sense of frustration. The news out of Iraq was devastating as the American body count grew, and the officially "uncounted" number of Iraqi deaths overwhelmed us.

We participated in activities with our local peace group PeaceWorks, which held a vigil every week and offered various educational programs. I was a member of Maine Veterans for Peace and Peace Action Maine. We were plenty busy, but we needed something more. We needed to stop "life as usual" to reflect – and provoke reflection by others—on all the lives lost in this illegal and shameful war and occupation in Iraq.

Once we opened the conversation, it took us no time to craft a decision to do a 48-hour vigil and fast here in Brunswick at the Naval Air Station. The perfect time was fast approaching—the third anniversary of the 9-11 tragedies.

Mary Beth and I wrote an op-ed that our local newspaper, *The Times Record*, published on September 10, 2004 in a half-page spread that included a picture of billowing smoke from the attack on the twin towers in New York. We offer the article here:

# PEACE VIGIL & FAST PLANNED AT NASB

When the terrorism of September 11, 2001 occurred, there was a time when much of the planet stopped to mourn. The tragedy deeply touched our souls. We grieved and tried to grasp the magnitude of the events. People around the world symbolically held hands with the American people.

We are among the millions who worked to prevent the rush to war in response to 9-11. Nevertheless, since the traumatic losses of that horrific day, our nation has unleashed a military force that has resulted in an overwhelming number of deaths. It is official policy of the U.S. government not to count the dead of our "enemy." The unofficial numbers are staggering: greater than 3,100 civilians in Afghanistan and at least 11,500 Iraqi civilians dead (before the recent fighting in Najaf). American soldiers are bearing the burden in incomprehensible numbers as well, as each day brings us closer to 1,000 deaths in Iraq, at least 130 in Afghanistan, and by now greater than 6,000 wounded physically. There is no end in sight.[82]

As Americans, what are we to do? We read the daily news, sigh with despair over the mounting losses that we cannot absorb, and then carry on with our daily routine. But in truth, it weighs heavy. We see clearly that each death leads to a deeper desire for revenge and attack, thus breeding rather than diminishing terrorism. Violence begets violence.

We've decided our way to honor the incomprehensible losses in the last three years is to simply stop. For 48 hours we will vigil and fast. We will stand in front of the Brunswick Naval Air Station (NASB). We will spend our time reflecting on the madness of war, the cost to our national treasury, and the sadness of loved ones lost. We will look to engage others to envision alternatives to war.

The NASB is our choice because we cannot ignore the fact that our community's economy is dependent on a base that aids the war and occupation in Iraq. Recently, three NASB squadrons were given "Battle Efficiency" awards for their surveillance and reconnaissance missions that helped direct attacks over the Iraq war zone. The war has hit close to home.

We acknowledge that we also have a role in this war. Our tax dollars pay for the reconnaissance missions, the satellite technology, the cluster bombs, the "smart" bombs, the bombs encased in toxic depleted uranium, and the private contractors' graft as they "rebuild" a country that has been virtually destroyed.

This war and occupation in Iraq should never have happened. The Bush administration acknowledges Iraq had nothing to do with the attacks on 9-11, and it had no weapons of mass destruction. Yet, we are supposed to accept that this "pre-emptive" war is justified. Meanwhile, Halliburton, its subsidiaries, and other corporations are making massive profits from war spending, and *Reuters* reports that $8.8 billion of our tax dollars are unaccounted for by the new government in Iraq. Just imagine how many teachers, nurses, childcare workers and the like could be hired here at home with that wasted money.

War also directly impacts members of the peace movement. We comfort friends and co-workers who have lost family members in Iraq, who live with the daily stress of waiting for the next e-mail from the son in Iraq, or who live knowing that it's only a matter of time before their loved one is sent off to war. Our friends include many who live with the physical or psychological wounds from their own experiences in wars past.

We know we will hear that our country is doing its best to help bring democracy to Iraq. But we have spent too many hours reading our military's documents and studying history to believe that is our true mission. Protecting corporate "interests and investments" is the fundamental purpose of our massive military spending, and of our occupation of Iraq. The only democracy our government will allow in Iraq is one that protects U.S. access to resources, and U.S. continued military presence in the region.

The rest of the world seems to understand that the U.S. has become an empire. One thing empires do is take over other countries' resources—like their oil or water. History shows us that empires, and the wars they make, are ultimately doomed to failure.

We will go to NASB on September 10 at 6:00 pm, and stay through Sunday, September 12 at 6:00 p.m. Members of Veterans for Peace and other peace groups will join us throughout the weekend, and we invite concerned citizens to join us by bringing a candle to our vigil. This vigil is not about blaming the troops. Rather, it is our way to express that the Iraq war policy is wrong. War is terror for everyone involved. We feel that we must publicly take a stand to say enough is enough.

# FLORIDA BOMBING RANGE FIGHT

*"It is time to speak your truth, each of you. Do not look outside yourself for the leader. There is a river flowing very fast. Trust the river has its destination. You must let go of the shore, push off into that river. Keep your eyes open and your heads above the water. See who is in there with you and celebrate. The time of the lone wolf is over. Gather yourselves. We are the ones we have been waiting for...."*

—Message from Hopi Elders in Arizona

On October 6, 2004 I returned from a one-day trip to Perry, Florida to speak to a gathering of concerned citizens who are organizing to stop the placement of a new bombing range in their rural community.

Perry is up in the Florida Panhandle, just south of the capital city of Tallahassee. The region is called the "Nature Coast" as Taylor county touches the Gulf of Mexico and has several key rivers that run through its pine tree forests to the Gulf. The county has a relatively small population as Florida goes, and that is one reason the Pentagon sees it as an ideal place to put a bombing range.

There is a bombing range already in the region, just a couple hours further west at Eglin A.F.B. near Fort Walton Beach. I lived there while in high school while my stepfather was stationed at Eglin, and I hiked through the middle of the bombing range as an Explorer Scout. It is one of the largest military bases in the nation, but population has grown around the base to the point where the noise from the bombing range has begun to draw complaints. Most recently, the Mother of all Bombs (MOAB) was tested at Eglin. The MOAB is the most powerful non-nuclear bomb ever created and forms a mushroom cloud and shockwaves similar to a small nuclear explosion.

Rural Taylor County, where Perry is located, already has huge problems. The Buckeye paper mill has been contaminating the Fenholloway River that flows into the Gulf. Long ago classified as an industrial river, it is essentially dead and dumps toxic pollution into the Gulf. Groundwater contamination in Perry has long been a result, and one local activist, Joy Towles Ezell, has been working to organize people in her company-controlled town for years. Joy is a fifth-generation Taylor County resident who has now taken on the military over the bombing range.

I met Joy years ago when I worked for the Florida Coalition for Peace & Justice. We tried to support her work around the paper mill and she supported our efforts to alert people when cruise missiles were fired from Navy ships positioned in the Gulf. The missiles flew over the Panhandle, and then crashed onto the Eglin AFB bombing range. Before the meeting Tuesday night, Joy showed me a letter she wrote to then Gov. Lawton Chiles in 1991 on our behalf, protesting the cruise missile tests. Years later, when I organized a 700-mile *Walk for the Earth* from the Everglades to Tallahassee, we camped on her land outside of Perry and held a rally at the paper mill.[83] My son, Julian, had a great time riding one of her prized mules.

Fifty local residents gathered on October 5 in the back room of the Chaparral Restaurant. The first thing Joy did when we arrived was make two of us go out front and put up on the portable advertising sign the words "Don't Bomb Nature Coast Meeting 7:00 p.m." just below the words "Country Buffet."

The first speaker was Dr. Ronald Saff from Florida State University in Tallahassee who is an expert on coal-fired power plant pollution. In addition to the paper mill and the bombing range, there are also plans to build a coal-fired power plant in Taylor County. Obviously, a decision has been made sacrifice the area by turning it into a wasteland.

Taylor County is your basic southern, rural, conservative community. People vote Republican and they don't take to outsiders very well. They don't do radical politics, either. That is what made the meeting so special.

The 50 folks who gathered were retired school teachers, good church-goers, the local industrial development officer, well dressed, quiet and concerned. One of them, a refined southern, Republican, Episcopalian woman had been in the group that the Air Force recently flew to Eglin to show how nice the bombing range looked, though she was totally unconvinced by the show-trip. The Taylor County delegation was promised that depleted uranium would not be used in their county. Joy was not invited to go along.

The Eglin AFB Bombing Range started testing depleted Uranium (DU) in 1973. Over 220,000 pounds of DU penetrators have been exploded there. Cruise missiles that crashed on the Eglin range carried DU as ballast in the nose cones in place of a warhead. After a so-called "clean-up" effort by the military, a public health assessment at Eglin estimates that 90-95% of the DU remains in the soil.

People in Taylor County have been told that cruise missiles will be tested over their heads and that the weapons will circle around in Alabama and come back to the proposed bombing range to crash land. The military says it "needs" the Taylor County range because it needs to practice firing cruise missiles off ships in the Gulf of Mexico. The Pentagon has been telling the residents that the tests are practice for "missile defense" as part of Homeland Security. A pro-bombing range group called "Citizens for Homeland Security" has been organized, but residents say it consists of just a couple of people who are involved in the money trail behind the bombing range and the coal plant.

I told the residents it was time to redefine the term "homeland security." I asked how secure they were when their water, air and land were becoming so contaminated that future generations could not live there. I also told them cruise missiles were first-strike, sneak attack weapons that have nothing to do with "defense." Cruise missiles, I said, are part of a preemptive military policy that violates international law. I asked them how they'd feel if another country launched sneak attack weapons into the U.S..

The local Rotary Club was offered a gift of $10,000 to support the bombing range. The county government was offered $40 million. Local hunters were promised continued access to the range so they can hunt deer and wild boar on the land. In spite of all that, the local residents organized a non-binding referendum on the question to be placed on the November ballot. They think they will win the vote, but fear the county will agree to the range anyway.[84]

The folks have yard signs, buttons, bumper stickers and will have a booth at the upcoming "Forest Festival" that draws 20,000 from the region. They keep letters to the editor flowing into their local paper in order to combat new rumors put out by the military.

The meeting ended with Joy calling Vieques, Puerto Rico to speak with Robert Rabin, one of the leaders of their long and successful campaign to close down the military bombing range on their beautiful island. I can't describe the feeling of listening to Robert as Joy held the microphone to her cell phone. I looked around the room. People were listening attentively as Robert told the story of how the Navy dropped a bomb on a Navy building, killing one of their own security guards, a young man much loved by the community. A moan went through the room. It felt like a knife through the heart. The Taylor County community had been assured by the military that they never have accidents. It was incredible to hear Robert use the word "love" a dozen times to describe the core of their campaign against the Navy, and explain how they used non-violent civil disobedience. The people listened and, after his 15-minute talk, they applauded vigorously.

There is nothing like life experience to change people. The folks in Taylor County are changing rapidly. One woman, a life-long Christian and good Republican, told me she'd never vote for another Republican again. (I couldn't help but think how stupid the Bush administration is to bring this bombing range issue up right before the November election in a state where EVERY VOTE really counts.)

At the end of the meeting, the people asked me two things. What more can we do, and do you think we can win? I told them the people in Vieques won because they became a "pain in the ass," and Taylor County had to do the same. I also told them they could not do this alone, that they needed to send folks out around the state to educate others about the issue. I acknowledged two people in the audience from the Florida Coalition for Peace & Justice, John Linnehan from Jacksonville and Bob Tancig from Gainesville. Bob is the new director of the organization. John had picked me up at the Jacksonville airport and drove me to Perry. They pledged the support of the Florida Coalition.

I urge others to send a message of solidarity to Joy and the folks in Taylor County. They could use some encouragement and some hope. I know they gave me a huge amount of both. You can reach Joy Towles Ezell at hope@gtcom.net

This is how America will change.

# SUPPORTING CANADIANS' OPPOSITION TO STAR WARS

This report covers the period of October 12-21, 2004 on my recent speaking tour of Nova Scotia, Canada. The tour was organized by Global Network board member Tamara Lorincz who is a leader in the Halifax Peace Coalition that sponsored my trip.

Mary Beth (MB) and I made the 10-hour drive from Maine to Halifax where the tour began. Tamara arranged for an op-ed I wrote about Canadian participation in "missile defense" to be placed in the *Halifax Daily News* and the *Cape Breton Post* before I arrived. The Canadian government, under intense pressure from the Bush administration and its own aerospace industry, is on the verge of making a decision about participation in the U.S. Star Wars program. Newly-elected Canadian Prime Minister Paul Martin (Liberal party) has publicly stated that Canada would not participate in the program if it led to the weaponization of space, and maintains that the present "missile defense" program would be strictly defensive. The Canadian peace movement is doing an admirable job of creating national debate and pressure on its government to stay out of the program. During our recent *Keep Space for Peace Week* there were more than 30 protests across Canada.

Tamara arranged for me to speak in Halifax, Wolfville, Annapolis Royal, Sydney and Truro. This included talks at Dalhousie University, Acadia University, University College of Cape Breton, and the Nova Scotia Community College. On the student union building marquee at Dalhousie, my talk was advertised as "U.S. World Domination."

One highlight of my Halifax visit was a live one-hour radio talk show interview on *CJCH*, which broadcasts across the province of Nova Scotia. I reminded listeners that the primary reasons behind U.S. pressure on Canada to join Star Wars were: (1) help the U.S. pay for the very expensive program; (2) use Canada's good name and reputation as a neutral nation to bring legitimacy to Star Wars; and (3) bring Canada's aerospace industry into the effort, thus ensuring Canadian government support. The eight callers who phoned in were opposed to their country's joining the U.S. space domination effort.

As we prepared to leave Halifax, we got an invitation to have tea with the matriarch of the Canadian peace movement, 96-year-old Muriel Duckworth, and Quaker activist Betty Peterson. Ever sharp, Muriel told stories of her first days creating a national women's peace organization and opposition to the Vietnam War. Betty, a former American citizen, one of many we would meet during the trip, was following the U.S. election closely and was particularly interested in talking about the growing strength of the Christian fundamentalist movement. As it turned out, Betty had been at a space center

"WHAT'S WRONG, PEOPLE? YOU WANNA BE
SOOPER-DOOPER SAFE, DON'T YOU?"

protest I organized in 1987 at Cape Canaveral, Florida. The visit with these women was quite special and will be treasured by MB and me.

Our next stop was Wolfville, and on the way we stopped at Grand Pre national historic site, the place where the French Acadian population had been rounded up and from which it was expelled by the conquering British in 1755. Over 6,000 Acadians were deported and their villages burned to the ground. It was hard not to see that the same things are still happening today as people are pushed off their lands in Palestine, Iraq, Sudan and other countries across the globe.

In Wolfville, we were hosted by Janet and Peter Eaton. Janet is a wonderful multi-issue activist and professor at Acadia University. Her home saw a constant flow of visitors and one of the most exciting for us was Colin Bernhardt, the director of the Acadia University Theatre Company. For over an hour, Colin enchanted us with his vision of using theater to help expand the public consciousness around political issues. For me, it was like attending church. The spiritual sparks were flying in every direction as Colin rose from his chair and began performing for us. It was particularly encouraging for me as I now chair the Action Committee of Peace Action Maine and we recently decided to undertake the task of organizing a multi-year campaign to convert the war industry to peaceful production. One of our first strategies will be to enlist the artistic community in a campaign to help people "see" the conversion message. Colin's inspiration felt like a good sign.

After a talk in Annapolis Royal, one of the most beautiful spots on the trip, MB had to return to Maine. She was taken by a local peace person to Yarmouth where she boarded the Scotia Prince for a rough ten-hour sea journey back to Portland. I, then, made the six hour drive to my next talk in Sydney, located on Cape Breton.

Tamara scheduled a day off for me so I could drive the incredible Cabot Trail in Cape Breton. Full of fall colors and rocky coastline, I was dazzled as I made each winding turn on the day-long trip. At Ingonish, I took a one-hour hike out to the rock cliff point where I saw a whale. Just south of Cheticamp I parked along the water and listened as the wind howled all around me. Nearby, I watched the sleek tall white windmill slowly turn wind into electricity, remembering that weapons production facilities could be building these rather than instruments of death and destruction.

That evening, I had the pleasure of staying in the home of Maria and Brian Peters in the Margaree Valley. Brian had come to the valley from Ontario 30 years before to live in a "hippie" commune and was the only one to stay. He married the Maria, a local girl, and they built their own lovely home in the woods where today they use water from the mountain stream to power their electricity. They also have a composting toilet. Brian builds all their furniture from the wood on their land, and they grow most of their own food. Maria, a public health nurse, had just returned from several wrenching months in Haiti delivering health care to the victims of a collapsing Haiti. Her sad stories again reminded us that U.S. policy toward that nation has done everything to obstruct real solutions to its difficult existence.

My last stop on the trip was in Truro where I was hosted by the Rev. Margaret Sagar from the United Church of Canada. Margaret had run for parliament in the last election on the New Democratic Party (NDP) ticket, a progressive party that has been a leader in opposition to Canada's participation in Star Wars. She arranged for a local reporter to interview me before my talk at the community college which was attended by students and local community folk.

The eight-hour drive home gave me plenty of time to reflect on this 2,000 mile long trip. I was quite proud to be a bit of help to the dedicated Canadian peace movement that is working so hard to keep their country from jumping into the dangerous and destabilizing space arms race. As I was leaving Canada, I learned Prime Minister Martin was calling for a debate in Parliament on the issue, but was instructing his Liberal party members that they had to follow him in voting for participation with the U.S. in "missile defense." The peace movement's response was an immediate demand for public hearings all across the nation so that the people could have input into the decision.

As always, I leave a region where good people are making huge efforts to educate the public and to participate as fully-engaged citizens, demanding democracy. The Canadian peace movement is proud of its efforts to prevent its government from supporting the U.S in its war with Iraq. The movement to reject Canada's participation in Star Wars is growing stronger every day.

# ORGANIZING
# TRIP TO FRANCE

Between October 28-November 4, 2004 I attended an anti-nuclear conference in Saintes, France and then traveled to St. Pierre and Toulouse for speaking events.

I was invited to speak at a conference called "Rally for International Disarmament: Nuclear, Biological & Chemical," organized by the French peace group ACDN, a member of Abolition 2000. I flew into Paris and then took the train south through wine country to Saintes. Along the way, I passed the town of Cognac. On the train with me was Russian anti-nuclear activist Natalia Mironova who was also scheduled to speak at the event. We discovered we shared similar concerns: our two countries are moving in authoritarian directions working to limit democracy and surrender to multinational corporate interests.

Organized by Jean-Marie Matagne, the conference included talks by two veterans who are now physically ill; one was contaminated by France's Pacific nuclear testing and the other was exposed to Depleted Uranium during the Persian Gulf war. A moving presentation by activist Andre Bouny showed chilling photos of Vietnamese children with various physical mutations, whose parents had been exposed to U.S. Agent Orange spraying during the war. Andre organizes medical aid for the Vietnamese and has adopted two children from the country. Andre himself is disabled, but is unstoppable as he climbs stairs and quickly moves around with crutches.

Saintes, the place where the conference was held, is steeped in history. Roman arches overlook the river that runs through the middle of the town which once served as an imperial outpost along the Roman road. On a day off, I toured a 1,000-year-old abbey that was built as a training ground for the daughters of the rich. It was turned into a prison following the French revolution and today serves as a cultural center for the community.

The U.S. Presidential election was a hot topic during the trip. I had voted absentee before I left Maine. Everyone wanted to know who I thought would win. French TV and *BBC World News* were doing extensive coverage of the pre-election buildup. It was clear to me that the U.S. election was really a global one. The rest of the world had strong opinions, and indeed, would be impacted by the outcome. Of course, the French, like many African-American voters in Florida and Ohio, had no say in this election.

Following the conference, Jean-Marie and Andre took me to St. Pierre, an island tourist community, along the Atlantic coast. There, we spoke at a cinema that showed the BBC film *The Bomb*, a graphic story about the likely effects of nuclear war. From there, we headed further south to the city of Toulouse, also known as the *cite de l'espace* (city of space) where a NASA-like space center tourist facility has been created to promote the French role in space to unsuspecting citizens. Toulouse is the center for France's aerospace industry. It is where Airbus and the Ariane rocket are built.

As we entered the space tourist center I saw that the electronic marquee was flashing my and Andre's names with details of our 3:00 p.m. talk. First, a friendly public relations specialist treated us to a fine three-course French meal and then took us on a tour of the center, including a walk through the MIR space station that France purchased from Russia. (I had to admit that treatment like this would never be offered to me at the Kennedy Space Center in Florida, where I organized many protests over the years.) One person who came to our afternoon talk was a reporter with the French astronomy magazine *Ciel Espace*. He handed me the latest edition of the glossy magazine that included a story he had written called "NASA's Reliance on Nuclear Propulsion," and included extensive quotes from me. His English was so good we immediately enlisted him as my French interpreter during my talk.

Later that same evening, Andre, Jean-Marie, and I did a talk at a local cinema called *Utopia* following another showing of *Le Bomb*. By now the election in the U.S. was over and the results known. The audience was shocked, angry and amazed that the American people had returned Bush to office. I was asked over and over again, "Don't the Americans know that there were no WMD in Iraq?" When I responded that the media in the U.S. are now under the control of a hand full of big corporations, they acknowledged they now have the same problem in France. The well-known left-wing paper *Le Monde* had recently been bought by a large French weapons corporation. It underscored my constant theme that the multinational corporations are taking over the world and don't have allegiance to any one nation any more. It is all about maximizing profits, and the world's media are being bought up in order to facilitate the process of manipulation of the public mind.

Having lived in Europe for almost six years as a young boy, I saw my share of castles. My own way of looking at the world is shaped by those early experiences. During the conference in Saintes, while sitting in a plenary session, I found myself writing a poem that came from the intense emotion I was feeling about the U.S. election, the global weapons buildup, and being once again in the presence of the ruins from past empires. Here it is:

### HISTORY LIVES

History lives in the present
The Kings, the Lords, and the peasant.
The power still remains
The people know but play the game
in hopes it won't be true.
What else are they to do?
Better to go along, pretend,

in hopes they won't have to defend
themselves from the treachery.
The fortress walls of the past change, crumble,
are today rebuilt with steel and atomic blasts.
But the barriers to the future
live like in the past.

Thanks to all my kind hosts. By the way, it is true, French desserts are wonderful!
See you on the streets, dear friends.

# BIG SKY AND STAR WARS
# DEBATE IN WESTERN CANADA

*"I have come to the conclusions that politics are too serious*
*a matter to be left to the politicians."*

—Charles De Gaulle

From November 25—December 3, 2004, I traveled in Manitoba and Saskatchewan provinces in Canada on a speaking tour. The trip was coordinated by the No War Coalition in Winnipeg, Manitoba.

As it turned out, the timing for this long-planned trip could not have been better as George W. Bush made his first visit to Canada on November 30 and December 1 and dramatically increased the interest in the "missile defense" issue.

When I arrived in Winnipeg, I almost did not make it out of the airport. Canadian customs discovered that I was carrying a load of videos and books and they diverted me to a side room where they calculated the tax on the items and charged me $63. Then, they asked if I'd ever been convicted of a crime, and when I said I had been arrested for non-violent civil disobedience, they wanted to know how many times. They also asked me how many times I had been arrested in the last five years. "Twice," I replied. The immigration officer then told me to have a seat while he ran a background check on me. When he returned, he told me they had a rule that if you have been convicted of a crime twice in the last five years you cannot enter Canada. Then, checking the long computer printout in his hand, he said "Oh, one of these was by the military and that does not count." He was referring to my last arrest at Vandenberg AFB in California.[85] So, they let me in.

I spent three days in Winnipeg speaking at several places including the University of Manitoba, a church Sunday school and the planetarium. The latter drew 200 people and was covered by three local TV networks. I also did a one-hour live radio talk show on CBC. The show was aired throughout Manitoba and was simultaneously broadcast on cable TV across the whole country. During the first half of the show, I debated a university professor who wants Canada to join Bush's "missile defense" program. I used my time to talk about how the program was not about "defense." Bush's upcoming visit to Canada, I said, was for the purpose of using Canada's good name to legitimize the program. Star Wars is going to be so expensive that Bush is out rounding up the posse to help pay for it, I said. Of the nine people that called in, eight opposed Canada's participation.

Newspapers reported that recently-elected Canadian Prime Minister Paul Martin was saying that Bush's visit would not be dealing with "missile defense." Twenty months ago, while campaigning for the Liberal party leadership, Martin favored Canada's joining the program. But, with recent national polls showing that a majority of citizens opposed Canadian involvement, Martin was trying to avoid the subject during the Bush visit. Instead, Martin wanted to focus on the beef ban (due to a short bout of Mad Cow Disease) that the U.S. had imposed on Canada, which was destroying its beef industry.

Before the trip, I had been asked what I would like to do during my free time. I replied that I'd like to see anything to do with Indian culture as I knew this region of Canada was rich in Native traditions. While in Winnipeg, my hosts took me to the Aboriginal Centre of Winnipeg to meet with First Nations leaders and get a tour of the place. The Centre turned out to be a huge former railway station, built in 1905. The building had come vacant in the early 1990's and was purchased by Aboriginal leaders in 1992. Between 1993-1997 hundreds of people restored the magnificent rotunda area of the building and today it houses clinics, children's centers, healing programs, employment services, educational programs, an art gallery, legal aid offices, and a restaurant that serves buffalo burgers. Wayne Helgason, the first president of the coordinating board, shared with us the joys and struggles of the long campaign to bring much-needed human services to the large but neglected First Nations population in the area. The Aboriginal population, once relegated to barren reserves, has been moving into the urban areas, and the Centre has proved to be a great service to the people. Just across the street, a spiritual roundhouse had also been constructed, but I was not able to visit it that day.

One other great experience I had while in Winnipeg was a lunch meeting with key leaders of peace and religious groups, union leaders, and civic activists. We shared the latest on the space issue and they oriented me on key political issues in Canada. One item was the fear about "deep integration" with the United States. A task force, consisting of government representatives from Canada, U.S.A. and Mexico, had been assigned to draft a plan to create a common border, common currency, military integration (including participation in Star Wars), and common policies on energy, law enforcement and refugees. Canadians were rightly concerned that the corporate takeover of the continent will mean a loss of sovereignty for their nation. The NAFTA-PLUS plan would lead to a loss of control over Canada's water supply and the opening up of their health care system to American insurance corporations.

My next stop was Brandon, a farming community in western Manitoba, where I was hosted by City Council member Errol Black. Errol interviewed me on local community access TV and then took me to the one commercial TV station in town where I was interviewed by the anchor-person for the evening news. My speech in Brandon was organized by the District Labor Council and drew a powerful and positive reaction from the audience. The question and answer period could have gone on forever as the assembled questioned why the American people allow the destruction of their democracy.

I was driven the long distance across the western prairie by veteran activist Darrell Rankin, a key leader in the Canadian Peace Alliance and the Winnipeg No War Coalition. The trip west ended up being about seven hours long as we headed through the cold and freshly snow covered land. But, it was the big sky, from horizon to horizon across the flat prairie of barren wheat fields and burnt brown grasses, that filled me with soulful memories of early years in South Dakota. As Darrell drove west we picked up the local paper and I read sections aloud about Bush's coming visit while Darrell filled me in on the layers of background behind the Canadian political scene.

When we arrived in Saskatchewan I was taken to the city of Moose Jaw for a talk. First, I did a community cable TV interview and then a group of us had dinner at the local truck stop restaurant owned by one of the peace group members. The evening talk at the local library was well attended and people left determined to stop Canada's participation in moving the arms race into space. After the talk, we drove to Regina where I would be speaking the next day.

The next morning I did a rush hour live interview on *CBC radio* in Regina. It lasted about seven minutes and I was able to address all my key points. I was staying at a local bed & breakfast and the man of the house phoned from his car on the way to work saying he liked that I reminded the audience it was the U.S. that was the only country to have ever used weapons of mass destruction, at Hiroshima and Nagasaki. I told the audience that Bush's fear mongering around the "rogue states" was intended to frighten people into supporting the weaponization of space.

This was the day Bush made his big speech in Halifax, Nova Scotia. He had declined to speak to Parliament in Ottawa, as is tradition, for fear that members of the body would heckle him. Instead, he simply had a meeting with Prime Minister Martin in Ottawa the day before, and then attended a state dinner. The Canadians were delighted to note that he ate "mesquite smoked medallion of Alberta beef" — the very meat he banned from entering the U.S. (People were watching Bush closely to see if he developed any symptoms of Mad Cow Disease, but, then again, how would we be able to tell the difference?)

Bush's speech in Halifax was greeted by about 5,000 protestors (about 20,000 had protested him in Ottawa). Activists in Halifax only had a few days to organize as Bush handlers had announced the visit at the last minute. During the event, Bush mentioned that he hoped Canada would join "missile defense." This set off a chain reaction of news headlines and opposition party howls. Bush, it seems, was not supposed to bring "missile defense" up while in Canada. According to an editorial in *The Globe and Mail* "a cozy little pact had been reached in advance between Mr. Bush's people and Prime Minister Paul Martin's people. The President was not, repeat *not*, to utter the two deadly words 'missile defense' in any of his public utterances. To do so would complicate things for Mr. Martin, who heads a minority government and has trouble in his own caucus regarding the missile defence scheme..."

At noon on that fateful day, I was taken to the University of Regina where an event was organized in the student "pit" at lunchtime. The Raging Grannies[86] sang some songs opposing Star Wars and then I briefly spoke to students and faculty who were watching the show. We also passed out leaflets advertising my talk at the university that evening. *CBC-TV* covered the event as did the French *Radio-Canada*. That evening as we watched the news on national *CBC* we heard Global Network board member Tamara Lorincz interviewed from Halifax during the demonstration outside Bush's speaking event. Then, following the national news, *CBC* switched to local coverage and the news anchor announced that, "We have two Americans in Canada today speaking about missile defense. Besides President Bush, we have Bruce Gagnon speaking in opposition..." and they went on to interview me and showed the footage of the Raging Grannies. I later told people I deeply appreciated George W. Bush's decision to plan his trip to Canada to coincide with my speaking tour!

That evening, my talk at the University of Regina was well attended; many students came. The next morning, Darrell and I drove seven hours drive back to Winnipeg. Upon arrival in Winnipeg, I was taken by Margie Warner to the First Nations roundhouse that I had not been able to visit earlier in the week. Wayne Helgason had made arrangements for his cousin, Clarence Neepinac, a spiritual leader, to give us a tour.

The beautiful building, in the shape of a teepee, has a star in the middle of the floor and is used for pow-wows and other sacred events. Outside is a sweat lodge which is used each week for spiritual cleansing and prayer.

On my last night in Winnipeg, a potluck supper was held to bid me farewell. I received gifts, including a book called *Indian Fall*, that tells of the last days of freedom for the Aboriginal peoples on the Canadian prairie. Much to my delight Clarence Neepinac also showed up and gave me sweet grass to take home to commemorate by visit to the First Nations roundhouse.

I'd like to share a couple things of note from the media. One Canadian journalist satirically wrote about the four reasons why it was great having Bush visit Canada. Her number one reason was "Because it's better to have Bush visit than the 4th Mechanized Infantry Division." Another editorial writer talked about the harsh treatment of Canadian society on U.S. TV during Bush's visit. She recalled watching the "O'Reilly Factor" show on the *Fox* network and quoted Bill O'Reilly as saying the reason Canada did not do well in the Olympics was because of a "culture of entitlements" (meaning they have national health service). Unlike Canadians, O'Reilly said Americans are committed to hard work and personal achievement. (Of course, Mr. O'Reilly did not say that over 40 million U.S. citizens don't have health care of any kind.)

Finally, the conservative *National Post* had various people of note comment on sections of Bush's speech in Halifax. In justifying the preemptive invasion of Iraq, Bush told Canadians that *"If, 20 years from now, the Middle East is dominated by dictators and mullahs who build weapons of mass destruction and harbor terrorists, our children and our grandchildren will live in a nightmare world of danger."* The newspaper had Jack Chambers, professor of linguistics at the University of Toronto, analyze this statement. He said, "On the phrase 'nightmare world of danger' Bush is referring to our worst fantasies, the part that comes from the deepest id. He's trying to get our worst fears into the front of our minds. He had 'weapons of mass destruction' in the same paragraph, so it comes out like little needles that get right into your mind."

To sum up: I was in a country that was not fooled by the fool on the hill. Bush did not succeed with his mental manipulations and in the end he put "missile defense" on the front page of every newspaper in the country. He invigorated the Canadian debate on national sovereignty and ensured that our friends in the peace movement there will have a more receptive national audience in the coming days. It was a great honor to be a small part of their resistance to Star Wars. Canada is the one country in the world today putting the issue front and center. We all wish them the best.[87]

# RETRACING MEMORIES
# ACROSS FLORIDA

*"One man can be a crucial ingredient on a team, but one man cannot make a team."*

—Kareem Abdul-Jabbar

Mary Beth and I traveled to Florida from December 24—January 11, 2005. The trip was part-vacation and part-speaking tour.

After spending a few days with our families in Sarasota and Titusville, we drove north to St. Marys, Georgia for the peace witness held each New Year's Eve outside the Kings Bay Submarine Base. For the last 24 years, peace activists have gathered at the Atlantic Ocean homeport base of the Trident nuclear submarine to hold a New Years midnight peace vigil at the gates of the installation. I've attended most of the annual events over the years and it was a good chance for Mary Beth and me to see friends again since our move to Maine. Over 60 people crowded into five cabins at the Crooked River State Park just down the road from the sub base. There, we shared food and held discussions over the course of three days. Twice we did three-mile peace walks through St. Marys, one of them leading us to the base gates for the New Year's midnight ceremony.

From the submarine base, we headed south to Melbourne, just below Cape Canaveral, where I spoke on Sunday, January 2 at the Unitarian Church. Old friends Cathy Stanton (descendant of suffragette Elizabeth Cady Stanton) and Smitty Hooper had arranged for me to deliver the sermon at the church. Over the years, Cathy and Smitty have been two of the most loyal activists in the Space Coast region in our efforts to protest the nuclearization and weaponization of space. In my talk, I outlined the growing effort of the Bush administration to move the arms race into space and concluded by calling for the conversion of the military industrial complex if we ever hoped to end war. The reception at the church was mostly positive, though one man stood up during the question period after my talk and read an editorial from the local newspaper proclaiming the wonders of the Cassini nuclear space mission that I led protests against in 1997. A woman stood up and said, "2004 was a bad year for us, with the hurricanes and all. We come to this church to feel better. And your talk was depressing. I wish you had not come."

Mary Beth and I next visited our old home in Gainesville and spent a few days there connecting with friends. We stayed at the home of Eve and Richard MacMaster. Eve is the pastor of Emmanuel Mennonite Church in Gainesville, and organized my speech at her church on January 7. It was attended by people from several different churches and peace groups. My talk was entitled the "Battle for America's Soul" and I raised the question, what does it say about our nation's soul when weapons are our number one industrial export? It was wonderful to see old friends like Julie Netzer, Miriam Welly Elliot, and Bill Warrick (my doctor and fellow member of Veterans for Peace). Bill's wife Sally, who works at the University of Florida public radio station, taped my talk for later rebroadcast at the station. My friend of many years John Hedrick drove down from Tallahassee to be at the event. He and I had created the People's Transit Organization in the early 1980's and were successful in getting Orlando to double its funding for public transportation at that time. While we love to share our latest organizing stories with each other, our visit was much too short.

After my talk that evening in Gainesville, I had to leave and immediately head south because I was to speak early the next morning to the Deerfield Progressive Forum near Ft. Lauderdale. As I was driving, I got a call on my cell phone from Ian Johnston who has a show on Pacifica radio station *KPFK* in Los Angeles. Ian had just read my article from our latest *Space Alert* newsletter and wanted me to be on his show. So, as I drove south, I did a half-hour live interview and took a couple of calls from listeners. Needless to say, it felt like a good night.

My plan that evening was to drive as far as Melbourne and get a hotel room. Mary Beth had already headed back to Sarasota for a visit with her family before returning to Maine. As I crossed the center of Florida, just south of Orlando, I passed through the rural region of the state that used to be part of the Everglades. Before white settlers came to Florida, the Everglades, the "sea of grass," had extended as far north as Orlando. At the time, the Seminole Indians lived in the northern part of the state, near Gainesville. General, later President Andrew Jackson, became famous as an Indian killer for pushing the Seminoles deep into what remains of the Everglades today, in south Florida. The majority of the sea of grass was drained and turned into grazing land for cattle. Today, overpopulation and development are turning these lands into large housing tracts and the newspapers are beginning to report that water scarcities are expected to worsen in the coming years throughout the state.

I often drove through this part of the state at night when I coordinated the Florida Coalition for Peace & Justice. For fifteen years in that job, I drove an average of 30,000 miles per year visiting our membership in every corner of the state. I'd often speak to a group in the evening and then make the long drive back home, marveling at the big starry sky so visible when out in this vast countryside, far from city lights. I always felt a spiritual connection to the Earth and sky as I made this drive and came up with some of my best ideas during these trips. Once, having just spoken to a group of senior citizen activists in Delray Beach who had asked me what the Florida Coalition was doing to get young people involved, I kept hearing their voices as I made the late-night drive. It was then that I formulated the proposal for the summer youth peace camps that are now a tradition with the Florida Coalition.

This trip to Florida was hugely emotional for me. I lived in Florida for 30 years, but always longed to return north to the seasons and cold that I loved when I was young. My favorite places were the cold-weather ones in South Dakota and Germany. Our visits to family in Maine and Connecticut, in between our moves, were always thrilling for me — especially in the winter. But Florida is really where I became an activist, where I developed my skills working with the United Farm Workers Union, and where I cut my teeth on the space issue. So, my time in the state was crucial to my career as an organizer. Now, visiting the state once again, brought back a flood of images and memories of peace walks, demonstrations and conferences, that I had organized and visits to family and friends.

My talk to the Deerfield Progressive Forum on January 8 was well received. It was held in a clubhouse at a huge senior citizen condo village that houses over 10,000 people. Essentially a city unto itself, this village of retired folks is just one of many in south Florida where peace groups are sprinkled. Progressive activists from the north retire and create groups so they can stay involved.

Next stop was St. Augustine, several hours drive north on I-95. Here, I went to the home of 94-year-old activist Peg McIntire, a woman who became a second mother to me during the 20 years we worked together. Peg, long a leader in the Florida Coalition, was one of our most effective activists and has been arrested several times at the Space Center in Florida protesting various launches of military rockets and space craft with plutonium on-board. Peg arranged for me to speak at her Unitarian Church on January 9 and expertly led the service herself. A lively discussion followed my speech and I was pleased that Peg felt good about the reception.[88]

Next on the reunion tour, I drove further north to Jacksonville to speak to the Wage Peace group there. Jacksonville is a conservative Navy town and a tough place to be a peace activist. Here, I saw Mary Claire Vanderhorst, and her husband Bill Quinlivan, dear friends from the Florida Coalition days. Al and Wendy Geiger were there, too. Al had given the Florida Coalition a sizeable piece of land north of Gainesville years before. It was to be used to build a permanent peace camp so we wouldn't have to rent one each summer. Another Florida member had donated money to build a meeting hall, and now the Florida Coalition uses the place as a center to teach a culture of peace in the state.

My last event was on January 11 as I headed south again on I-95 to Delray Beach. Here, I was to speak to the Delray Citizens for Social Responsibility, another senior-citizen-run peace group that was founded in 1981 and continues today even though the aging process is taking a toll on its membership. I probably have spoken to the Delray Citizens more times over the last 20 years than to any other group. Led by Eleanor and Irving Rempell, it is always like coming home to be with these folks. Old friend Nat Kaplan was too ill to come to my talk, but familiar faces like Bobbie Graff, author of a new book on the McCarthy period, were in the audience.

It has been hard for many of these aging veteran activists to watch America become the promoter of endless war around the world. You can see the pain in their faces as they witness a lifetime of work for social justice and peace being destroyed by the Bush administration. In my talks to the Deerfield and Delray folks, I told them they were needed now more than ever. I suggested they consider gathering up hundreds of senior citizen activists and occupying the offices of Florida Senators Bill Nelson and newly-elected Mel Martinez to protest the war in Iraq and the privatization of Social Security. I asked them to imagine the reaction of the media and the public to legions of elderly folks risking arrest in order to speak out. I even promised Eleanor Rempell I'd come back to join them if they did it.

The new senator in Florida, replacing retiring Democrat Bob Graham, is Republican Mel Martinez from Orlando. As I mentioned earlier, I have known Mel for many years. He became the Chair of the Orange County Commission and then was appointed by George W. Bush to be his cabinet secretary at Housing and Urban Development (HUD) in Washington during his first term.

So, that was my visit to Florida. It was good to see old friends, but the warm weather in January reminded me why I had long wanted to move back North where the seasons change. My trip to Florida turned out to be over 1,600 miles long and brought tears to my eyes more than once. But, it was a good chance to say to my old friends that even though I have moved North, I am still with you all and always will be. Keep resisting, dear friends. I love you all.

# LETTER TO A NEW SENATOR

## February 2, 2005 • Sen. Mel Martinez, U.S. Senate, Washington DC 20510

Dear Mel:

I write this letter to you this morning as I watch the Senate debate on *C-SPAN* about the nomination of Alberto Gonzales for Attorney General of the United States.

I saw what you described as your first-ever speech from the Senate floor, as you tried to create a groundswell of support in the Hispanic community for the controversial appointment. Seeing you, as you can imagine, brought back a flood of memories from our days coaching our kids in baseball in Orlando years ago.

One memory from that time was the frequent debates you and I had over Castro and U.S. policy toward Cuba. I remember one time, while we were pitching batting practice to the kids, we got so involved in debate that we left the kids standing for some time as we carried on.

One of your chief arguments against Castro was his record on human rights abuses in Cuba. You were quite eloquent about the many who had been locked up in Castro's prisons and who had suffered from torture and abuse.

You can imagine my surprise and dismay to hear you defend Mr. Gonzales. It is now well known that as George W. Bush's in-house attorney, Mr. Gonzales has been a primary party to the creation of legal and rational justification for U.S. torture in Iraq and at the U.S. prison base in Guantanamo, Cuba. The FBI and the Red Cross have concluded there is torture at Guantanamo. Yet the administration persists in denying the obvious.

I find it so ironic that your first speech would essentially try to provide a rationalization for the appointment of a man who has basically disavowed the Geneva Conventions. You, who come from the Cuban soil, now in a position of power in the U.S., turn away from U.S. torture in Cuba and Iraq. Not a good way to start your time in the Senate.

I seriously doubt any of your children, especially John, will ever end up in the military. But, I do wonder how many of those working class kids we coached on the Twins might now be in the military fighting this illegal and immoral war in Iraq. I wonder if any of them were ever captured, how you would feel if they were subjected to torture. By ignoring the torture by our own government, we make it more likely that U.S. troops captured in any combat situation will eventually face such a reality.

I have always been fond of you, as a person, but I am afraid your desire to become part of the power structure has always allowed you to justify making decisions that, in your heart of hearts, you knew were not right. But your operating principle, as you told me the last time we met in the New York airport is that, "You have to do what you have to do." This is the principle that now controls our government and has led to the use of torture by our military.

I hope that when you stand up to speak in the Senate you will think of people like me. Think of the people in your state and around the world who care about real justice in the world. Think about those of us who believe that a government by the people and for the people cannot coexist with secrecy, corruption, deception, and unlawful acts. Think of us as you vote to deny democracy to the vast majority of the people so that the oligarchy can consolidate its power in the U.S. You know how this works. You know the history of pre-revolutionary Cuba.

It is interesting that you have come to the Senate at the very time that the U.S. oligarchy moves to diminish democracy in our land. You will constantly be faced with the question, which side are you on? Do you stand for real justice, democracy, and rule of law? Or do you stand with those who believe they are above the law?

In peace,

> Bruce K. Gagnon
> Coordinator
> Global Network Against Weapons &
> Nuclear Power in Space

# HILLARY JOINS THE WAR

*"One must change ones tactics every ten years if one wishes to maintain one's superiority."*

—Napoleon Bonaparte

Hillary Clinton, who hopes to become president, is on the Sunday morning talk shows (February 20, 2005) saying our troops might be in Iraq for some time to come. "We've been in Korea for 50 years," she said. "We are still in Okinawa," she told the TV cameras. Right-wing Sen. Lindsay Graham (R-SC), sitting next to Hillary during the interview on *Faze the Nation*, chimed in that even though "Sen. Clinton and I are on different ends of the political spectrum, we both agree that our troops will be here for a long time."

That is it. Pack up your bags, peace movement, and just go home. Hillary has made the pronouncement. She is in sync with George W. Bush, the neo-con crowd, Halliburton, Bechtel....she wants to be president and she knows the road to the White House has to pass through the gates of the military industrial complex....and the oil corporations....and the globalization crowd that intends to create a "market economy" in Iraq (read privatization of everything there). Hillary has totally sold out.[89]

The war on Iraq, and the very long presence of U.S. troops there, will bleed America to the bone. The Democratic Party, with a few very noble exceptions, is on its knees, in loyal complicity with the war machine. How can any self-respecting peace activist contemplate for a moment supporting such a party in the next election?

Hillary will try to rehabilitate herself with progressives by talking about social programs. But how can we have social programs when we are spending our national treasury on a bloated Pentagon and a disastrous war in Iraq?! How long will we be fooled by those "progressives" who claim that we can afford "guns and butter?"

The peace movement will get very little help from the Democratic party in putting a stop to this "endless war" we are in now. We are going to have to step up the pressure on Congress by committing to a steady flow of opposition to our senators and congress members. We've got to sit in their offices, call out their names in our letters to the editor and public meetings, point out their inconsistencies when they claim we can have endless war and social progress at home. We are on our own now. Local activists are going to have to run against war supporters in upcoming elections. The Democrats might have let Howard Dean become the chair of their party, but they will not stand up against this illegal and costly war in Iraq. They have sold their souls to the Big Corporations.

It was no different during the Vietnam War. Lyndon Johnson, the good Democrat, abandoned his own "war on poverty" in order to escalate the war in Vietnam. Republicans and Democrats climbed into bed together to bring "freedom" to the Vietnamese people. In the end, they killed millions of them and tens of thousands of American GI's too. The use of Agent Orange in Vietnam, to defoliate the jungles, still today negatively impacts the people there. Children are born with mutations because parents were exposed to the deadly toxin. The same thing is happening in Iraq today, the country is being contaminated by depleted uranium that will cause severe health effects for thousands of years. And we hear no concern by either corporate political party.

It is up to the peace movement and we'd better get serious fast. We can't be so concerned about being nice and not offending people. We'd better stop being so worried about what our neighbors think of us. We'd better step it up quick and begin to resist this insanity that our government is perpetrating with our tax dollars. We'd better make a commitment to be a real part of the global movement for peace before this war spreads to Iran, Syria, and even North Korea.

The U.S. is being turned into a military culture. Our role, in the new world corporate order is going to be to export security. That means we won't have well-paying industrial jobs in America anymore. We will send our kids off to foreign lands to suppress opposition to corporate globalization. The military is where our kids will find work as endless warriors. You think we are hated now in the world....you haven't seen anything yet.

We've got to use every opportunity to bring this resistance message to the public. We can't sit on our fluffy laurels and fancy titles any longer. We've got to get into the garden and get our hands dirty. We've got to get into the soil of this nation and mix it up. We can't wait for our hired gardeners, like Hillary Clinton, to do it for us. We can't trust that Hillary will plant the kinds of seeds we want in our garden. We've got to take on the job ourselves. The time has come to get real.

# LIFE IS LIKE A ROSE
# BEAUTY AND THORNS

*"Each friend represents a world in us, a world possibly not born until they arrive, and it is only by this meeting that a new world is born."*

—Anais Nin

Sad news came to us today (February 25, 2005) that our dear friend, Satomi Oba, in Hiroshima, Japan has died. Only 54 years old, Satomi was as active and vital as anyone. You can imagine the total shock it was to hear this news. Satomi was on the board of our Global Network and has been with us since our early days. She translated two of Karl Grossman's space videos into Japanese and then distributed them all over her country. Two years in a row, she translated our *Keep Space for Peace Week* poster into her language and again made sure it was spread all over Japan. No one could be kinder, gentler, have a more loving spirit than Satomi. Most of us last saw her when she came to Portland, Maine in 2004 for the Global Network's annual Space Conference. In 2002, when we had our annual meeting in Berkeley, California the organization gave Satomi our annual *Peace in Space Award* for her tremendous efforts on behalf of the peace in space movement.

The image that will always stay with me about Satomi is the vigil she would hold each year during our *Keep Space for Peace Week* at the famous dome in Hiroshima that remains as a symbol of the U.S. nuclear bombing of her city. She and friends always held the banner reading *Keep Space for Peace*, written in Japanese and English. Her presence there was a chilling reminder that creating new arms races has consequences, something she lived with every day in her beloved Hiroshima. We will miss her dearly, but we will never forget her.

Life is like a rose: The beauty and the thorns. Just as we got the bad news about Satomi, we got a loving e-mail from another one of our board members, Tamara Lorincz in Halifax, Nova Scotia. Tamara has been a key activist in her country during the past couple of years of intense organizing to prevent Canada from joining the Bush Star Wars program. Tamara wrote today to thank the Global Network board members for their active support of our Canadian friends during their historic organizing effort. But all the credit really goes to the Canadian peace movement. When some thought it a certainty that the Canadian government would join Bush on "missile defense," the peace workers there dug deeper and pushed their government harder.

Canadian Prime Minister Paul Martin wanted to join Bush on Star Wars, but he was stopped. The peace movement throughout Canada organized big protest events, conferences, speaking tours, and media events. But most importantly of all, peace people were determined that Canada would not turn over its national sovereignty to the U.S. Neighbors and friends—yes. Underlings to the U. S.? Never! They've taught us all a lesson about determination, tenacity, outreach, and belief in a high ideal. They have inspired us all.

Today was, indeed, one filled with emotion. The tears still come easily as I write these words. They are tears of sorrow for a lost dear friend and tears of joy in seeing the positive outcome of hard work and fierce will power. Let us all remember these moments and be inspired by the examples of these lives.

# NAZI PAST, OUR PRESENT

*"The high stage of world-industrial development in capitalistic production finds*
*expression in the extraordinary technical development and*
*destructiveness of the instruments of war."*

—Rosa Luxemburg

A woman called tonight (February 28, 2005) who had seen our video, *Arsenal of Hypocrisy: The Space Program and the Military Industrial Complex*. She was very moved by the part that tells the story about the Nazi rocket scientists brought to the U.S. after World War II in the secret military program called Operation Paperclip. I first learned about the story when I read the book *Secret Agenda* by former *CNN* investigative reporter, Linda Hunt. The book detailed how 1,500 top Nazi scientists were smuggled into the U.S. through Boston and West Palm Beach, Florida. One hundred of them, along with 100 copies of Hitler's V-2 rocket, were brought to Huntsville, Alabama to create the U.S. space program. Wernher von Braun, the head of Hitler's team that built the V-1 and V-2 rockets, was made the first director of NASA's Marshall Space Flight Center in Huntsville.

In Germany, during World War II, the Nazis had a concentration camp called Dora where 40,000 Jews, French resistance fighters, homosexuals, communists and other prisoners of war (including a black American GI) were brought to build the V-1 and V-2. By the time the slaves were liberated by the allies, over 25,000 had perished.

Hitler's military liaison to von Braun's rocket team was Maj. Gen. Walter Dornberger. Several times Dornberger and von Braun met with Hitler to request more money and more slaves so they could step up the rocket production effort. Hitler was anxious to use the rockets to terrorize the cities of London, Paris and Brussels toward the end of the war as the Nazi army began to lose. Dornberger and von Braun showed Hitler motion pictures of the V-2 rocket test launches to prove they were making significant progress.

Dornberger came to the U.S. along with von Braun's rocket team during Operation Paperclip. According to author Jack Manno's book, *Arming the Heavens: The Hidden Military Agenda for Space, 1945-1995*, Dornberger was appointed vice-president at Bell Aviation Corporation and went on to serve on the first military oversight committee. This ensured that NASA was controlled by the Pentagon from the first days. It was Dornberger who first came up with the idea of "missile defense" as an offensive program that would have nuclear-powered satellites orbiting the planet, able to hit targets on Earth.

Kurt Debus, the chief of V-2 launch operations in Hitler's Germany, later became Chief of Operations for NASA at Cape Canaveral. When tourists converge on the

Kennedy Space Center, they will pass a portrait of the former German SS member that hangs in the entrance. It honors Debus's service as the Center's first director.

In a recent book, *The Hunt for Zero Point*, respected military journalist Nick Cook talks much about the "black" (the Pentagon's secret) budget. For 15 years, Cook has been a defense and aerospace writer for *Jane's Defence Weekly*, which some consider the Bible of the international weapons community. Cook spent the last 10 years researching secret military programs in the U.S. and believes that over $20 billion a year is spent on these programs outside the purview of Congress. Cook states, "It [black programs] has a vast and sprawling architecture funded by tens of billion of classified dollars every year. The height of its powers was probably in the Reagan era. But it has not stopped since then. In fact, under the Bush administration it is having something of a resurgence. Stealth technology is a primary example...research into anti-gravity technology...has been going on for quite some time."

Cook traces the roots of the U.S.'s secret programs back to the Nazi scientists brought to the U.S. after World War II in Operation Paperclip. He states, "We know the size and scope of Operation Paperclip, which was huge. And we know that the U.S. operates a very deeply secret defense architecture for secret weapons programs... it is highly compartmentalized... and one of the things that's intrigued me over the years is, How did they develop it? What model did they base it on? It is remarkably similar to the system that was operated by the Germans—specifically the SS—for their top-secret weapons programs."

"What I do mean," says Cook, "is that if you follow the trail of Nazi scientists and engineers who were recruited by America at the end of the second world war, the unfortunate corollary is that by taking on the science, you take on—unwittingly—some of the ideology...What do you lose along the way?"

Could this be what former President Dwight Eisenhower was talking about just a few years after Operation Paperclip, in 1961, when he warned the American people to "beware" of the power of the military-industrial complex? Could Eisenhower's prophetic warning have been that an ideological contamination had come from America's embrace of the Nazi operatives?

The woman who called me tonight recently wrote a letter to the editor telling her community that the Nazis created the U.S. space program. Those who responded called her crazy. Even her own son, a local firefighter, was outraged over the letter and told her that she must support George W. Bush or not talk politics with him ever again. She called me to ask for more evidence, which I gladly provided her.

I was impressed by this woman's great courage in stepping out and telling a story that America wants to bury with the rest of our dark past. But the woman was right; this story informs the present—maybe more than that—guides and directs the present. This is a story that must rise from the dead if we are to halt U.S. plans for global empire. We must face our collective national demons. Let the telling begin.

# TOWARD A SUSTAINABLE
# MAINE ECONOMY

## Winter, 2004-2005 (Written for Peace Action Maine Newsletter)

During the past 100 years, Maine's economy has experienced dramatic changes. The two largest employers, textile mills and shoe factories have all but disappeared. Paper mills are on the wane. Our largest industry today is based on military contracts. But those contracts are diminishing. Bath Iron Works, our largest employer, and the maker of our most deadly product, the Aegis Destroyer, now faces the possibility that the Navy will cut back on the number of ships it is planning for the future. Layoffs are continuing. The economic status of a privileged layer of middle managers, engineers, scientists, and skilled workers is tied to war-making institutions. How will these men and women make a living once these jobs are gone?

Conversion of war industries to peaceful purposes has in recent years been a low-priority issue for peace and justice groups. At this time, however, Peace Action Maine sees conversion as part of a strategy that creates positive results directly affecting three communities: the peace community through reduced dependence on military contracting; organized labor through security of high wage, skilled jobs; the environmental community through use of clean energy. This is a win-win alliance that will engender further cooperation for positive material and political change in the state.

If we want a robust 21st Century economy, manufacturing jobs, and a high-quality environment, we need to invest in domestic renewable energy supplies and more efficient energy systems. Developing these new energy systems can be a powerful driver for economic revitalization and family-wage jobs. The clean energy market will amount to $3.5 trillion over the next 20 years, according to a 2001 study. Other states and regions in the U.S. (like the midwest & northwest) are now getting on-board this idea.

The U.S. gets only six percent of its energy from renewable energy sources today. But wind power and solar energy are the fastest-growing energy sources in the world. Wind power has become cost competitive with other electricity options in regions with good wind speeds. Solar energy technologies are rapidly advancing and are becoming more economical every year. If U.S. energy policy emphasized increased use of renewable energy as well as energy-efficiency improvement, the U.S. could obtain more than 15 percent of its energy from renewable sources by 2020 and even more over the long run.

These are not theoretical solutions. European countries, taking the global warming threat seriously, are not building new nuclear power plants. Instead, they are focusing on improving energy efficiency and increasing renewable energy production. Denmark and Germany are the world's leaders in wind power production. The European Union has set a goal of getting more than 20% of its electricity from all renewable sources by 2010.

With a fraction of the wind and solar resources of the U.S., Germany now has almost three times as much installed wind capacity (38% of global capacity) and is a world leader in solar photovoltaics, as well. In fact, Germany has done something NASA says is impossible: it has created solar technology that will even work in deep, dark space.

Germany now generates 4.5% of its electricity through wind power, and appears on track to meet government targets of 25% by 2025.

Denmark has a clear, long-term energy policy with renewables, particularly wind power, set to supply 50% of electricity by 2030. The Danes have been pouring money into researching wind power ever since 1972 when the Danish government turned against nuclear power.

At a converted shipyard in Copenhagen, wind turbines are now under construction. The windmills, a joint project of the local utility and a co-operative of shareholders, are headed for the ocean. When in place in the shallow waters off Eastern Denmark, they'll be the world's largest offshore wind farm. The rotation of their giant blades will generate enough electricity to power 60 thousand households.

Danish turbine manufacturers already sell thousands of windmills abroad. In fact, they've built more than half the world's turbines. Germany and Spain are especially big clients. And so is the United States, although, relative to its size, the U.S. is moving at a snail's pace. In this country, energy policy is largely controlled at the state level, and some states are more inclined to subsidize ideas like wind power than others.

In Mars Hill, Maine there is a plan to create a wind farm. The 33 turbines will likely be built in Denmark. When completed, the 50-megawatt (MW) project will generate sufficient electricity to meet the needs of up to 25,000 homes. Why can't these windmills be manufactured in Maine?

## CONVERSION PLANNING NEEDED

Over the past dozen years, the number of countries and facilities producing antipersonnel landmines (APMs) has declined dramatically around the world. Recently, this trend has been a direct result of the International Campaign to Ban Landmines (ICBL) and the Mine Ban Treaty. Decisions to end landmine production have necessitated action to close or to convert manufacturing plants, as well as to address community economic, social, and environmental impacts of ending production.

The U.N. Conference on the Relationship Between Disarmament and Development asked governments to do studies on the conversion of military industry to civilian production and to publicize the benefits that could be derived from the reallocation of military resources. While studies have shown that a much higher percentage of jobs are created from investment in civilian production than in military production, governments as a whole have not publicized research to show the economic and social benefits of converting military expenditures to human needs.

Just one small example for taxpayers in Maine: Mainers are paying over $589 million for our share of the Iraq war. That same amount of money could provide health care for 79,627 people in our state.

We have come to realize that we can't leave this job to government. The profits from war-making are too great and the military-industrial complex ensures, through its control of Congress, that the status quo will prevail. The U.S. weapons industry is the second most heavily-subsidized industry, after agriculture. The U.S. dominates the international arms market. When weapons are the # 1 industrial export what is the global marketing strategy going to be?

If we are to end war and if we are to help create a sustainable and better life for the citizens of Maine, then we must create a grassroots movement that understands this conversion issue and begins to make demands on the political system. There has never been a better time for change. People are thinking and talking about jobs. They are worried about their economic future. They are losing faith that the political system will provide real answers. They are looking for leadership.

A sustained statewide campaign to create education and debate about the benefits associated with conversion of the war industry will be hard work. But over time it could have a real and positive impact as the public begins to realize our tax dollars, now being wasted on an unwinnable war in Iraq, could be used in our state to build products that we can be proud of and would help give life and hope to future generations.

Economists say that the collapse of the Soviet Union's economy was largely due to the concentration of production resources on the military. In the end, sustained concentration of resources on military goods yields a third-rate economy. A declining economy leads to social collapse with the concomitant rise of poverty, drug use and crime.

Peace Action Maine is now undertaking a multi-year campaign around the conversion issue. We are now working with artists and others to find ways to help raise the consciousness of people in our state around the conversion issue.[90] Unless we convert, our country will continue to hop from one war to the next in the service of our addiction to military spending and violence.

# SIMPLY RIDICULOUS!

George W. Bush was quoted in the news today (February 22, 2005) as saying it is "simply ridiculous" that the U.S. is ready to attack Iran. He then went on to conclude: "And having said that, all options are on the table."

Bush is likely to have Israel do the bombing, but the U.S. will provide satellite technology to direct the attack. After all, now that Israel is going to give back some Palestinian land, Bush had to give Sharon something in return. "Ok, Ariel, you can blow up Iran," Bush likely said. "Just don't do it while I am at the ranch in Texas."

When I was a kid I wanted to be an FBI agent. I wanted to fight organized crime. I took an FBI correspondence course when I was about 14 so I could get a head start on my new career. In it, I learned about fingerprints — how to read them, etc. I also learned a bunch of definitions I have long ago forgotten, except for one. "Modus operandi" ....method of operation. Every criminal has one.

So what is the M.O. of those in power today? They lie, they cheat on elections, they steal the public tax dollar, they mislead foreign governments, they plan a takeover of the world on behalf of their corporate overseers. Oh yeah, they invade other countries on false pretenses.

So, when Bush says we won't be invading Iran, I find it hard to believe him. It is a matter of trust. My detective instincts tell me to keep an eye on him. Park outside the White House to see who comes and goes. Who is he hanging out with? Stuff like that.

The Belgian peace group, For Mother Earth, did a preemptive strike today while Bush was in their country. They went to the Brussels headquarters of one of Bush's primary collaborators in crime, Lockheed Martin. A number of them in Bush masks entered the lobby of the HQ building and started playing some music. That was the diversion while 15 more of them in G.W. masks went upstairs and took over the office of Lockheed Martin. They began asking questions of the office staff, interrogating them about recent crimes against humanity that the corporation, along with Bush, had been perpetrating. No arrests were made and they were evicted after about 30 minutes.

I am still gathering evidence of Bush crimes.[91] Surely what he has already done is worse than pulling a "Monica Lewinsky?" In my little detective notepad I have written the following so far. See what you think—maybe you can help me gather more evidence:

* Bush proposes cutting $489 million of clean-up funds at the Environmental Protection Agency
* The U.S. now ranks 17th in the world in high school graduation rates
* The U.S. is 49th in the world in literacy

* Jobs are leaving the nation like crazy, and being replaced by virtually nothing except Burger King hamburger-flipper jobs
* Bush used homophobia to get out the vote in the last election.
* Bush cheated on two national elections
* Bush and Condi knew about 9-11 before it happened
* The water quality in America is worsening dramatically
* The air quality in America is worsening dramatically
* The cars in America are getting bigger while public transit is being defunded by Bush
* Bush allowed a pretend journalist, who runs male prostitute websites, into his press conference and picked him to ask a question
* Bush orders the torture of innocent people who have no access to legal counsel
* Bush is deploying "missile defense" systems that can't even get off the ground
* Bush lied to the public about the justification for the war in Afghanistan and Iraq.

Anyway, it's getting late. The list could go on. Really, please help me gather evidence for Bush's criminal prosecution. I think he did it.

# BACK TO WILLIAM MCKINLEY'S TIME?

**FEBRUARY 24, 2005** The Republicans are, at last, after four years of Bush administration deficit creation discovering the growing debt crisis in America. I've been monitoring "conservative" politicians' statements in recent days and they are all following the pack, calling for massive cuts in social spending. "We can't saddle our children with this huge debt," they say. Funny, they never worried about it when they were voting to create the debt by giving huge tax cuts to the rich, massively increasing Pentagon spending, and throwing money at the war in Iraq like they were playing the Monopoly game.

The Republicans have, of course, done this on purpose. They created the debt crisis so they could then go to the people with their "final" solution. "We've got to cut social spending across the board because we must rein in big government spending," they say. They knew if they followed Ronald Reagan's prescription—cut taxes on the rich, and increase military spending—they could finish the job that Reagan had begun in the 1980's. The right-wing sees this as its best chance ever to kill social progress in America and bring back the days of corporate domination of the people. I call it 21st Century feudalism.

Bush's political advisor/guru Karl Rove says that his favorite president was William McKinley. Why McKinley? McKinley was the last president before we began to get social progress in America. Back in McKinley's day, all we had was the poorhouse or the street. You lost your job—tough. You are sick and can't afford a doctor—too bad. You want public education for your kids so they can advance—no way. You need Social Security so you can survive in your old age — tough luck. This is the vision for America that Rove and Bush and their team of greedy corporate operatives have.

Let's face it. The big corporations figure, why pay some American $20 an hour to make TV's when they can go to China and pay someone 50 cents a day? So, they move to China. Americans are left jobless and, most importantly, our local communities begin to feel the pressure as the local tax base dries up. No money for road repairs, no money for schools, etc... Then Bush cuts federal social spending and within one generation you have the "Third Worldization" of the U.S. It will happen before most people know what hit them. Bush keeps saying, "I'm optimistic," and about half the country believes him. Then one day they wake up to the whole shell game, but it is too late. They are f_ _ ked.

I think most people, in their heart of hearts, understand what is going on. They can see the writing on the wall. But they were taught early on to keep their nose clean, don't rock the boat, climb the corporate ladder. They know that if you stick your neck out and say anything about all this you might get it chopped off in this corporate-dominated society. They want someone else to do the dirty work for them.

It's what I call the "success mythology." Folks are more committed to "success" (fancy house, big-paying jobs, expensive car, gigantic color TV, hot vacations) than they are to making sure their kids can breathe clean air, drink clean water, or attend schools that are sufficiently funded. They go along to get along. They tell activists quietly, behind closed doors, "Hey, I am so glad you are out there working on these issues, but I can't do it. I've got three kids to put through college, you know." The problem, though, is that because they don't get involved, they are getting ready to put their kids through the wringer of hell.

So what is the answer? We've got to start talking about the success mythology and the responsibility of parents and grandparents to work NOW to protect the future generations from this impending economic and environmental tsunami. We've got to urge folks to muster up the courage to think of their KIDS first.

# AMERICA IS ADDICTED
# TO WAR AND VIOLENCE

*"Our enemies are innovative and resourceful, and so are we. They never stop thinking about new ways to harm our country and our people, and neither do we."*

—George W. Bush

**FEBRUARY 15, 2005** People often ask me if I get depressed seeing all that is going on in the world, with Bush's endless war to control the resources of the world and the war at home against social progress.

Well the answer is yes. Of course I do. Who wouldn't? But how long can I wallow in misery before I have to get moving again?

There is just so much that needs to be done. We need to get folks out of their misery and depression into some kind of action. Can we get them to write a letter to the editor? How about helping organize a small delegation of friends and neighbors to our senator's office to speak out against the war in Iraq? Can we get them to contemplate doing civil disobedience? How about forming an affinity group to begin discussing what they might do together?

What about our economy? The U.S. is in such debt and Bush has now intentionally created the conditions whereby we have to cut the budget. Of course we can't cut military spending, he says. Instead we have to go after things like home heating assitance for poor people in the north, social security, low income housing assistance...you all know the list.

I heard recently that the public libraries in Salinas, California were slated to close because the local community has no money. Outside of one of the previously-functioning libraries is a statue of the great author John Steinbeck, who often wrote about farm workers, the same kind of people who live in Salinas today. These are the forgotten people. They are no longer needed in a society where computerization, mechanization, and robotics have taken over. They are a superfluous population. Defund their public education....defund their health care.....what happens to them next? Who really cares? They can join the military and fight endless wars. There are always more of them crossing over the Rio Grande to replace those who are used up.

America is addicted to war and violence. America is addicted to mythology, too. Addicted to the mythology that at any moment you might strike it rich. So, don't raise taxes on the rich, because it might come back to haunt you when you win the lottery next week! Yeah, right.

We have to pull the veil off America's mythology. We have to begin to share with our friends and neighbors the reality of what America is, and what America is not. We are not a sharing and caring society. Of course there are many Americans who do care and do share. But, as an organized society, we are a greedy, power-hungry culture. We have been trained by several hundreds of years of acting out "manifest destiny." There is a battle for America's soul underway now.

In fact that is the title of my latest video, *Battle for America's Soul*. In it, I talk about how we've been like this from Day One when the Native Americans were slaughtered so the new empire could be built in North America. From the first days of the American "revolution" at Valley Forge, the military contractors stole from the peasant army as they froze in the cold night. The food, blankets, and weapons paid for by the Continental Congress were not delivered. During the Civil War, the contractors delivered guns that did not work. And now, in Iraq, the big boys like Haliburton and Bechtel steal from the taxpayers, steal from the troops, and fatten their already-overstuffed pockets with profits.

The challenge for America is to come to grips with this addiction. Will America take the step and enter a collective 12-step program where we say, "Hello, my name is America and I am addicted to war and violence?" Will the American people be able to face the sad reality that as a nation we have become dependent on weapons and war to provide significant portions of our population with jobs? Will we have the courage to make a political demand that begins to turn us away from exporting war around the world?

# WHICH PILL WILL YOU TAKE?

**March 14, 2005** The news these days is all about oil. We are running out of it. Experts estimate we are now on the downward spiral in terms of oil availability. With the emerging economic development of China and India, the global supply will decline very rapidly.

Imagine the consequences to life as we know it today. How much will gas come to cost per gallon? Maybe $5 or $15 or $20. Maybe more. How much will electricity and home heating oil cost? Think of the costs of highly mechanized agricultural production and delivery. All done with oil-based equipment. Only the rich will be able to afford to eat.

The U.S. answer to all of this is to begin planning for war in Africa. The Pentagon is now setting up military bases throughout Africa in anticipation of making a move on the continent's oil in the near future. Arms sales to African countries have increased. This will create more internal conflict which the U.S. will use as justification to intervene.

Again, the U.S. is willing to destablize another region in order to satisfy its heavy oil dependence. We did the same thing in the Middle East. For years the U.S. destabilized that region with arms sales. Then, in order to save the people of Iraq, George W. Bush had to invade. Permanent U.S. bases are now being set up there because "we can't cut and run." But, the war in Iraq was "set up" long before it happened. We have to learn to watch the left hand, as well as the right hand. The shell game is now being run in Africa.... Watch Venezuela... Watch Mexico.... Colombia..... Watch the Caspian sea region.... even watch Canada that sells a lot of oil to the U.S.

The solution to all of this is the development of new and sustainable technologies in the U.S. Solar, wind power, and public mass transit (Bush is cutting back on Amtrak as I write this) are alternatives that we must advocate for loudly while there is still a chance. This will take federal investment. The oil/weapons mafia that runs our government wants to drain the oil fields and get every last dime it can, as prices inevitably rise. The American people had better wake up to the game very quickly.

Life is not a pretty picture these days. We have two choices. We can close our eyes, hoping it will go away, and leave it to our kids to sort out. Or we can get engaged. The red pill or the blue pill. Which will you take?

# A MONTH OF SUNDAYS

Winter, 2004-2005
A Play
By Bruce K. Gagnon

*"A very great vision is needed and the man who has it must follow
it as the eagle seeks the deepest blue of the sky."*

—Crazy Horse

Characters: Mom, Dad and Daughter (high school age)

**Setting**—Somewhere in a red state or a blues state. A kitchen table is surrounded by 3 chairs. One light is overhead.

## FIRST SUNDAY

| | |
|---|---|
| **Mom:** | Time to eat |
| **Dad:** | What are we having? |
| **Mom:** | The usual, chicken |
| **Dad:** | What ever happened to roast beef? |
| **Mom:** | Have you seen the price of a roast lately? Anyway, eating red meat so often is not good for you. |
| **Dad:** | You are starting to sound like one of those new age hippies they told us about at church. |
| **Daughter:** | What's wrong with watching what you eat? |
| **Dad:** | A man works hard and wants to eat. Do you think the owner of the plant has to go without meat on Sunday? Why should I have to? |
| **Mom:** | How are things going at the plant? |
| **Dad:** | About the same. Pushing us harder. They are talking about more layoffs again, but the union says not to worry about it yet. |
| **Mom:** | How are we not supposed to worry? |
| **Dad:** | We'll be all right. Jamison was late again a couple of times this week and they pulled him into human relations and chewed him out. He says his car battery died, but I think he's been drinking heavy again. |
| **Mom:** | He needs to get back to church. |
| **Dad:** | He'll never come to church. |
| **Mom:** | He will one day. God has a way of working miracles when they are most needed. |

**Dad:** It would take a real miracle to get Jamison straightened out. Anyway, we were told to watch out next week because a bunch of peaceniks are expected to come and protest outside the plant at the shift change.

**Mom:** What are they protesting now?

**Dad:** The usual, saying we are a bunch of baby killers. Want us to disarm. Hand the country over to the terrorists. Why can't they just go move to Iraq or Russia? Here we are trying to keep the country safe and they want us to just *(Says it like he imagines a "pacifist" would say it)* lay down our weapons. Where do these people come from?

**Mom:** I bet they've not been in a church anytime lately.

**Daughter:** What's wrong with protesting? In social studies they told us all about Martin Luther King and protesting stuff. Mr. Gordon said protesting was part of the tradition.

**Dad:** Those goddamned liberals are taking over the schools now, too. What the hell am I paying taxes for? No wonder you kids can't read or write anymore. We didn't have all that King crap when I was in school, and it never hurt me.

**Daughter:** But Mr. Gordon said that is what democracy is all about. Being able to....

**Dad:** Enough of that! Anyway, I've told you before, children should be seen and not heard at the table.

**Mom:** Here, honey, have some more potatoes.

**Dad:** This whole country is falling apart. Cost me almost $50 to fill up the truck today. If it wasn't for the credit card, there is no way in hell I could drive the damn thing.

**Mom:** I'm going to have a yard sale next Saturday with Jean next door. I want you both to go through all your junk and pick out what you don't want anymore and give it to me so I can sell it. We should make at least $100 from it, and that will help.

**Dad:** All right, honey, but it's gonna take more than that.

**Mom:** It will at least help. Don't worry though, the Lord will provide.

**Dad:** He'd better provide damn fast, that's all I can say.

**Mom:** The Lord works in mysterious ways. He has a plan for all of us.

**Dad:** Yeah, He's planning to send us to the friggin' poor house.

**Mom:** Watch your language, especially at the table!

**Dad:** I'm gonna go watch the football game. Bring me a beer.

**Daughter:** I'm gonna go to my room.

**Mom:** Young lady, you clean the table before you go anywhere. Is your homework all done for school this week?

**Daughter:** Yes Mom, it's all done.

**Mom:** *(Mutters to herself)* God help me. How am I going to make it? What are we going to do?

## SECOND SUNDAY

**Mom:** Come and get it. Dinner is on the table.

**Dad:** What are we having? Chicken?

**Mom:** No, I made a roast for you.

**Dad:** About time.

**Mom:** I made corn on the cob for you, too. They had a special on it at the store, so I bought enough to freeze. Stock up while you can. I think it's good corn.

**Dad:** This roast looks kind of dried out. You cooked it too long. It's supposed to be moist.

**Mom:** *(Ignoring him)* Pass the potatoes, honey.

**Daughter:** Here, Mom.

**Mom:** How was school this week, honey?

**Daughter:** Boring as usual. The football team won, though, and the dance afterward was great.

**Mom:** Did you dance any?

**Daughter:** I danced with Sue and Becky some.

**Dad:** Don't boys and girls dance together anymore? Girls dancing together is not natural.

**Daughter:** Oh, dad. We do that all the time. It's normal. Anyway, most of the guys are too shy and half of them can't shake it.

**Mom:** What happened with the protesters at the plant? Was there any trouble?

**Dad:** Naw, they stood out there holding signs and shooting peace signs at us. We gave 'em the finger. It was pretty harmless except the damn media was out there crawling all over the bastards. Now, they get to spread their "disarm" message all over the liberal media.

**Mom:** Don't worry; no one pays any attention to them, anyway. I don't think anyone even notices they were there. *(pause)* What did their signs say?

**Dad:** Some shit about converting the plant. They want us to make windmills or some crap like that. Who the hell do they think they are? The government? Just because they decide they don't like what we're doing, they think we should all just up and change!?

**Daughter:** I heard in school that windmills were good for making cheap electricity. They are good for the environment. Mr. Gordon said some countries in Europe are using windmills a lot to make electricity so they don't have to use oil, which creates global warm.......

**Dad:** There you go again with that Mr. Gordon crap. What the hell is he doing talking about what Europe is doing when he should be talking about America. It sounds like a bunch of nonsense. Windmills to make electricity. I ain't going to make no windmills. I make goddamned weapons that kill people and keep us free. I ain't gonna make no damn windmills.

| | |
|---|---|
| **Daughter**: | But Dad, if they help with the environment, what is wrong with that? |
| **Dad**: | There is nothing wrong with the environment. Rush says all this global warming shit is a pack of lies. Look how damn cold it is out there right now. Supposed to snow this coming week. How can that be global warming? |
| **Daughter**: | But, Dad, global warming is true. Mr. Gordon said that the Artic is melting because of global warm.... |
| **Dad**: | That's bullshit. More liberal media propaganda. |
| **Daughter**: | But, Dad, it's true. The icecaps are melting! The polar bears are losing their food. It's like really bad! You just don't know what you're talking about! |
| **Dad**: | That's enough of that. You will not speak to me that way. |
| **Daughter**: | But Daddy.... |
| **Dad**: | Enough! Anyway, how are the rest of your studies? |
| **Mom**: | But, maybe there is something to this global warming. Our weather is getting kind of crazy these days. It's all messed up. |
| **Dad**: | I don't believe it. |
| **Mom**: | Ok. Here sweetie, have some more corn. It's fresh. |
| **Dad**: | *(Changing the subject)* How did the yard sale go? Sell anything? |
| **Mom**: | Yes, I made over $100. Going to put it aside. Jean made about the same. It was fun. We met a lot of new people. Some new folks moved in a couple doors away. They seem nice. I invited them to come to church with us, but they didn't show up this morning. Maybe I should invite them again. Pastor says we have to keep witnessing to new people. We have to share the joy of the Lord with them. So, I guess I should try again. |
| **Dad**: | Yeah, good idea. |
| **Mom**: | We are going to have a special program at church for new people. Pastor says we need to bring in more people so we can get them registered with the Lord. He says we need to get more people to pray for the President, especially in times when terrorists are trying to attack us. This could be the End Times. If the terrorists succeed we could have the Rapture and those that are not saved will be left behind. |
| **Dad**: | I'd like to leave some people behind. Like them peaceniks. They want us to lay down our arms. Hell, that is just what the terrorists want us to do! They want us to make those damn windmills. That would make their day! I can't believe it. Windmills. Sissy shit. I'm gonna go watch football. Windmills.......... |

### THIRD SUNDAY

| | |
|---|---|
| **Mom**: | Time to eat. Come on. |
| **Dad**: | What are we having? |

| | |
|---|---|
| **Mom:** | Fried chicken, salad, mashed potatoes and string beans. |
| **Dad:** | Alright, I'm coming. |
| **Mom:** | Pastor said today that we need to expand the church, so I am going to give them the $100 I made at the yard sale. He says we need to build a new sanctuary. |
| **Dad:** | What the hell for? The place is only half full now. |
| **Mom:** | He says we need to build a house the Lord would be proud of. He says we need to think big and that if we build it the people will come because they want to be part of something big and growing. He said the reason people don't come now is because they don't think we are something special. |
| **Dad:** | Something special all right. Sounds like a waste of money to me. Then after you build a big place, you have to keep it up and that will cost money. Where the hell will the money come from? |
| **Mom:** | Well, he says we'll get new people. He said it was like the President. By cutting taxes the president grows the economy. So, by building the church bigger we get more people. We've got to at least try. |
| **Dad:** | Yeah, maybe. They announced they might have to lay off some folks at the plant. They said the government was cutting back on money for the company because of the national debt. Maybe 200-500 of us might get laid off. Where the hell we supposed to find work? All the damn industry in the area is moving overseas. Third Worlders working for damn near nothing, taking our jobs. Now they're even saying they might "outsource" the defense industry overseas. Imagine that, damn Chinese building our weapons. Makes no sense to me. What the hell is happening to this country? How are we supposed to put food on the table? How are we supposed to pay the bills? What the hell are they thinking in Washington? |
| **Mom:** | Pastor says the gays are taking over the country. He says they want to make their marriage legal so that they can take over the schools and teach the kids about being gay. He says we've got to stop the gays. And, he said we've got to call our Senators right away about the vacancy on the Supreme Court. The President has nominated a God Fearing, strict conservative judge who wants to enforce the law, not make laws. We've got to call the Senators right away. |
| **Dad:** | Yeah, ok. You do it for us. |
| **Mom:** | We have to support what the President is trying to do. He's trying to make us a more moral country. Without God in our lives we have nothing. The liberals even want to get rid of the Pledge in the schools. |
| **Daughter:** | No one cares if they do. We don't really say it, anyway. We just like mumble when we do it. Kids are saying "big deal." What good is a Pledge when we ain't got no jobs when we graduate. Most of my friends are joining the Army next year. There ain't no jobs! Or they're moving to Texas or Florida. |

|           |                                                                                                                                                                                                                                                                              |
|-----------|------------------------------------------------------------------------------------------------------------------------------------------------------------------------------------------------------------------------------------------------------------------------------|
|           | They say there are lots of jobs there working like at Disney. I wanted to go to college, but I don't know.                                                                                                                                                                      |
| Dad:      | Nothing wrong with defending your country. I did it and it sure didn't hurt me. Taught me discipline. How to take orders from above. Nothing wrong with that. Too damn many kids today have no discipline. That's what's wrong with the country.                                 |
| Daughter: | I don't know Dad. I think the future looks kind of dark. I don't think most kids have much hope.                                                                                                                                                                              |
| Dad:      | Hope? No damn hope? Of course, there is hope. Don't talk like that. I don't want you to give up.                                                                                                                                                                             |
| Mom:      | There is always hope in the Lord. They need to come to church.                                                                                                                                                                                                                |
| Daughter: | Most kids don't go to church, Mom. They don't care about all that.                                                                                                                                                                                                            |
| Mom:      | Well, they should. If they got right with the Lord everything would be fine.                                                                                                                                                                                                   |
| Daughter: | What good is the Lord, if there are no jobs? What good is the Lord if there is no future? What good is the Lord....                                                                                                                                                            |
| Mom:      | Now, stop that!                                                                                                                                                                                                                                                                |
| Daughter: | No, I mean it. What good is the Lord if I can't go to college? What does the Lord care about me?                                                                                                                                                                               |
| Mom:      | The Lord loves you! And, you should love the Lord!                                                                                                                                                                                                                            |
| Daughter: | If the Lord loved me, he'd answer my prayers. I want to go to college. I don't want to go to the Army just to kill people!                                                                                                                                                     |
| Dad:      | Enough of that! Killing people is what they do in the Army. If it was good enough for me, then it's good enough for you. That's what made America great. We made the world free. Freedom! That's what the Army does, it brings freedom. And sometimes you have to kill people to make them free. Look at Iraq right now. We are giving those damn people freedom, even if they don't want it! |
| Daughter: | Yeah, freedom for the rich. Freedom for the oil corporations. Mr. Gordon says that the whole war in Iraq is about oil. He says it is all for the oil corporations .......                                                                                                       |
| Dad:      | Enough of that damn talk. That's a bunch of bullshit put out by the liberals. If we don't kill the terrorists in Iraq then we'd have to kill them here. Better we kill them over there. The President has my support! He might not sound like he knows what he is doing, but he does! |
| Daughter: | Well, he doesn't have my support. He's messing up the whole world. People hate us all over the world.....                                                                                                                                                                     |
| Dad:      | All right, enough!                                                                                                                                                                                                                                                            |
| Mom:      | All right, All right! *(dead silence)* What are we going to do if you get laid off?                                                                                                                                                                                            |
| Dad:      | Don't worry, it'll be all right. They aren't going to lay me off. I've got 18 years in that plant. They will lay off the new guys first. I'll be ok.                                                                                                                           |

| | |
|---|---|
| **Mom:** | I hope so. I'm worried about it. My job doesn't pay enough for all of us. And I hear they are cutting back on unemployment. |
| **Dad:** | Don't worry. Everything will be fine. |

### FOURTH SUNDAY

| | |
|---|---|
| **Mom:** | Come and get it. Time to eat. |
| **Dad:** | What are we having? |
| **Mom:** | Salad, glazed potatoes, string beans, rolls. |
| **Dad:** | What about meat? |
| **Mom:** | I'm trying to conserve. Anyway, it's all good for you. |
| **Dad:** | Christ! Now, your trying to turn me into one of those God damned vegetarians. What's next? Going to teach me yoga or make me eat yogurt? A man is supposed to eat his meat. |
| **Mom:** | Sit down and eat. You act like you are starving. I'm doing the best I can. You told me to cut back on what I spend at the store. I'm trying. Give me a damn break. Eat it and shut the hell up! *(Long uncomfortable pause)* What are they saying at the plant about the layoffs? |
| **Dad:** | Looks like it might be more than 400 of us. If so, that means some of us that have been there a while might have to go, and I think I am going to be one of them. The word is that the contracts might not be renewed. They say the Pentagon is over budget because of Iraq. How the hell can they have a war and not need the weapons we build? I don't friggin' get it! What kind of a damn war is this? I thought war was supposed to be good for the economy. How the hell can you have a war and lay off the weapons makers? They want to send our jobs someplace else. What the hell are we supposed to do for work now? And then them God dammed protesters were out there at the plant again yesterday. They had this big windmill they made by the gate, as we drove out. They have to know we are getting laid off. It's in all the papers. And they are just gloating at us! They want us to get laid off so they can have their God dammed PEACE! So, they show up with windmills. What kind of a job is building a windmill? |
| **Mom:** | It would be a job. Better that than nothing I guess. At least we could pay the bills. |
| **Daughter:** | What's wrong with making windmills? They are good for the environment. They'd help stop global warming. I asked Mr. Gordon about windmills and he said they could create lots of clean energy. He said.... |
| **Dad:** | I don't want to hear anymore from that God damned Mr. Gordon. Why the hell doesn't he move to France if he thinks they are doing such a great job? |
| **Daughter:** | It's not France, Dad. It's Denmark. They are the ones making the windmills. Mr. Gordon said they converted a shipyard to build windmills and |

|         |                                                                                                                                                                                                                                                                              |
|---------|------------------------------------------------------------------------------------------------------------------------------------------------------------------------------------------------------------------------------------------------------------------------------|
|         | now they are making them for countries all over the world. Even some places in the U.S. are buying windmills from Denmark. Why couldn't you make windmills? At least you'd still have a job.                                                                                    |
| Mom:    | She might be right, honey. At least you'd still have a job.                                                                                                                                                                                                                    |
| Dad:    | Well, I guess it would be better than nothing. But they won't do it. They'll just lay us off and we won't have anything. Sometimes I think they just want us to have nothing. The whole damn country is falling apart right before our eyes and there is nothing we can do about it. I feel so...... |
| Mom:    | Oh, honey, don't say that. It will be ok.                                                                                                                                                                                                                                     |
| Dad:    | I'm not so sure. I'm worried about it.                                                                                                                                                                                                                                        |
| Daughter: | That's why I want to go to college. I want to learn about how to make all this better. I want to be able to help our country.                                                                                                                                               |
| Dad:    | That's what I said when I joined the Army, and look what it got me. A big fat nothing. The only thing I learned was how to run a floor buffer and salute sorry ass officers. I had hopes, too. I had dreams. Now, they are all going out the door. I thought if I just did what I was supposed to we'd be all right. I tried to do what I was told. I got a good job. I got married, had a family. Bought a house. Now look. It's all going up in smoke. What am I supposed to do? |
| Mom:    | Now, honey, don't give up. We've made it this far. We will be all right. The Lord will take care of us.                                                                                                                                                                       |
| Daughter: | My friends sometimes talk like that, too. But I won't give up. I think we have to stand up and fight for what we think is right. I think I'm going to go join them peace people and hold signs saying we need windmills and rail cars for mass transit. We need jobs! |
| Dad:    | Like hell you will!                                                                                                                                                                                                                                                           |
| Daughter: | You always taught me to stand up for what I believe, didn't you? Well, I believe that guys like you, Dad, deserve more than just getting laid off. You've worked hard for all these years. You deserve more than this. |
| Dad:    | That's for damn sure.                                                                                                                                                                                                                                                         |
| Mom:    | That's right.                                                                                                                                                                                                                                                                 |
| Daughter: | What right do they have to just throw you out the door? Do you think the big corporation guys will be thrown out? Mr. Gordon says the salaries of the corporate executives are going up at the very same time they are laying off workers. Like that is not right! |
| Dad:    | He's right about that.                                                                                                                                                                                                                                                        |
| Mom:    | Doesn't seem right to me.                                                                                                                                                                                                                                                     |
| Daughter: | But, if you don't speak up, then nothing changes. Maybe those peaceniks have a point about how the corporations control the whole government. |
| Dad:    | Now, don't start talkin' like a peacenik.                                                                                                                                                                                                                                     |

**Daughter:** I mean it, Dad. Like, maybe they are right. Maybe the big corporations are running the country now and don't care about the people.

**Mom:** Lord knows that might be true.

**Dad:** Well, Miss Smarty-Pants; what are we supposed to do about it? What if what you say is true? What if they don't give a God damned bit about any of us? What if the big corporations are moving the jobs overseas and we are left with nothing? How the hell can we pay our credit cards off? Who is going to pay the mortgage? How the hell can we make the payment on the truck? How will we eat? What are we supposed to do, honey? What is a man supposed to do? I just don't know anymore. *(Dad buries his face in his worn, weathered hands in frustration as the light goes out.)*

# NEW PENTAGON VISION
# TRANSFORMS WAR AGENDA

## *Space Alert Newsletter,* Winter, 2004-2005

*"The right to swing my fist ends where the other man's nose begins."*
—Oliver Wendell Holmes, Jr.

Pentagon transformation is well underway. The U.S. military is increasingly being converted into a global oil protection service. Secretary of War Donald Rumsfeld has a "strategy guy" whose job is to teach this new way of warfare to high-level military officers from all branches of services and to top level CIA operatives. Thomas Barnett is a former professor at the Navy War College.[92] He is author of the controversial book *The Pentagon's New Map,* that identifies a "non-integrating gap" in the world that is resisting corporate globalization. Barnett defines the gap as parts of Latin America, Africa, Middle East and Central Asia—all of which are key oil-producing regions of the world.

In what Barnett calls a "Grand March of History," he claims the U.S. military must be transformed in order to preemptively take control of the gap so the U.S. can "manage" the global distribution of resources, people, energy, and money. (As the Pentagon has predicted for a long time, the gap between rich and poor around the world will continue to widen. I've said that the Pentagon will be used to keep the boot on the necks of the people of the Third World to the benefit of corporate globalization.)

Barnett offers that U.S. unilateralism will lead to the "inevitability of war." Referring to Hitler in a recent presentation, Barnett reminded his military audience that the Nazi leader never asked for permission before invading other countries. Thus, the end to multilateralism and on we go to endless war.

Barnett argues the days of arms talks and international treaties are over. "There is no secret where we are going," he says as he calls for a "new ordering principle" at the Department of Defense (DoD). Barnett maintains that as jobs move out of the U.S., the primary export product of the nation will be "security." Global energy demand will necessitate U.S. control of the oil-producing regions. "We will be fighting in Central Africa in 20 years," Barnett predicts.

In order to implement this new military "vision," Barnett maintains, the U.S. military must move away from its often-competing mix of Air Force-Navy-Army-Marines toward two basic military services. One he names *Leviathan,* which he defines as "kick ass," wage-war special operations, and not under the purview of the international criminal court. Give us your angry, video game-playing 18-19 year olds, for the *Leviathan* force Barnett says. Once a country is conquered by *Leviathan*, Barnett says the U.S. will have to have a second military force that he calls *Systems Administration*. This force he describes as the "proconsul" of the empire. It will be the "boots-on-the-ground" police force to control the local populations. This group Barnett says "will never come home."

Barnett's plan is essentially underway today. New, fast, flexible, and efficient projection forces with "lily pad" bases are now being developed for control of the gap. Over the next decade, the military will abandon 35% of the Cold War-era bases it uses abroad as it seeks to expand the network of bare-bones sites in the gap. The planned changes, once completed, will result in the most profound "reordering" of U.S. military forces overseas since the current global arrangements were set 50 years ago.

According to Michael Klare, professor of Peace Studies at Hampshire College, "American troops are now risking their lives on a daily basis to protect the flow of petroleum. In Colombia, Saudi Arabia, and the Republic of Georgia, U.S. personnel are spending their days and nights protecting pipelines and refineries, or supervising the local forces assigned to this mission."

Klare continues, "The DoD has stepped up its arms deliveries to military forces in Angola and Nigeria and is helping to train their officers and enlisted personnel; meanwhile, Pentagon officials have begun to look for permanent bases in the area, focusing on Senegal, Ghana, Mali, Uganda and Kenya." The *Wall Street Journal* has reported that "a key mission for U.S. forces (in Africa) would be to ensure that Nigeria's oil fields, which in the future could account for as much as 25% of all U.S. oil imports, are secure."

National Guard units across the U.S. are now being assigned the task of developing on-going basing relationships[93] with each nation on the African continent.

## ROLE OF SPACE TECHNOLOGY

The Bush administration is also exploring the possibility of expanding the emerging missile defense system into Eastern Europe as an element in the strategic containment of Russia, China and the Middle East. The Pentagon has been negotiating with Hungary, Romania, Poland, and the Czech Republic about one or more of them hosting new missile defense bases. Oil-rich Iran is to be encircled by missile defense posts in Azerbaijan, Turkmenistan, Iraq, and Afghanistan.

In order to pull all of this together the Pentagon claims it will need "a God's eye view" of the world. A new "Internet in the sky" is now being built for the wars of the future. Costing well over $200 billion, the new web would give war machines and military forces a common language, instantly emitting an encyclopedia of lethal information about all enemies.

According to Art Cebrowski, director of the Pentagon's Office of Force Transformation, "What we are really talking about is a new theory of war."

The military wants to know "everything of interest to us, all the time," says one Pentagon insider. Military intelligence—including secret satellite surveillance covering most of the Earth—will be posted on the war net and shared with troops. "The essence of net-centric warfare is our ability to deploy a war-fighting force anywhere, anytime. Information technology is the key to that."

Thus, U.S. military and economic control of the gap will be dependent on a system of networked computers. Fusing weapons, secret intelligence, and soldiers in a global network—what the military calls net-centric warfare—will, they say, change the military in a way the Internet changed business and culture. [94]

# WHERE YOUR MONEY IS GOING

## *Space Alert Newsletter,* Winter, 2004-2005

> *"A government that robs Peter to pay Paul can*
> *always depend upon the support of Paul."*
>
> —George Bernard Shaw

The Pentagon budget for fiscal year 2006 is $417 billion, 12% higher than the average budget during the Cold War. The Bush administration intends to seek about $82 billion in emergency funding for the wars in Iraq and Afghanistan in early 2006, pushing total war costs close to $225 billion since the U.S. invasion of Iraq.

A civilian contractor force of about 20,000 personnel has supplemented the current force of 150,000 military personnel in Iraq.

New high-tech weapons systems have brought record sales to the U.S. aerospace industry. In the U.S. today the industry product line is 50% military and 50% civilian. This is quite different from aerospace corporations around the world which generally have 80-90% commercial business and only 10-20% military accounts.

Thus, the Pentagon, has no incentive or pressure to be cost conscious. According to one industry analyst, "There is not a single [military] program out there that isn't behind schedule and over budget."

It's only going to get worse. The Pentagon's space czar and director of the National Reconnaissance Office (NRO), recently told Congress that, "We need more flexibility to be able to move funds from one program into another program" without Congressional oversight.

Private contractors are taking over many military operations, and the government lacks the expertise to control the contractor workforce. What we get is essentially a privatized foreign and military policy, removed from the purview of the public and Congress.

In fact, the Pentagon can't provide the most basic information on its contractor workforce. Poor data goes hand-in-hand with inadequate management.

In 2002, the last year such data are available, the top six U.S. weapons corporations donated more than $8.5 million to candidates and political parties. Armies of lobbyists and public relations people swarm Washington promoting weapons systems that don't work and are not needed.

During the last six years, forty-one military contractors have collectively won $266 billion in contracts from the Pentagon. Well over one-half of these contracts were awarded without "full and open" competition.

NASA has failed to account for billions of dollars spent on the Space Shuttle and the International Space Station. The General Accounting Office (GAO) has found that NASA has yet to comply with a 2000 law that requires the agency to verify how much it spends each year. The GAO report says the space agency's accounting systems are so convoluted they could not tell what money was spent where. Former Sen. Ernest Hollings (D-SC), a member of a NASA oversight committee recently said, "In my mind, this raises questions about NASA's ability to manage programs of the scale the President wants to undertake in the future."

# GROWING POVERTY AND
# NO MONEY TO DEAL WITH IT

## *Space Alert Newsletter,* Winter, 2004-2005

*"More and more of our imports are coming from overseas"*
—George W. Bush

Massive Pentagon waste should be viewed in the context of expanding national debt and growing poverty in the U.S. For the third straight year, the number of Americans living in poverty has increased. It is now over 36 million. Nearly 45 million Americans, or 16% of the entire population, lack health insurance. Over two decades, the income gap between the richest Americans, who own homes and stocks and get big tax breaks, and those at the middle and bottom of the pay scale, whose paychecks buy less has steadily increased.

The tax burden is now shifting dramatically onto the lower and middle classes. In 2003 alone, 46 corporations with combined profit of $42.6 billion paid no federal income taxes and instead received rebates totaling $5.4 billion.

According to economist, and former Secretary of Labor under Clinton, Robert Reich,

"The wealthy have shifted their Washington portfolios. A lot of the money they used to send to Washington in the form of tax payments they now send to Washington in the form of loans, through treasury bills and bonds. The big difference, of course, is that loans have to be paid back, with interest. So far in 2004, interest payments on the federal debt have totaled over $290 billion. And who pays that interest?"

# MARKS ON CONGRESSMAN'S
# WALL REPRESENT DEAD IN IRAQ

*"There's an old saying in Tennessee—I know it's in Texas, probably in Tennessee—*
*that says, fool me once, shame on—shame on you.*
*Fool me—you can't get fooled again."*

—George W. Bush

Today (March 18, 2005) thirty-five people occupied the office of our Congressman Tom Allen (D-ME) in Portland. We entered the office at 11:30 a.m. and Karen Wainberg, the board president of Peace Action Maine, read a prepared statement. It read in part, "Your recent vote in favor of $81.4 billion more for the war was a heartbreaking thing for us to witness...We have come to your office to strongly urge your sponsorship of the Woolsey resolution that demands the Bush administration develop an exit strategy immediately.... Rep. Allen we want to see leadership from you on this war issue. It is not acceptable for you to just sit back watching to see which way the wind blows.....We strongly request that you hold a public town hall meeting on the war so that people in your district can give you their feedback on your current position."

As we entered the office, a cameraman from one local TV station as well as a reporter from the *Portland Press Herald* newspaper were waiting for us. Doug Rawlings, president of Maine Veterans for Peace, did interviews with the media explaining why we had come. The *Brunswick Times Record* also had a front-page story about the occupation today, having done the interview yesterday in advance of the action.

As we previously did when we organized similar occupations in the offices of Maine's Republican Senators Snowe and Collins, we began reading over 1,500 names of American soldiers killed in Iraq and an equal number of names of Iraqi civilians. One thing we immediately noticed as the names were read is the high number of children killed in Iraq from cluster bombs and other U.S. bombing raids.

We sat in the office and inner hallways of the congressman's office while each person read two pages of names, and then passed the list on to the next person. Allen's staff was forced to step around us to get to the fax and copy machine, and our voices, as we read, were surely a hindrance as they tried to talk on the phone. From time to time, one office worker would just stop typing at her computer and listen closely to the names. Hour after hour the names were read...a seemingly endless string of deaths. Business as usual was interrupted today.

Artist Pat Wheeler brought along a large cloth banner she had made. The words "Iraqi war dead" were written in the upper left hand corner.[95] The rest of the banner was empty. As each name was read an X was made in either red or black chalk on the banner. By 2:00 p.m. the entire banner was full of the marks. Then, folks began to put X's in between the existing X's. We took turns holding the banner up against the wall so those marking the X could use the wall as a backboard.

At some point we discovered that the chalk was bleeding through the banner onto the freshly painted white walls of the congressman's new office. By the end of the day, virtually the entire wall was covered with the X's.[96]

We finished reading the names by 4:00 p.m., and gathered in a large circle in the front room of the office where we stretched the banner out so everyone could see it. It was covered with over 3,000 X's. We invited the Congressman's four staff persons to join our circle, and they did. I began by saying that we had not come to criticize them, we knew they were just doing their jobs. I said that we had come because we were heartbroken over the Congressman's vote on the Iraq war appropriation and we were now more determined than ever to keep coming back to the offices of Maine's congressional delegation until the war was brought to an end. Pointing to the banner I remarked that it looked chaotic with all the X's. The Congressman, I said had just voted to give even more money to make Iraq even more violent and chaotic. I told the staff to tell Rep. Allen that in a truly democratic society it would be his job to serve the people. In a truly democratic society, I said, he would care what the people had to say. In that regard, I reiterated our demand for a public town hall meeting on the subject.

As we were preparing to leave, one of the staff women said her husband was a Vietnam veteran and had died in the last year. She told us if he were alive he would be with us today.

One reporter asked me yesterday what we expected to accomplish by occupying Congressman Allen's office. I told him, "we have no rosy expectations. We understand that we've had a takeover of our government by Big Money. But we must do something."

Today we did something. It was something good. Even the Congressman's staff, in their hearts, agree.[97]

# GOD'S WARRIORS: SPACE WEAPONS & CHRISTIAN FUNDAMENTALISM

*"I trust God speaks through me. Without that, I couldn't do my job."*

—George W. Bush

On April 4-7, 2005 I traveled to Colorado to attend protests at the *21st National Space Symposium* in Colorado Springs. In addition, I traveled to Denver and Boulder for speaking events.

Each year Global Network's co-founding group, Citizens for Peace in Space, organizes vigils outside The Broadmoor Hotel in Colorado Springs where the Space Foundation holds its annual conference. This year, over 6,500 military personnel and aerospace industry representatives gathered to plan for moving the arms race into the heavens. The conference organizers brought in eight hundred students from 46 states in order to indoctrinate them about "everything space." Speakers at the four-day event included Gen. Lance Lord, Commander of the Air Force Space Command and Lt. Gen. Thomas Goslin, Deputy Commander of the U.S. Strategic Command. A host of speakers from aerospace corporations like Raytheon, Arianespace, Lockheed Martin, Boeing, and General Dynamics were also on the agenda.

Colorado Springs is a military town. There are five military installations there, including the headquarters of the Air Force Space Command at Peterson Air Force Base. Over 40,000 active duty military personnel are assigned to those five bases. I was told that 47% of those living in the city, with a population of 357,000, now work for the military industrial complex. How will we ever end America's addiction to war and violence as long as our communities are increasingly dependent on military spending for jobs?

My first day there 20 of us activists gathered outside the building for a news conference which was covered by two local TV stations and two newspapers. The next day a story appeared in the local Colorado Springs newspaper under the headline, "Don't use space for war, protesters say." Amazingly, the reporter used virtually all of the statements I made in the news conference: "He blamed the 'corporate dominated' media for not informing Americans of the military push into space and its consequences." I learned years ago, from watching Dr. Michio Kaku handle the media, that it is wise to challenge them to print the statement that you think the media is under the control of the corporations. Sometimes they print the statement just to prove you "wrong."

After the news conference we vigiled for a couple of hours. One banner I especially liked was "Space Domination, Group Think = War." Apparently, the news editor liked it too because they showed a picture of it. Group think is the right way to describe what goes on at events like this. The people pile into the event, listen to the generals say the U.S. must deny other countries access to space, they fill up their plastic bags with fancy posters of rockets and satellites, grab handfuls of Lockheed Martin pens and mouse pads, and head to the hotel bars. All in a day's work.

The following morning, my host, Bill Sulzman, and I returned to the symposium early in the morning because he wanted to be there when Lt. Gen. Goslin arrived to speak. Goslin works for the U.S. Strategic Command, which was newly created with the merger of the Strategic Air Command (SAC) and the U.S. Space Command. So, now the old bomber command, SAC, and the new space jockies are together and head-quartered in Omaha, Nebraska. The Air Force Space Command is still based in Colorado Springs at Peterson A.F.B. Bill got to say a word to Goslin as he passed right by us on his way into the symposium. We were standing at the main entrance where security guards were screening every civilian who went inside. Anyone in a military uniform was allowed to just walk into the symposium without any screening. Did anyone ever consider that all a "terrorist" had to do was put on a uniform and strut in?

After our short vigil, Bill took me to see the two big religious fundamentalist "campuses" in town. First, we stopped at the huge, 87-acre *Focus on the Family* facility run by Dr. James Dobson. The place includes a visitor center, it even has its own exit off the interstate highway. Bill and I watched a film inside their 172-seat theater that showed Dobson getting accolades from former president Ronald Reagan and George W. Bush as well as his father. A TV inside the lobby continuously played an appearance of Dobson on *CNN's Larry King Live* where Dobson made the claim that gay people had a secret plan to destroy the institution of marriage.

The Dobson "ministry" has a global radio program that is aired more than 18,000 times each week on about 2,000 outlets in the U.S. It is said Dobson's message is now heard on more radio stations around the world than any other message on the planet. His broadcast is played in Russia, China, and 157 other countries.

Next, Bill took me to the nearby *World Prayer Center* that is for Pastor Ted Haggard's base. Haggard is the President of the National Association of Evangelicals. The center-piece of this operation is an enormous church where Haggard preaches international outreach. I later watched a videotaped interview with Haggard in which he said of Colorado Springs, "This city is a light on a hill, devoted to protecting people worldwide...thank God we had a strong military to help the Iraqi people make their own choices."

It was interesting to me that Haggard's "church" looked more like a basketball arena. It was round, with exits all around it, and had the exposed steel rafters in the roof just like the ones at major indoor sports stadiums. Inside there was not one typical sign of a church. No Jesus on a cross, no cloth banners hanging from the rafters, no candles, no stained glass. In a video interview I was later to see of him, Haggard described his Sunday services as "kind of like a rally...with music and very simple Bible teachings.....we do what we can to encourage free markets."

Haggard appears to focus on young people. There was a Christian rock band performing in another part of his campus with about 20 young people dancing with their arms raised to the sky. While there I picked up some literature entitled "The World Prayer Team—Prayer Points" and read the following: AFGHANISTAN—Pray for the continual efforts to rebuild and stabilize this country. Pray for the protection of the soldiers accomplishing this work. IRAQ—We thank our Heavenly Father for the work he has accomplished in this country as insurgent attacks continue to drop. Pray that stability will grow in ever increasing measures over the next few months and on into the future."

As we were leaving Haggard's campus, I picked up a schedule of upcoming conferences. One scheduled for July, 2005 in Dallas, Texas is called "Taking Back the Spoils from the Enemy" and another for November, 2005 in Greensboro, N.C. is "Prayer and Spiritual Warfare Conference—East Coast."

As we drove away I asked Bill what the connection between Colorado Springs' massive military presence and the Christian fundamentalist operations was. He responded that, "Fascist theology in this town sees God on the side of the U.S. The U.S. government is an agent of evangelization that provides a security cover for them. Haggard says that without the protection of a dominant U.S. military they would not be free to practice or evangelize others." Bill knows a bit about religion. He was a Catholic priest who was defrocked from the church after getting arrested inside "Our Lady of the Skies" chapel at the nearby Air Force Academy, while protesting the Vietnam War.

That evening, I spoke at an event organized at a local church. The other speaker was Kelly Dougherty of Colorado Springs. Kelly was recently in Iraq serving with the Colorado National Guard. She now belongs to the Iraq Veterans Against the War and told of the many Iraqi men, women and children she saw killed by "smart bombs" directed to their targets by space technology. One young man in the audience revealed he was AWOL. After having already served one tour in Iraq he is now refusing to go back.

During the next two days, Bill drove me to Denver where I spoke and then we returned to the space symposium for more vigiling. He also took me to Boulder where I talked at the University of Colorado. On the last morning of the trip he arranged for me to speak to a political science class at Colorado College back in Colorado Springs. The talk was supposed to last for one hour, but the class of about 25 students had so many questions the professor extended the session by a half hour. Upon returning home I got an e-mail from the professor telling me I won some converts that day and that several of his students thought my ideas were "cool."

While I was vigiling outside the space symposium, I ran into a Wing Commander, Chris Knapman, from the United Kingdom. We had met a couple years before when I was on tour in England. Friends had taken me to the U.S. Star Wars radar facility in Yorkshire called Fylingdales. My friends asked the commander to come talk with me outside the front gate at Fylingdales and he did. When I got back to where I was staying in Colorado Springs, I wrote up the story about seeing Chris on my web blog and added a photo of us talking outside his base. The next day, while vigiling again at the space symposium, Chris walked by and said, "You work fast. I saw the photo on your blog." I was a bit taken aback that he saw my blog and later asked him how he had known to look at it. He told me that he regularly checks the websites of anti-Star Wars groups in the UK and the U.S. Nice to know they are watching us. Just goes to show that our actions are under scrutiny and the government fears the work we do enough to keep a close eye on it. Keep watching, Chris!

# LETTER TO NASA

Mr. Kurt Lindstrom
Mission and Systems Management Division
Science Mission Directorate
NASA HQ, Washington DC

April 11, 2005

Dear Mr. Lindstrom:

I write on behalf of our organization, the Global Network, to offer comments about NASA's *Draft Environmental Impact Statement* on the New Horizons mission to Pluto. Since the 1989 Galileo mission we have been opposed to the launching of nuclear power into space for any purpose.

We know that a joint committee decides on the kind of power source to be used when NASA and the Department of Energy (DoE) identify a new mission. It is our understanding that the nuclear industry, which views space as a new market, has been quick to place its operatives right in the middle of this process. So, at the very outset, this is a rigged game.

We also know that NASA and the DoE have been defunding the research and development of alternative space power concepts in recent years. It is clear that the nuclear industry intends to make sure that there are no other significant players in the process.

Our concern and opposition is, of course, centered around the fact that space technology can and does fail. We have seen rocket explosions on launch. We remember the 1996 Russian Mars mission, which carried plutonium on-board. It failed to achieve proper orbit and fell back to Earth, burning up over the mountains of Chile and Bolivia, and spread plutonium over that region. At the time, the *Boston Globe* reported those governments requested assistance from the U.S. to send in radiological teams to help identify the plutonium contamination belt, but then-President Bill Clinton refused to respond. Two years ago, we witnessed the Columbia shuttle disaster; I myself saw NASA operatives on TV dressed in haz-mat suits using Geiger counters to take readings of people in Texas and Louisiana who had come in contact with debris from that accident. Local police forces were heard on *National Public Radio* warning the public to stay away from Columbia debris. They were told by NASA that "radioactive" sources were on-board that mission. Just what was the radioactive source on Columbia?

In addition to space accidents, we are also concerned about the entire nuclear production process and its contamination of workers and communities. We have very little confidence in the DoE. It is a matter of public record that nuclear labs across the country have been contaminated for years. *The New Mexican*, in Santa Fe, reported in 1996 that, "Mishaps in which workers and equipment have been contaminated with radioactive sources are on the rise at Los Alamos National Laboratory." The reason? "Lab officials say the rise in radiation exposure and radioactive mishaps since 1993 has one primary cause: the [NASA] Cassini project and an ongoing effort to build radioactive heat sources." So, even if there is no launch problem, the production process is already contaminating, and, likely, killing people.

Now NASA and DoE are saying that they have so many plans for space nuclear power in the coming years that they must ramp up production of plutonium. It appears that DoE will center its operations for these missions at the Idaho National Laboratory. A $230 million proposed facility expansion is now underway. Citizens across Idaho have expressed opposition to this expansion. They fear, with good reason, that they will not get the truth about contamination from the DoE. In a recent article in the *Boise Weekly* newspaper, Jeremy Maxand, director of the nuclear watchdog group, The Snake River Alliance, says the following in regard to this issue: "The DoE is proposing a project that could leave Idahoans breathing plutonium for the next 80 years, and they won't tell us what it's for. Let's talk about something they can't hide from the public. Plutonium-238 is lethal and difficult to contain. Is this secrecy going to benefit Idahoans, given the DoE's well-documented and abysmal track record for worker, community, and environmental safety?"

Maxand goes on to say, "It makes me highly suspicious that, on one hand, they sell this extremely hazardous process to Idahoans via sleek NASA space batteries, when in fact we've made them for decades using plutonium purchased from Russia's stockpile. Then, in the next breath they'll say that the plutonium-238 produced in Idaho will be used for classified national security missions...."

Forgive us for thinking that you all have no credibility. One example is Kodiak Island in Alaska. The U.S. government built a rocket launch facility there and promised the citizens of Alaska it would only be used for civilian launches, never military. But, in reality, the only missions that have yet been launched have been Missile Defense Agency (MDA) tests. We are convinced the expansion of nuclear power into space for missions like New Horizons is a Trojan Horse. We are convinced NASA, DoE and the Pentagon are setting up the nuclear space infrastructure to eventually build nuclear reactors for warfare in the heavens. New Horizons is an ice breaker.

For all these reasons we demand that the New Horizons mission be cancelled. NASA and DoE must develop new non-nuclear power sources for space exploration. We will oppose the New Horizons mission in the same way we opposed Galileo (1989), Ulysses (1990) and Cassini (1997). Project Prometheus, the nuclear rocket, will also be a target of our organization. NASA has been taken over by the military and the nuclear industry.

The time has come for the public to reject plans to move war and nuclear power into space. Our money is being wasted on these dangerous projects, while schools and libraries close across the nation, and people can't afford health care. Jobs are leaving the U.S. by the millions and we are told there is no money for job training. The public is turning against NASA and its gee-whiz plans for nuclear launches, because the public understands the dangers involved. NASA and DoE are out of control and must be restrained by the taxpayers of the nation and the citizens of the world.

In anticipation of a nuclear space accident, the U.S. Congress has created the Price-Anderson Act that limits the liability of the U.S. for nuclear contamination clean-up. This law would not have been passed if NASA did not expect a space nuclear accident at some point in the future. We will not wait until the tragedy happens before we speak out. Cancel New Horizons and all other space nuclear missions today, before it is too late.

In peace,

Bruce K. Gagnon
Coordinator
Global Network Against Weapons &
Nuclear Power in Space

# SPACE WEAPONS MEDIA BRIEFING TRIP

I made a two-day (May 16-17, 2005) trip to northern Virginia where, along with Global Network board member Loring Wirbel from Colorado Springs, we attended an event organized by Dr. Helen Caldicott called *Full Spectrum Dominance*.

Helen's Nuclear Policy Research Institute gathered key media representatives from news outlets like *CNN, NBC, Space News, Reuters, Financial Times, San Francisco Chronicle, Defense Daily, Washington Post, Cape Cod Times, Toronto Globe & Mail, UPI* and others, to hear the two-day briefing from scientists, policy makers, space strategists and activists. The event took place at a conference center in a beautiful rural setting where 25 briefers sat down with 45 members of the media to discuss the latest developments in military space issues.

The event began with Gen. Charles Horner, retired commander of the U.S. Space Command. He described his career as one of "destroying things and killing people" and told the assembled that the Pentagon does not "want to talk about space control because they are afraid of groups like you that will be protesting in the streets." He went on to defend plans for missile defense by saying that "ones [nukes] that we shoot down are going to fall on Canada" rather than the U.S.

Since World War II well over $130 billion has been wasted on research and development (R & D) for the Star Wars program. The Pentagon's Missile Defense Agency (MDA) is now spending about $10 billion a year on space weapons R & D. The Bush administration is expected to announce its new national space policy in June, 2005 and the *New York Times* reported on May 18 that the new directive will likely include language giving the Pentagon the green light to move forward with offensive technologies for space control and domination.

Dr. Richard Garwin, Senior Fellow for Science and Technology at the Council on Foreign Relations, talked about the benefits of U.S. military control of space and said "It would be a disaster for U.S. military capability to lose our current space resources." It was commonly agreed that the U.S. today has sole military control of space and that current Pentagon satellites give the U.S. the ability to wage war onto the Earth with unrivaled power. Peter Hayes, former Air Force officer, reported that nearly 70% of the weapons used in the recent U.S. "shock and awe" invasion of Iraq were guided to their targets by space satellites. Thus, he maintained, the U.S. must control the space medium.

As the public becomes more aware of U.S. plans for space dominance, the military seeks to water down some of its previously provocative language. One example is replacing the word "deployment" with the phrase "test-bedding" when describing new space weapons technologies. This will make it harder for Congress to vote against a particular program because it is sold as a benign R & D effort.

Even some people that you would consider "peace activists" support the notion of U.S. space control. Mike Moore, former Editor of the *Bulletin of Atomic Scientists*, stated he is "in favor of full spectrum dominance," but urged the U.S. not to reject the notion of treaties that could bring stability to space. Moore, and others from traditional arms control organizations, argued that using weapons in space would create larger space debris problems for the Pentagon, thus putting existing U.S. military space assets in jeopardy. One representative of an arms control group implied that using "reversible" anti-satellite weapons (that only temporarily blind an opponent's satellite) might be more acceptable as they leave an attacked satellite intact but inoperable, thus eliminating the debris problem.

Much time was spent debating the merits of National Missile Defense. Will it work or not? Can a bullet hit a bullet in space or is the technology incapable of ever working? Ted Postol, Professor of Science, Technology, and National Security at MIT offered strong evidence that the missile defense "kill vehicle" could never effectively discriminate between actual warheads and dummies thus enabling any attacking nation the ability to overwhelm the system. During one back-and-forth debate on this issue (what I call "inside baseball") several arms control advocates responded to a question from missile defense proponents saying they would support the program if indeed it would work.

One program offered by many as an alternative to an unworkable National Missile Defense system (whose job would be to protect the continental U.S. from attack) is Theatre Missile Defense (TMD), or a boost-phase defense system that would have a "better chance" of performing the desired result of destroying a launched "enemy" missile. This could be done by deploying TMD systems near North Korea (who today has zero nuclear weapons capable of hitting the North American continent) and "taking out" their missiles soon after launch. Dr. Hui Zhang, a Chinese scientist now studying at Harvard University, reminded the audience that China views TMD systems as highly destabilizing and believes they would negate China's current deterrent stock of 20 nuclear missiles. TMD deployments by the U.S., on Aegis destroyers, are planned in Japan, South Korea, Australia, and possibly Taiwan. China has responded that TMD deployments, as well as other U.S. moves to "deny" space access to potential enemies, could force them to build more nuclear missiles.

Dr. Everrett Dolman, Professor of Military Studies at the Air Force School of Advanced Air and Space Studies at Maxwell AFB in Alabama, emphatically stated that the U.S. "will not give up its right to use force as long as it is the hegemon." Formerly on active duty in the Air Force, Dolman began his career as an intelligence analyst for the National Security Agency, and later moved to the U.S. Space Command. At one point, during a discussion about the need for a new international space treaty to prevent an arms race in space, Dolman responded derisively, "Mice always vote to bell the cat."

One of the "mice" in the meeting was Vladimir Yermakov, Senior Councellor at the Russian Embassy in Washington. (He was closely watched by an FBI agent who monitored every move he made while he was at the event.) Yermakov stated that Russia has sworn off first-deployment of weapons in space. In reference to Russia's strong support for a new, space weapons treaty he said, "We fail to understand the position of the U.S. in this matter. We ask what is wrong with our approach and get no answer." He referred to the U.S. refusal to negotiate a new space treaty. The official position of the U.S., during both the Clinton and Bush administrations, has been that there is no problem and thus no need for a new treaty banning weapons in space.

On the second day of the event Loring Wirbel and I had a chance to make presentations to the assembly. Loring went first and did a fabulous job of describing how space technology today is used to coordinate virtually all warfare on Earth. He began by challenging the tendency of some arms control groups to offer compromises on the space weapons issue, suggesting they strengthen themselves by developing some "outside the beltway thinking." (Loring is a long-time member of the Colorado Springs-based Citizens for Peace in Space, a founding affiliate of the Global Network. He makes his living as an editorial director for a high-tech magazine and is an effective spokesman for the peace movement position that allowing a "little bit" of space weaponization will lead to more of it over time, thus creating the eventual spark for a dangerous new arms race.) Loring estimated that about $70 billion a year is spent on "military space" development once the combined space budgets of the MDA, the National Reconnaissance Office, the National Security Administration, NASA, and the Department of Energy (now developing the nuclear rocket) are factored in.

I began my presentation by referring to the heated debate over whether missile defense will work or not. I proposed to widen the discussion and suggested we look at Christopher Columbus and Spain. I reminded everyone how Queen Isabella began the 100-year process of building the Spanish Armada after Columbus' "successful" return voyage from the Americas. Spain's naval armada helped create the global war system, that we suffer from today, as all the European powers were soon building navies to "compete" for control and domination of the sea lanes for resources and markets. I suggested we were now debating the size of the cannon balls on Spanish armada ships rather than discussing the long-term implications of creating a new arms race in the heavens. I talked about the long-range plan of the space command to build a military highway from the Earth out to the planetary bodies and showed the congressional study called *Military Space Forces: The Next 50 Years*. I suggested that "missile defense" was a Trojan horse that didn't really have to work — it had already allowed the Pentagon and the aerospace industry to move tens of billions of dollars into research and development programs for space offensive warfare — all the while hyping up North Korea's "puny" missile capability. I talked about the mission of the Global Network to create an international citizens constituency to stop an arms race in space, and detailed the efforts of our affiliated groups across the U.S. and around the world. I shared how TMD deeply concerns our members in Japan and South Korea because they understand how this program **will** be a provocation to China and destabilize the Asian-Pacific region. Could it be, I asked, that is what the weapons industry really wants? A new arms race partner in China? I concluded with several solutions. I suggested America is addicted to war and violence and that local economies in the U.S. are addicted to military spending. I suggested people want jobs, and that both Democrats and Republicans are not addressing the issue because both parties are committed to massive military spending. I called for the defunding of all space weapons R & D (something many of the arms control groups will not say), and suggested our hard-earned tax dollars should be used to develop alternative sustainable technologies in a much needed conversion of the military-industrial complex. I urged religious leaders to raise the moral and ethical questions about war in the heavens. I called for more public debate about the legal question on the ownership of space as aerospace corporations make a move to grab planetary bodies for eventual "resource extraction."

My presentation ended with a quote from NASA's new director, Mike Griffin, who appeared before a Senate committee on May 12, 2005. Griffin, who worked on Ronald Reagan's SDI program in the 1980's, told Congress, "For America to continue to be preeminent among nations, it is necessary for us to be the preeminent space faring nation." I told the assembled room of journalists and space enthusiasts that just as nuclear weapons are today unacceptable, so too is the philosophy outlined by Mike Griffin.

Helen Caldicott took the floor after I finished and reminded us all, as she so powerfully does in these moments, that our planet is in the intensive care unit and that we must change our way of thinking if we are to save life for the future generations. She underscored that we cannot continue to play the little boys game of tit-for-tat that was so evident among many at this unique gathering.

It was an honor to have been invited to attend this event and I came away convinced that our work to keep space for peace is more important than ever. We must step up our efforts and ensure that when Bush releases his new space policy directive, it is met with a resounding global chorus that says we will not allow this plan for space warfare to go forward. We must raise our voices now.

# HEALING OUR VIOLENT SOULS

Growing up, my family was at times chaotic and violent. My stepfather would occasionally beat my mother and regularly beat me. I was a good kid, rarely caused any trouble, but my mother would use me to keep the rest of the kids in check. If I did anything to get out of line, she would say, "Wait until your father comes home. You are going to get it." And I did. He often would tell me, while he was beating me, "This hurts me more than it does you." I now believe that he meant it. He had to administer the beatings, he thought, to keep peace in the home. In order to get my mother off his back, he had to whup my ass. It was his job, whether he liked it or not. Just like being in the military. In a way he was drafted to kick my ass.

Imagine generation after generation of Americans whupping the world's ass, in a series of wars, not being fought because the American working class GI wanted to but because they had to—they were told to do so by those who ran the country. The whupping often hurt the GI's as much as it hurt those they administered it to.

Post traumatic stress disorder (PTSD) has just become known since the Vietnam War. In earlier wars, GI's were ridiculed when they got battle fatigue or became gun shy. Virtually every family in America has been touched by the trauma of war. These generations of soldiers have come home, most of them never talking about their experiences, and gone on to try to put their lives back together in a country that did not want to know about how they felt.

I once had a friend up in rural north Florida who was an old farmer. One day his wife called me and told me to come visit them soon because her husband was going to die. When I arrived at their house he began to tell me horrific stories about his time in the Army during World War II. He went into his room and retrieved his combat medals and wept like a baby as he described the painful memories that had been locked inside him for over 40 years.

In many cases, when those stories get locked inside the GIs they turn to rage and self destruction. This is what happened to my stepfather, Wes. He had been in Korea and Vietnam, but was not "allowed" by our culture to cry and to grieve about his experiences. His only option was to go to the Veterans for Foreign Wars (VFW) hall, get drunk, and glorify the wars with wild stories of heroism. These stories also put down, dehumanized, the cultures that had been subdued by U.S. violence. The souls of the GI's were sealed shut with liquor and denial.

Generations of this practice have deadened the souls of our entire nation. A veteran of George Washington's Army, in 1779, said, "I really felt guilty as I applied the torch to huts that were homes of content until we ravagers came spreading desolation everywhere....Our mission here is ostensibly to destroy but may it not transpire, that we pillagers are carelessly sowing the seed of Empire?" The solider wrote this as

Washington's Army set out to remove the Iroquois civilization from New York state so that the U.S. government could expand its borders westward toward the Mississippi River. The creation of the American empire was underway.

From there we had war with Mexico and then it was off to the Philippines, Puerto Rico and Guam. Soldiers were sent to Russia, Africa and the Caribbean. Marine General Smedley Butler[98] who led his troops into battle many times, remarked, "I spent 33 years and 4 months in active military service…And during that period I spent most of my time as a high-class muscle man for Big Business, for Wall Street and the bankers. In short, I was a racketeer, a gangster for capitalism….Thus, I helped make Mexico and especially Tampico safe for American oil interests in 1914. I helped make Haiti and Cuba a decent place for the National City Bank boys to collect revenues in. I helped in the raping of half a dozen Central American republics for the benefit of Wall Street….I helped purify Nicaragua for the international banking house of Brown Brothers in 1902-1912. I brought light to the Dominican Republic for American sugar interests in 1916. I helped make Honduras right for American fruit companies in 1903. In China in 1927, I helped see to it that Standard Oil went on its way unmolested."

Next our American fathers fought in World War I and World War II. When they came home no one helped them heal their broken souls. Then they came home from Korea with PTSD but no one knew what PTSD was. In 1965 our fathers swept into the Dominican Republic and gunned down 3,000 innocent people in the streets of Santo Domingo. In Vietnam almost 60,000 American GI's were killed and two million, mostly civilian, Vietnamese died. Our fathers came home angry, frightened, and deeply scarred from the experience. Lebanon came next to be followed by the invasion of Grenada in 1983. In 1989 the U.S. attacked Panama, killing several thousand innocent civilians. Next came the Persian Gulf War in 1991 and the Kosovo war in 1999. Today, GI's, men and women alike, are coming home from Afghanistan and Iraq filled with a pain they can't talk about.[99]

What happens to the pent-up violence inside these American GI's when they return? They feel guilt but have been told they are "heroes," so they hold the conflicted feelings inside and turn on their loved ones, erupting like molten volcanoes. The corporate culture does not care about what they feel. The corporate culture does not want to talk about the pain and suffering of the GI's because the corporate culture has plans for endless war in order to subdue the world for its benefit.

Well known journalist Seymour Hersh wrote in *The Guardian,*[100] "Amid my frenetic reporting for the *New Yorker* on Abu Ghraib, I was telephoned by a middle-aged woman. She told me that a family member, a young woman, was among those members of the 320th Military Police Battalion, to which the 372nd [Military Police Company] was attached, who had returned to the U.S. in March [2004]. She came back a different person—distraught, angry and wanting nothing to do with her immediate family. At some point afterward, the older woman remembered that she had lent the reservist a portable computer with a DVD player to take to Iraq; on it she discovered an extensive series of images of a naked Iraqi prisoner flinching in fear before two snarling dogs. One of the images was published in the *New Yorker* and then all over the world."

"The war, the older woman told me, was not the war for democracy and freedom that she thought her young family member had been sent to fight. Others must know, she said. There was one other thing she wanted to share with me. Since returning from Iraq, the young woman had been getting large black tattoos all over her body. She seemed intent on changing her skin."

After awhile this proclivity to violence turns to ugly addiction. We, as a culture, begin to celebrate it and brag on our prowess. We romanticize the wars and the warriors. We idolize the weapons and stand in wonder as the warplanes fly overhead in celebration of our collective insanity. And insanity it is. If you doubt it, just ask some of the people whose countries we have invaded.

We must climb out of this deep, dark hole. In order to do so we must first admit our addiction and then we must get treatment for it. Just like any other addict, we must begin a collective, national 12-step program to recover from our passion for war.

The peace movement in America is the mirror. We hold up the mirror so the country can gaze into the glass and see what we have become. Most Americans don't want to look. They know what is there, but if they look deeply into the mirror then they might have to do something about it. And the reality in America is that this is one subject we don't touch. Domestic violence is always denied by the family. I know all about that. I remember vividly the days after my mother was beaten and I had to walk to school with a heavy heart and no one to share it with. I was taught to keep it quiet. So we do.

I thank god for the peace movement. It has helped me find my way back to some semblance of sanity. It has given me a safe place where I can tell my story to people who deeply care. The peace movement is the conscience of America. We need more of it.

## NOW AND THEN

In the beginning of it all there was the land
And the sea and the sky
Then into the middle of it all there came man
To live on the land.
And then a great nation
Put into operation an evolutionary plan
Now mighty corporations and politicians rule the land
Wish I could remember when
We were more innocent
Than all of those violent bitter men.
The world was much younger then
But we were much wiser then.
Before we were full of discontent.
It's too bad the simple ways came sadly to an end
I guess that's the difference between now and then.
In the beginning of it all there was the land.
We were much younger then
But we were much wiser then
We never questioned why or when
One day we'll be born again

Our lovers and friends will remain
To live in a world without suffering and pain
And I can see a day when enemies are friends.
And there'll be no distance between now and then.
In the beginning of it all there was the Land.

By Ray Davies
The Kinks

## GOD'S CHILDREN

Man made the buildings that reach for the sky
And man made the motorcar and learned how to fly
But he didn't make the flowers and he didn't make the trees
And he didn't make you and he didn't make me
And he got no right to turn us into machines
He's got no right at all
'Cause we are all God's children
And he got no right to change us
Oh, we gotta go back the way the good lord made us all
Don't want this world to change me
I wanna go back the way the good lord made me
Same lungs that he gave me to breathe with
Same eyes he gave me to see with
Oh, the rich man, the poor man, the saint and the sinner
The wise man, the simpleton, the loser and the winner
We are all the same to Him
Stripped of our clothes and all the things we own
The day that we are born
We are all God's children
And they got no right to change us
Oh, we gotta go back the way the good lord made
Oh, the good lord made us all
And we are all his children
And they got no right to change us
Oh, we gotta go back the way the good lord made us all
Yeah, we gotta go back the way the good lord made us all

By Ray Davies
The Kinks

# FOOTNOTES

1  One night in the spring of 1985 I had a dream. There was a knock on my door and when I answered it a man was there holding a book. He asked me if I was Bruce Gagnon. He told me my father had died and wanted me to have the book. A couple weeks later I got a phone call. A woman was on the line and asked if I was Bruce Gagnon. She told me she was married to Kenneth Gagnon, my father, and that he had recently died. She said they lived in Tucson, Arizona and had been married for the past eight years. My two older sisters, Karen and Joan, joined me as we immediately flew to Tucson to find out more about our father. He had died from complications after the removal of a stomach cancer. He had told his wife that he had three kids and when she asked why they never visited he told her I was an airline pilot who was very busy. His wife told me how much I looked like him, how I walked liked him, and how I laughed like him. She gave me his personal belongings including his trophies for being a shuffleboard champion on the Tucson senior citizen circuit. She told us he was a good man and they had met at a senior citizen dance. In the past I had tried to find him but had given up hope I ever would. Now he was gone for good. I had always felt a spiritual connection to him though and realized that the dream was evidence that we had been connected throughout the many years of our separation.

2  My mom and Wes would have three children together in the years to come—Laura, Lynn and Leslie. I would have five sisters.

3  The native people called the Black Hills the paha sapa, or the heart of the Earth.

4  I had heard of marijuana before but had never smoked it. Of course, I never inhaled.

5  Vietnam was divided at the 17th parallel. All French and South Vietnamese forces were moved south of the demarcation line. All Viet Minh forces moved to its north. France was to leave the country completely. National elections to reunify Vietnam under a single government were to be held in July 1956. Vietnam was officially reunified as the Socialist Republic of Vietnam on July 2, 1976. Saigon was renamed Ho Chi Minh City.

6  To this day I am a strong believer in getting out on the streets to hand out leaflets. I do it for several reasons. First, it is good to pass on important information to people. Secondly, it inspires people who agree with us when they see someone else doing something—they don't feel so alone and isolated. I also use it as a way to gauge the depth of public concern about an issue. And finally, it is a good way to meet new people who might become active in issues I am working on.

7  The UFW held onto the Coca-Cola contract for many years but eventually, bit by bit, Minute Maid sold off its Florida orange groves to competitors and moved its citrus

operation to Brazil and Costa Rica. The loss of Minute Maid groves in Florida, bought up by non-union corporations, slowly led to the demise of the UFW stronghold in Florida.

8   Minute Maid orange juice is a subsidiary of the Coca-Cola Corporation.

9   *Writings and Speeches of Eugene V. Debs*, 1948, Hermitage Press

10  On June 16, 1918 Debs made his famous speech in Canton, Ohio that got him prosecuted and jailed under the Sedition Act for interfering with the draft. In the speech he said, "Wars throughout history have been waged for conquest and plunder. In the Middle Ages when the feudal lords who inhabited the castles whose towers may still be seen along the Rhine [river] concluded to enlarge their domains, to increase their power, their prestige and their wealth they declared war upon one another. But they themselves did not go to war any more than the modern feudal lords, the barons of Wall Street go to war....They have always taught and trained us to believe it to be your patriotic duty to go to war and to have yourselves slaughtered at their command. But in all the history of the world you, the people, have never had a voice in declaring war, and strange as it certainly appears, no war by any nation in any age has ever been declared by the people....You need at this time especially to know that you are fit for something better than slavery and cannon fodder. You need to know that you were not created to work and produce and impoverish yourself to enrich the idle exploiter. You need to know that you have a mind to improve, a soul to develop, and a manhood to sustain...Do not worry over the charge of treason to your masters, but be concerned about the treason that involves yourselves. Be true to yourself and you cannot be a traitor to any good cause on earth." These words by Debs had great meaning to me as I began to work with one group of disposed people—migrant farm workers.

11  Today John is a lawyer with the Public Defender's office in Tallahassee. In his spare time, he is organizing an effort to stop the St. Joe Paper Company from turning its enormous land holdings along the Florida Panhandle gulf coast into an urban development. Developers hope to essentially build a new city in the remote region now largely used for pine tree farming. John, as always, has been successful in organizing a hugely controversial campaign to protect the land. John and I remain friends and see each other when ever possible to share organizing tales.

12  This phrase, "royal pain in the ass," is what my supervisors at Travis AFB in California used to call me. I was a hard worker, and always got good performance reports for my work, but my "attitude" was not up to their standards due to my anti-war posture.

13  Read Holly Sklar's book called "Trilateralism: The Trilateral Commission and Elite Planning for World Management"

14  The application process was a snap. What was difficult was the political process. We had to ensure that the city and county community development block grant citizen's advisory groups would support us. We had to identify those on the committee and

make sure we got people with influence to talk with them on our behalf. In these kind of internal governmental systems you have to be sure to cover all the bases. There are always lots of competing interests trying to go after the same money.

15  By this time I was making sure our local CCBO newsletter was connecting growing military spending to cutbacks in social programs. I was also making sure that people heard about the efforts nationally to oppose the military build-up.

16  Dr. Manning Marable teaches history at Columbia University. He is author of many books including "How Capitalism Underdeveloped Black America."

17  This was the same donor who would years later give $100,000 to the Florida Coalition to build a building on the organization's land north of Gainesville. The building made it possible for the Florida Coalition to hold its summer youth peace camps on the "teaching farm," land that had also been donated to the organization by Quaker Al Geiger from Jacksonville.

18  Over the years, whenever the Florida Coalition would have a significant financial need, I would call a small group of big donors who would gladly make a special gift to the organization. They had learned to trust and appreciate the work I was doing. A couple of years after I left the Florida Coalition one of these donors died and left the organization over $100,000 in her will. I learned a long time ago that if you do good work by bringing good people together, the money will come.

19  The key to the success of this demonstration was the traveling I did around the state to promote the event. This was my first big demonstration and I learned the important lesson that personal visits to groups to invite them to participate was a key to determining the success of such an event. To this day, I time my travels to promote Global Network annual events like space conferences and our Keep Space for Peace Week. The human touch is always important. You can't just rely on e-mail or a leaflet to get people out. They have to feel the passion that only a personal visit can relay.

20  On August 11, 1984, during a radio broadcast sound check, Ronald Reagan, thinking that the microphone was turned off said, " My fellow Americans, I'm pleased to tell you today that I've signed legislation that will outlaw Russia forever. We begin bombing in five minutes."

21  It is the same story that we saw with Agent Orange in Vietnam and now depleted uranium in Iraq where the U.S. refuses to acknowledge the health affects of these weapons. This way the government avoids legal liability.

22  Gar Alperovitz. *The Decision to Use the Atomic Bomb.* New York: Alfred A. Knopf, 1995.

23  Once the cruise missile testing program began, the military had several mishaps where the missiles went out of control and their flights had to be "terminated." I first heard about depleted uranium (DU) when we learned that it was used in the nose cone of the cruise missile as ballast in place of a warhead. When the cruise crashed and burned

after flight termination, the highly toxic DU was released and scattered by the wind in the Florida panhandle.

24    The Trident II was developed to be launched from nuclear-powered submarines that would be home ported at the Kings Bay Naval base in St. Marys, Georgia—just above the Florida-Georgia line. President Jimmy Carter built the Kings Bay nuclear submarine base during his term in office. (Trident is also homeported at the Bangor, Washington Naval Submarine Base.)

25    Mobe took responsibility for doing the national promotion for the event. I was to coordinate the state and local effort, including the big rally on January 17.

26    The Great Peace March was organized to help bring the disarmament and peace message to America as it made its way across the country. The original organizer ran out of money and abandoned the march, just as it was set to begin in California. The march participants immediately took over. Some flew home to get their cars and upon their return, teams set out ahead of the peace march to handle day-to-day organizing of places to eat and sleep. Hundreds of activists stayed with the march and it became a symbol of the peace movement's determination to end war.

27    Walks are huge logistical undertakings. You need a place to sleep each night, people to feed the walkers, port-a-toilets to be dragged along the walk, support vehicles to carry walkers personal gear and camping equipment and lots of patience. When you bring people together for this kind of intense walking community all kinds of sparks fly. John and Martina did a great job pulling it together and between us we were able to raise enough funds to make it happen.

28    Affinity groups are small clusters of people who get together to do an action. They self select and make their action plans in private. Not all people in an affinity group get arrested, some stay in the background and do support before, during, and after the action. Jail support is always a big role for members of an affinity group.

29    Leslie Cagan now leads the New York city-based national coalition called United for Peace & Justice.

30    We had some wonderful folks, Barbara Buck (Miami) and Dave Hartgrove (Daytona Beach) were two of the best, who led our Peace Keeper team that day. They coordinated and briefed volunteers from across the state, before the demonstration began, ensuring that when we needed them they were ready. It was the most professional group of Peace Keepers I ever saw and it was the most volatile situation I've ever been in.

31    Many of us in jail refused to give our real names making it difficult for the Brevard County jailers to process us. I said my name was Joe Nagasaki. One jailer called me Joe Nag-ask-i as if I was of Polish origin. A few of the folks stayed in jail for a month or more. We kept our mini-office near the Cape open after the demonstration so those doing jail support had a place to hang out. Some folks who had nothing else to do

slept there and we got a $1,000 telephone bill for one month's use. The Florida Coalition quickly moved to close the office which made some people angry with me.

32   Mikhail Gorbachev was president of the Soviet Union when in December of 1991 the nation disintegrated into fifteen separate countries. By the time of the 1985 rise to power of Gorbachev, the Soviet Union's last leader, the country was in a situation of deep economic and political crisis. Recognizing this, Gorbachev introduced a two-tiered policy of reform. He initiated glasnost, or freedom of speech. He also began a program of economic reform known as perestroika, or rebuilding. What Gorbachev did not realize was that by giving people such freedom of expression, he was unleashing emotions and political stirrings that had been pent up for decades. Moreover, his policy of economic reform did not have the immediate results he had hoped for. The Soviet people consequently used their new freedom of speech to blame Gorbachev for his failure to improve the economy. While extremely popular around the world, Gorbachev was removed from power and to this day is a controversial figure in Russia.

33   Plutonium 238 is roughly 280 times more toxic than the Plutonium 239 which was released during nuclear weapons tests. PU-238 is used on space missions because it releases tremendous amounts of radioactive "heat" that can be turned into electricity on-board a space craft. Once in the body plutonium is absorbed in soft tissues, notably the liver, and in bone marrow. Plutonium may be ingested by accidental ingestion of plutonium-contaminated soil, or through eating and drinking contaminated food and water. Plutonium in dust form, which could be created in a space nuclear accident, can also be inhaled.

34   www.brianwillson.com/awolpanama.html

35   *The Panama Deception* (film) documents the untold story of the U.S. invasion of Panama; the events which led to it; the excessive force used; the enormity of the death and destruction; and the devastating aftermath.

36   *The U.S. Invasion of Panama: The Truth Behind Operation 'Just Cause,'* The Independent Commission of Inquiry on the U.S. Invasion of Panama, 1991, South End Press

37   While working for the United Farm Workers union I learned that inevitably those in power would almost always do something very stupid just at the right moment to make an organizers job easier. During union contract negotiations the Coca-Cola company would take some measure to clamp down on the fruit picketers, trying to intimidate them, only making it easier for us to organize them. Or in the case of local Central Florida police, they could usually be counted on to take some extremely ridiculous step that would end up getting us more media attention than we could have dreamed for. These kinds of blunders helped us reach more people and swell our final demonstration turnouts.

38　I am not suggesting that people should not write letters. I send them all the time to politicians and to my local paper. Letters are very important but I do understand that some people feel it is a waste of time. It can be a hard point to argue with when folks see time after time that the politicians are ignoring public opinion. But, in spite of that reality, we must keep writing and speaking up. Good letters don't have to be long and full of facts. Short, sweet and right to the point is my style. Speak from your heart. Tell them how you really feel. It can be therapeutic.

39　Those figures were for 1995. By 2005 we have 29,000 people at the top in America owning the equivalent wealth as the 96 million people at the bottom.

40　I've made three trips to Cuba over the years. I had to go pick the forbidden fruit. Had to see for myself what was really going on there. On two of those trips I led delegations of about 30 people to travel the country and return to report to others what they experienced. I can tell you Cuba is no danger to the U.S. Well, except for the fact that if the American people were to go there on vacation and discover that Cuba has free health care—that might be a problem. How come we can trade with China but not Cuba? Cuba is not a black and white issue. In Cuba there are many shades of gray. In the end I came away from Cuba with a deep love for the people, a deep respect for their independent spirit, and a clear belief that Castro had tried to serve the poor first. I will always remember one pastor, an old black man, who told me he had grown up a peasant in the sugar cane fields before the revolution. He had two sons, he said, one became a doctor and one an engineer. To him the Cuban revolution meant dignity and progress for the poorest of the people.

41　In fact in the job as coordinator of the Florida Coalition for Peace and Justice I used to drive an average of 30,000 miles each year across the state. Some of my best ideas sprouted in the car. I witnessed the environmental damage caused by over building and over population. My favorite bumper sticker that I saw was "Take a snowbird home with you when you leave." (For those who don't know, a "snowbird" is a person from the north that comes to Florida during the winter to avoid the northern cold. In the spring, the snowbird flies back north again.) Florida now faces a severe water crisis in coming years due to over population. Water is wasted on fancy green lawns that are not appropriate in a state that is essentially a sand pit. In all my years in Florida I heard only one prominent politician say that Florida had reached its caring capacity. His name was Buddy MacKay from Ocala. In 1998, Jeb Bush defeated his Democratic opponent Buddy MacKay (55% to 45%) in the governors race. Jeb Bush had been a developer before running for governor. When Buddy MacKay served in the U.S. House of Representatives he was the only Florida politician that I can remember who spoke out against Ronald Reagan's illegal war on Nicaragua.

42　The first thing I did was to make sure virtually every peace group newsletter in the U.S. ran a story by either Karl Grossman or myself about Cassini. If you want to create a national campaign your issue must be seen by activists as a "happening."

People tend to gravitate to issues that appear to be "hot" or to issues that they think can be used to get media attention. Thus, creating the perception that "everyone" was into the Cancel the Cassini campaign was important. Once that begins to take hold the campaign takes on a life of its own as people start jumping into the effort and the job of the organizer then switches to essentially reporting on the new energy flowing into the campaign. This only serves to make the issue even more popular. The final stage is when the mainstream media wakes up to the campaign, usually right before launch, and discovers a national and international grassroots effort underway and they are amazed because it was essentially organized without their help. How was this possible they often asked?

43    In this case we got people to write letters and to call because they were inspired to do so. They wanted to help because they felt like they were part of something bigger than normal.

44    The founding meeting of the Global Network Against Weapons & Nuclear Power in Space (GN) took place in Washington D.C. in 1992. We met in the D.C. city hall building and had about 40 people there. Each year since 1992 we have met in places like New Mexico, Colorado, Florida, Alabama, England, Germany, California, Australia, Maine and New York City. (See Karl Grossman's book *The Wrong Stuff* for a full report on the founding of the GN.) The GN has now grown to about 170 affiliated groups all over the world. The GN is governed by a very active board of directors and board of advisors. The creation of the GN was intended to serve as a vehicle to spur international consciousness about the costly and dangerous plans to move the arms race into the heavens. Pro-space organizations, heavily funded by the aerospace industry, lobby for "everything space" and support plans for the nuclearization and weaponization of space. The development of the GN has added a needed counterweight to the overwhelming influence of the space development industry who view space as a new market for weapons, nuclear power and ultimately strip mining of the planetary bodies for precious minerals. Plans to put bases on the moon, so the U.S. could control the pathway on and off the planet Earth, have long been on the agenda of the space warriors. The GN maintains that while it is inevitable that humans will move into outer space, we must do so in a way that does not carry the tragic environmental and warlike mistakes our species has made on the planet Earth. The GN believes that there must be a global debate about the kind of seed humans carry with us as we leave our home planet.

45    In May of 2005 NASA made public their Environmental Impact Statement for Project Prometheus, the nuclear rocket for Mars. Rep. Cynthia McKinney (D-GA.) contacted the Global Network to say that she intended to try to remove the $400 million allocated for the nuclear rocket in NASA's budget. Her first step was to send a "Dear Colleague" letter to all members of Congress inviting them to join with her.

46  Published in February, 1997 the U.S. Space Command spells out how it intends to "control and dominate" space and "deny" other countries access to space.

47  On May 1, 2003 the Navy transferred control of Vieques to the Department of Interior, ending a 62 year saga of bombing and contamination of the island. Now the fight turns to the clean-up issue and health related illness as residents of Vieques have been exposed to depleted uranium and other toxic contaminants for years.

48  Sen. Ted Stevens (R-AK) prides himself in bringing lots of federal money into the state. This process has long been called bringing home the bacon, or pork.

49  As it turned out the peace movement was right about no WMD in Iraq. How is it that with no access to intelligence data, the peace movement was able to know what Congress did not appear to know? Or was Congress just lying to the public when they maintained they had "secret" information informing them of the existence of Iraqi WMD?

50  On April 20, 2005 the ACLU informed me that NASA, the Air Force's Office of Special Investigations (OSI), and the Brevard County (Space Coast) Sheriff's department had infiltrated the Global Network in recent years. According to the ACLU investigation, NASA was particularly concerned about the 2002 Keep Space for Peace Week actions and particularly European participation in them. The ACLU found that Global Network members Mary Beth Sullivan, Maria Telesca and I were being heavily investigated—including extensive background checks. Even my son Julian was named as a "related subject" for investigation. The ACLU requested authorization to represent us in possible legal action. We, of course, gave our permission.

51  The Danish government would eventually reject Greenland's request to deny the U.S. permission to upgrade the Thule radar.

52  In April 2005 I met the Wing Commander, Chris Knapman, again while protesting at the 21st National Space Symposium in Colorado Spring, Colorado. I was holding a sign outside the event to which over 6,500 military personnel and aerospace industry representatives were attending. When I returned to my room that night I wrote about seeing him again on my blog and put a picture of us talking outside Fylingdales on the internet site. The next day when I saw Chris at the symposium he said, "You work fast." He had seen the blog. I later asked him how he knew about the blog and he said he regularly checked the websites of many peace groups working against Star Wars.

53  A publication reporting on the anti-nuclear resistance around the U.S. and internationally since 1980. Gives detailed coverage and support to those doing time in jail. Contact at PO Box 43383, Tucson, AZ 85733.

54  Undetected in nature, americium (as the isotope americium-241 ) was artificially produced from plutonium-239 in 1944 in a nuclear reactor. The isotope americium-241 is the most important because of its availability; it has been prepared in kilogram amounts from plutonium and has been used industrially in fluid-density gauges, thick-

ness gauges, aircraft fuel gauges, and distance-sensing devices, all of which utilize its gamma radiation. All isotopes of americium are radioactive. Americium is commonly used in home smoke detectors.

55    Actually, the driver of the rental car was a contractor for the U.S. Air Force whom we had met on the plane. He was a good man—we thoroughly enjoyed our New York to Maine "snow adventure," with the rental car paid for by the military.

56    In 2004, Mel was elected to become one of Florida's two senators. A former Democrat, Mel turned Republican some years ago when he saw the political winds shifting to the right.

57    The board of directors/advisers of the GN had authorized moving the office, as well, so the work of the organization would continue without interruption in a new location.  Just north of Portland, in the city of Bath, is the place where Aegis destroyers are now being built for the Pentagon's Theatre Missile Defense (TMD) program that will be deployed along China's coastal region provoking and encircling them and guaranteeing a new arms race.  We looked forward to joining the protests at Bath Iron Works in the future.

58    In March, 2005 Jackie Hudson was released from prison though it was not yet known what would happen to her when she refused to pay for "damages" that the military claimed the nuns had done to Pentagon property. Carol was released in May, 2005 and had become friendly with world famous criminal, Martha Stewart, as they shared the jail house in Alderson, West Virginia. Ardeth remains in federal prison in Danbury, CT. Bill Sulzman would later comment about the trial, sentencing, and appeal of the nuns, "There are injustices and there are injustices. This decision stands with the worst of them. Sisters Ardeth, Carol and Jackie were charged with sabotage and felony destruction of a weapon of mass destruction at the time that this nation was busily justifying its pursuit of a vicious and murderous war against the people of Iraq—a war with no limits, a war that defies every 'law of war,' a war in which the U.S. of A. is revealed as having no shred of decency. The nuns were tried as that brutal war advanced—'shock and awe' for the world. They were convicted by a jury-fed by 'Fox-News.' And now their illegal and immoral conviction has been upheld by Bush appointed judges of the 10th Circuit Court of Appeals. The decision of the judges exposes the U.S. courts and the legal system as existing to serve and justify the crimes of government. This ruling is in harmony with the Alberto Gonzales Injustice Department."

59    I was later to learn that one woman, Vicki Johnson, did run for Congress in the 2004 election after hearing my suggestion. In fact she even called me one day while in the middle of her campaign to review her campaign strategy. She did not win, and apparently unsettled some Democrats by speaking forcefully about war and peace issues, but in the end she stuck to her desire to use the campaign to educate the public.

60  Suggested readings on the subject are *The Secret Life of Bill Clinton* by Ambrose Evans Pritchard, *Whiteout* by Alexander Cockburn, and *Partners in Power* by Roger Morris.

61  ACORN, the Association of Community Organizations for Reform Now, is the nation's largest community organization of low- and moderate-income families, working together for social justice and stronger communities with neighborhood chapters in 75 cities across the U.S.

62  Another one of my favorite Debs quotes is "While there is a lower class I am of it, while there is a criminal class I am of it, while there is a soul in prison I am not free."

63  In fact, Bush did announce plans to return to the Moon and Mars in 2003. The enormous cost, hundreds of billions of dollars, was immediately met with ridicule and anger by the public. The Bush administration quickly stopped talking about it, but quietly plans are moving ahead.

64  I have been assembling this list ever since our first big space campaign in 1989 when we took NASA into federal court to block the Galileo plutonium launch. The media do not often focus on our issues, but when they do it can get quite busy.

65  The video features Noam Chomsky, Apollo astronaut Edgar Mitchell, and myself in an hour-long documentary that begins with the story of Nazi scientists being brought to the U.S. to create our space program. The video explains how "missile defense" is really a part of the overall plan for U.S. control and domination of space. At the time of this book's publication several thousand copies have been sold and the producer signed a contract with Free Speech TV to air the video regularly for one-year.

66  My maternal grandfather, Vincent DiCapua, was a Republican activist in Shelton, Connecticut. He was friends with Sen. Prescott Bush who was Connecticut's senator from 1952-1963. My grandfather was known to have been helpful to the senator in drafting immigration legislation. During his 1959 acceptance speech as the Alfalfa Club's presidential nominee, Sen. Prescott Bush quipped: "I recall here the immortal words of Granville Rice, when he wrote, *"The rules of life apply the same, To any sport you choose, It matters not how you play the game, So long as you never lose."* The Alfalfa Club is an exclusive Washington, D.C. club for the rich and powerful, founded in 1913. Its sole purpose is to hold an annual banquet each January to honor the birthday of Confederate General Robert E. Lee. No press coverage is allowed inside the banquet hall and the proceedings are ostensibly secret. The membership list of the club reads like a Who's Who of Republican and Democratic political leaders.

67  Alexandra Robbins, "Secrets of the Tomb: Skull and Bones, the Ivy League, and the Hidden Paths of Power"

68  See next entry called "Blueprint for World Domination" for the full text of my speech at the *International Citizens Inquiry into 9-11*

69  Check their web site at www.newamericancentury.org and note their letter to President Bill Clinton on January 26, 1998 which called on Clinton to invade Iraq. The

letter said, "Given the magnitude of the threat, the current policy, which depends for its success upon the steadfastness of our coalition partners and upon the cooperation of Saddam Hussein, is dangerously inadequate. The only acceptable strategy is one that eliminates the possibility that Iraq will be able to use or threaten to use weapons of mass destruction. In the near term, this means a willingness to undertake military action as diplomacy is clearly failing. In the long term, it means removing Saddam Hussein and his regime from power. That now needs to become the aim of American foreign policy."

70   This September 2000 report is also available on the PNAC web site in the Publications/Reports section.

71   Frances did come to the conference and when we protested at Bath Iron Works on the first day of the event, she and several other women, attempted to deliver a letter to the head of the weapons corporation stating our opposition to their building of the Aegis destroyer, which is being outfitted with Theatre Missile Defense systems. The ships will be used to surround China along their coastal region, being deployed in South Korea, Japan, Taiwan and throughout the Pacific. A representative from the company came out to accept the letter and, try as they may, the women were not arrested.

72   This speech delivered in San Francisco on March 26, 2004 at the *International Citizens Inquiry into 9-11*.

73   You can find this document on the Global Network's web site in the links section under "Military."

74    In early 2005 George W. Bush appointed Paul Wolfowitz to be the new head of the World Bank. Protests were heard from around the world concerning the appointment but Bush was not deterred.

75   The Warren Commission was appointed by Democratic President Lyndon Johnson to investigate the assassination of President John F. Kennedy. Despite much available evidence that Lee Harvey Oswald was not the "lone assassin" of Kennedy, the Warren Commission came to the controversial conclusion that there was no "conspiracy" to kill the president.

76   Check their web site at www.space-law.org

77   The study was authored by Congressional staffer John Collins and was published in book form by the Air Force Association. The study also proclaimed that "Nuclear reactors thus remain the only known long-lived, compact source able to supply military space forces with electric power.... Larger versions could meet multimegawatt needs of space-based lasers, neutral particle beams, mass drivers, and railguns. Nuclear reactors must support major bases on the moon until better options, yet unidentified, become available.... Safety factors, rather than technological feasibility, will remain the principal impediment to nuclear power in space, unless officials convince influential critics that risks are acceptably low."

78 Check their web site at www.ivaw.net

79 Check their web site at www.mfso.org and www.gsfp.org

80 Catholic Workers live a simple lifestyle in community, serve the poor, and resist war and social injustice. Most are grounded in the Gospel, prayer, and the Catholic faith. If you feel called to do something about poverty and homelessness in your community, your local Catholic Worker house would be a great place to start. If you don't have a Catholic Worker house in your community then start one.

81 The video is available from the Global Network. Send $10 to PO Box 652, Brunswick, ME. 04011

82 As of December 2005 the number of U.S. dead in Afghanistan and Iraq is over 2,130. More than 15,500 U.S. troops have been wounded. Iraqi civilian deaths are well over 100,000. How far must it go before the American people will react?

83 In 1991, Joy and friends were trying to get President Clinton's Environmental Protection Agency (EPA) director, Carol Browner, to resist lowering the dioxin standard for waterways in Florida. A hearing was held in Orlando so Joy and her buddies prepared seven fried mullet dinners (with fish caught in a net from the contaminated Fenholloway River) and took them to the hearing. They sat in the audience all day, public comment periods are almost always at the end of the meetings. When they finally got their chance at 5:00 p.m. one of Joy's friends got up and gave the "country dinner blessing" just like her Mama taught her while Joy served the dinners to Carol Browner and the other members of the hearing panel. The media loved it and Joy then went to the microphone and told them about all the poor people that live along the river and eat the fish that the corporate run pulp mill keeps polluting. One year later *CBS 60 Minutes* covered the story and then *CNN* did two environmental award —winning features stories about their efforts. Joy reports now that the regulatory agencies find ways around the rules to suit polluters, and help to write new rules which make the Clean Water Act and Clean Air Act almost totally moot.

84 The local citizens protest paid off when on election day (November 2004) Taylor County voters rejected the bombing range by a margin of 75% to 25%. The fight is far from over though as Gov. Jeb Bush (brother of George W. Bush) will try to find a way to help move the bombing range into the community despite overwhelming public opposition. But don't despair, good friends, Joy is on the case!

85 On October 7, 2000, as part of the Global Network's annual Keep Space for Peace Week, I was arrested at Vandenberg AFB in California. Twenty-one persons, including the actor Martin Sheen, were arrested for crossing the line onto base property. I was the first to be taken away as I tried to deliver a letter, signed by the 300 demonstration participants, that called on the base commander to "lead your troops out of Vandenberg AFB and into the real peace movement." After going to trial in Los Angeles I was sentenced to two years of supervised probation and fined $1,010. During

the two years of probation I had to get the courts permission to travel. The only time I was ever denied was when I made my last request, only two weeks before my probation period ended. I was refused permission to travel to Washington DC for a peace demonstration.

86    Raging Grannies have become a continent-wide phenomenon where elder women peace activists dress up in clothes from a bygone era and rewrite words to popular songs. The lyrics they come up with usually mock the powers that be and get a lot of laughs from the audience.

87    In February, 2005 the Prime Minister of Canada, Paul Martin, announced that their nation would not be joining the U.S. in the controversial "missile defense" program. Martin had hoped to partner with the U.S., he was under intense pressure from the aerospace industry in his country to do so, but the pressure generated by the peace movement all across Canada was even greater. We are all proud of our Canadian friends for their determined effort to say NO to Star Wars.

88    Peg McIntire was the treasurer of the Florida Coalition for many years and was one of our top volunteers helping to organize several walks, peace camps, conferences and other events. A woman of remarkable energy, Peg is universally loved across Florida and virtually everyone in the Florida peace movement aspires to be like Peg when they "grow up." After working with Peg in the kitchen for a week during one of the Florida Coalition's summer peace camps, I limped home and stayed in bed for several days recovering from the heat, humidity, and long hours in the kitchen. I began to worry about Peg and called her to see how she was doing. She said, "Oh, I haven't had a minute to rest since I got home. In fact, the night I came home from camp I went out dancing with friends." Peg was inspired into activism when her brother was killed during the Spanish Civil War while with the Abraham Lincoln Brigade in Spain. She lived in Italy for many years and worked as a technical assistant to the director of the famous movie *Ben Hurr*.

89    Actually Hillary is just one of a group called "National Security Democrats" who aspire to power. The group says that the party should be "more open to the idea of military action, and even preemption." Members of this groups include Sen. Evan Bayh (D-IN), Sen. Joe Biden (D-DE), Governor Bill Richardson (D-NM), and former senator and Vice-Presidential candidate John Edwards.

90    On April 1, 2005 I coordinated the "Fools No More" parade in downtown Portland that kicked off Peace Action Maine's Sustainable Maine Economy Campaign. Over 250 people joined stilt walkers, fire twirlers, people in costumes and others as we made our way through downtown during the evening rush hour. A group of Unitarian's brought up the rear of the parade singing "Down by the River Side"—we ain't gonna study war no more. A week later over 200 people gathered at the University of Southern Maine art gallery for the opening of "War Flowers: Swords into Ploughshares" art exhibit where over 70 artists entered images of what economic conversion would

look like. Following that exhibit the art show will travel throughout the state helping to raise awareness about the conversion idea.

91 In March, 2005, Veterans for Peace called for the impeachment of George W. Bush. The National Office sent a letter to every member of Congress urging them to introduce articles of impeachment into the Congress.

92 This article was written after I saw and ordered a copy of Barnett's presentation on *C-SPAN* (June 2, 2004.) He was speaking to an audience full of high level military officers and CIA operatives. Barnett told them if they wanted to get promoted in the future they had to buy into the new Pentagon "transformation" program and teach it to their subordinates.

93 I saw this on *C-SPAN* too. I watched a four star general in 2004 give a speech to the right-wing Heritage Foundation on Africa. He had a map of the continent and told how the Pentagon is now assigning each of the 50 state National Guards in the U.S. to a different African country. Each state National Guard will set up a military base in an African country.

94 Barnett later found out about this very article and did a critique of it on his web site in February, 2005. Needless to say he was not pleased that I was not an adoring fan of his work.

95 Pat also video taped the entire action and later created a powerful 35-minute video called "Iraq War Cloth" which shows footage of the occupation, as well as her later consecrating the cloth by tenderly pouring tea over it. The video ends with very moving music. Several local cable TV stations agreed to air the video.

96 We were later to learn that Rep. Allen's office had painted over the X's but they had used the wrong paint. Apparently the X's were still showing through the new paint job.

97 Rep. Allen finally agreed to hold a public town hall meeting on the Iraq war in Portland on July 17, 2005. Over 500 people turned out. The local newspaper chose not to cover the event.

98 *War is a Racket* by Gen. Smedley Butler (New York, Round Table Press, 1935).

99 *Addictred to War*, Joel Andreas, Third Edition 2004, AK Press.

100 *The Unknown Unknowns of the Abu Ghraib Scandal*, *The Guardian*, United Kingdom, May 21, 2005.

# APPENDIX

# RECIPES FOR FUNDRAISING

*"Lack of money is the root of all evil."*

—George Bernard Shaw

❏ Build a solid membership base. Stay in touch with your members regularly via e-mail and postal mail. Keep them informed about what your group is doing. (Some groups never communicate with their members yet wonder why they can't get them to do anything.) Some people are very good members, but never come to a meeting. They can give money, write letters, make phone calls. Keep them involved.

❏ Send a funding request to your list via the mail a couple times each year. Studies show mailings on behalf of organizations seem to do best in October, January, September, February and March, in that order. Include a news clip about your work to show your group is making news.

❏ Nurture your best donors by sending them something special your group has produced from time to time. (Booklets, videos, good news clips) This reminds them you appreciate them and helps build confidence as they see something tangible coming from the organization.

❏ Hold potluck dinners regularly for your membership. A key to organization building is creating community. Community builds a solid base of support.

❏ Create a video about your group's work and sell it. There are many talented people around who would be happy to produce a video. Get the video onto your local community access cable station.

❏ On every piece of literature you produce, try to add a line for people to say they would like to make a donation to your organization. Get in the habit of inviting people to help you.

❏ Don't become too dependent on foundations. While foundations can be very helpful, they can also create a sense of false security for an organization. With that said, my favorite foundations are *Resist* and *A.J. Muste Institute*. (*Resist* 259 Elm Street, Somerville, MA 02144 and *A. J. Muste Institute* 339 Lafayette Street, New York, NY 10012.) They give very small grants and have been supportive of my work for over 20 years.

❏ Take up a collection every time you hold an event or have a speaker. Don't be afraid to ask for money.

❏ Don't go it alone. Invite others groups to co-sponsor events and ask them to share the costs. It helps build turnout and movement growth.

❏ Hold an annual supper for your membership and use it as a fundraiser. Invite a well-known speaker who will help draw in other people. It might start out small, but will grow each year if you keep at it. Have some music there, as well.

❏ I've learned that events raise funds, things that inspire people bring in money. My biggest success in fundraising has come from our very public campaigns like the Cancel Cassini, the Walk for the Earth and Peace Camp. If you build it, they will come.

❏ I am a big believer in organizing an annual conference. The theme is generally tied into whatever campaign I am working on at the time. These events can be good fundraisers, they educate people, and also fulfill the need to bring people together for socializing. A win-win all the way around. I always include music, too.

❏ Sell T-shirts, hats, bumper stickers, buttons. Experiment at first to see what sells best. Be careful about ordering too much up front, until you know what sells.

# RUNNING A MEETING

❑ Start the meeting on time – or at least within 5 minutes after the advertised starting time. By doing this you show your members you intend to use their time wisely.

❑ Begin the meeting with introductions then go around and let people make their **short** announcements. Many people come to meetings with something on their mind. If you let them make their announcements early on, they can relax and become full participants in the meeting.

❑ I am not a big believer in setting times for each agenda item. By saying we have 30 minutes for an item most people will talk for 30 minutes. If you set 30 minutes for an item and it becomes possible to finish it in 15, then do it.

❑ Review the agenda with everyone right after introductions and announcements. (The agenda should have been created by the group's leadership in consultation with the membership. A facilitator for the meeting should also be set in advance and the person facilitating should be well-briefed on the agenda and purpose of the meeting.) Make sure everyone in the meeting understands what it is, and is not, about. See if anyone has any questions about the agenda. (Save paper by posting the agenda on the wall where everyone can see it.)

❑ If your group has a few "big talkers" suggest that each person has three matches in his or her hand. Each time they speak they use one match. Have people self regulate their talking habits. That way everyone has a chance to participate in the meeting.

❑ If the same people insist on speaking during the meeting, the facilitator should say, "Let's see if anyone who has not yet had anything to say would like to speak before we call on those who have already spoken."

❑ Consensus building is a great idea. I always try to build consensus in meetings. One way to do it is to look for common themes among the participants and focus on them as a possible solution, rather than focusing on the things that divide the group. In the end, after repeated attempts to reach consensus, I am in favor of asking those who disagree if they could step aside and not block consensus. In larger meetings, after repeated attempts to reach consensus has failed, I am in favor of taking a vote.

❑ A good facilitator should try to keep the meeting moving along. I am not afraid to cut off discussion once I see the agenda item has been accomplished. Some folks have a tendency to keep talking. A good facilitator should step in and say it is time to move on to the next item.

❑ If a particular person seems intent on holding up business then you should ask the group if they would like to hear more from the person or move on. Most times people say, "Let's move on." Let the group help regulate the "big talkers."

❑ People want to talk in meetings, but they also want to finish on time. It's always good to establish the end time as the meeting begins and then remind people you intend to stick to their desire for a timely finish.

❑ If you can finish the meeting early, you can give the group the option to end the meeting, or take some time to have an open discussion on X, Y, or Z topic. Most business meetings can be dull and boring and giving this reward to a group is often very much appreciated. It gives the group a chance to talk about things that may be on their minds, but were not part of the formal business meeting.

❑ Don't hold meetings unless you really need them. If there isn't much to talk about, have the group go out to dinner or do something fun together. Many people join a group, but never really get to know the people in it because no social time is created. Building strong community within the organization will get it through the hard times.

# WHAT'S A GROUP TO DO?

❑ At the start of each new year, bring the group together and spend some time reviewing the work of the past year. What went well? What did not? (It is best to spend the good part of one day doing this process.)

❑ Have people list on a sheet of paper on the wall what they think the group should do during the next year. Look for common themes and highlight them.

❑ After the list is made, go through it and take an informal, non-binding, poll of what are the top 3-4 priorities. Do this just to begin to get a sense of the thinking of the people.

❑ Knock the obvious items off the list that do not have much support from the group or see where they might fit into other more popular choices.

❑ Break into small groups and ask folks to talk with each other about what should be the top priorities for the group of the remaining items on the list.

❑ Come back together and ask them to make the decisions to pick the top priorities.

❑ Form committees for each item that is chosen as a priority and ask them to make a plan to implement the effort. Once the organizing plans are completed have the committees bring the plans back to the whole group for review and adoption. (This does not all have to be done the same day.)

❑ If you don't have enough people to fill the committees then you have chosen too many priorities for the year.

❑ Make it known publicly what your group's priorities are for the year and invite people from outside your organization to participate on a committee. Many people don't want to go to business meetings, but will be happy to serve on a committee to implement a program.

❑ Have a beginning and an end to any issue campaign you take on. Usually a 3-4 month cycle is best. At the end of the campaign have a pot luck, thank folks for helping, and celebrate your successes. Doing this helps create a sense of accomplishment, even though the ultimate goal (like ending the war) might not yet be achieved.

❑ If you've taken on an issue that will be a multi-year effort, then break the organizing plan into 3-4 month sections. Give folks a short break after each quarter is completed. This helps avoid burnout.

❑ Try to avoid jumping from one issue to the next. Some organizations have no focus and bounce around depending on whatever appears to be popular at the moment. Groups need to establish an identity. One group can't handle every issue that comes along and do it justice. Pick a few things and do them well.

❑ Learn to integrate issues into everything the group does. If you are organizing against the war, then also mention cutbacks in human needs programs as a result of the war. Weave in how space technology now coordinates all warfare on Earth. Mention the environmental consequences of war. This way your message connects to allies working on those issues, but your primary focus is still stopping the war. If we all did this in our work, we'd help each other out more and we would build the consciousness level of the public. By integrating these other issues we also give recognition to members of our groups who might have wanted those other issues to be a key focus.

❑ Be sure to take good care of people in your organization who are your spark plugs. Those who provide the vision for your group need to be recognized for their specific role.

# WHAT ABOUT THE MEDIA?

*"Karl Marx is wrong, Television is the opiate of the masses."*
—Tony Follari, Comedian

❏ Don't rely on the media. If they cover something, great. But if they don't, have another plan in motion that will help get the word out to the public.

❏ We have to create our own media. That means alternative local newspapers, cable TV shows, local radio shows where possible, and our own documentary videos. A regular e-mail report from your group's leadership sent to your members, with a request for them to share it with their lists, can be a very effective way to spread the word.

❏ Establish a "poster hanging" route in your community so every event you plan gets publicity through posters hung in public places.

❏ Regularly send local mainstream media contacts information about the issues you work on. Don't send them a lot of paper, just 1-2 pages at most on the subject. Don't expect anything in return. You are just showing them you are a resource on the subject. And, you are educating them. They are likely to contact you when they need someone to comment on the subject.

❏ Have people write letters to the editor on your group's stationery. Then, have others in the group write letters in response to the first letter after it gets published. This will build a discussion in the paper. It is amazing how many people never write letters to the editor.

❏ Create a web site and a blog for your group. The blog will allow people to give feedback, which can be very useful. If you don't know how to do it, ask around. Someone will be able to help you.

❏ Be creative when organizing your events. Use good visuals. When making protest signs make the statements short and the words **BIG** on the signs so they can be read by people driving by at 35 mph. Have artists help and make colorful banners and signs with images that relate to your event.

❑ When you have an event, make sure you have someone(s) picked out in advance to approach the media that come. These members don't have to do all the interviews, but they should direct the media to the appropriate people to do the talking.

❑ Learn to use days/events that are regular media draws. For example Tax Day, on April 15, is always a great time to do an action at the post office about how our money is being spent. The media will often cover the protest since they have to do a Tax Day story, anyway.

❑ If you are lucky enough to get media coverage, reporters will frequently ask you one of these questions at your event. "Are you disappointed that more people are not here?" or "What good do you think will come from this event?" The reporters are trying to get you to say something negative they will then use as your primary message. Never answer a media question in a way that has you appearing to complain about the public's "apathy" or the membership of your own group. It is my opinion that the corporate media has essentially been trained to "demobilize" the public by focusing on things that are not really important. I've learned over the years to basically ignore these questions. Have 1-2 key points prepared in your mind that you want to make, and keep finding ways to make those points. An example of a response you could give: "We are very happy people have come out today to publicly say what we all have been feeling. Our government has been taken over by the military-industrial complex and the big corporations. People are really fed up with our loss of democracy to the big corporations. More and more people now understand the big corporations have taken over our government. We will keep protesting and will keep publicly speaking out against our loss of democracy to the big corporations." This way if they only use one sentence in the newspaper or on the TV you will have still gotten your message out. Don't let the media control your message any more than possible.

# THINGS WE CAN DO

*"You gain strength, experience and confidence by every experience where you really stop to look fear in the face. You must do the thing you cannot do."*

—Eleanor Roosevelt

❏ Don't ever give up. Make a commitment to a lifetime of activism working for the future generations. Nothing in your life can be more important.

❏ Evaluate the level to which the power structure has colonized your mind. How much have you internalized the consumerist "success" mythology? (Climb the corporate ladder; Keep your nose clean; Every "man" for himself; Don't rock the boat; You can't beat City Hall.)

❏ Are you an independent thinker? Are you able to become critical of the Republican and Democratic parties? Are you able to acknowledge that conservative *and* liberal leadership in Congress generally supports the U.S. economic and military empire?

❏ Consider creating cooperative households that share resources and burdens as we face the likely downhill slide of the U.S. economy.

❏ Consider making political activism a priority in your life. A career. Could activism become as important as golf, tennis, TV, expensive vacations, bigger or remodeled homes, fancy clothes, luxury cars, or even graduate school?

❏ Help organize political study groups in your community. Learn more about corporate domination of our political system. Study our current corrupt voting system. Educate others.

❏ Read more history. Learn about past labor and progressive movement struggles in the U.S. and around the world. We have had victories in the past.

❏ Consider running for political office, in order to give voice to the issues you care about. Don't worry about money or winning. Use the campaign to teach.

❏ Consider giving more of your income to organizations you belong to.

❏ Become a self-starter. If no one is addressing an issue you feel strongly about, initiate something yourself.

❏ Don't be afraid of what others will think of you, if you become an activist. The future generations need you to act now.

❏ Surround yourself with other people of good spirit who share a desire to work for the common good.

❏ Don't think there is "one thing" that will be the magic bullet to make everything better. It takes lots of things. Be innovative. Don't be afraid to make mistakes. If at first you don't succeed, try, try again.

❏ Stop thinking those in power don't have a plan to stay in control. They do and they are implementing it. There is a lot of money at stake.

- Don't separate people. Just because someone does (or doesn't) go to church, like sports, eat meat, is young or old, does not mean you can't approach them and become friends. Be open to everyone.
- Don't think those who disagree with you are stupid or less than you. Remember, even the most conservative people can change.
- Keep a good sense of humor, even in the darkest moments. We are not the first people in human history to be engaged in a tough struggle. We won't be the last. Remember how stories of past heroes have inspired you. Become the inspiration for the future generations. You can do it. Si se puede!
- Share power and the limelight. The more you share, the more effective you will be at attracting support.
- Everyone has something they can do well. Find out what people want to do and help them do it. That is leadership.
- Be willing to admit when you are wrong.
- Keep your perspective. Remember we are nothing more than a grain of sand on the beach of time. Don't take yourself too seriously.
- Organize where you are. Raise the level of discussion at your church, office, classroom or social group.
- Start your own cable access TV show.
- Change your shopping habits. Skip the chain stores/restaurants and buy from local businesses.
- Lower your consumption habits. Learn to ask yourself, "Do I really need this?"
- Ride the bus or your bike as often as possible. Car pool to your next protest.
- Don't be an out-of-town activist. (One who only goes to protests in other communities for fear of being seen in your own.) Join the effort in your own hometown. Stand up and show courage.
- Don't think you know everything. Be open to new ideas and information. Listen to everyone and make up your own mind.
- Work cooperatively with others whenever possible.

# MY FAVORITE RESOURCES

❑ Global Network Against Weapons & Nuclear Power in Space PO Box 652, Brunswick, ME 04011 (207) 729-0517 www.space4peace.org and space4peace.blogspot.com for my blog.

❑ National Priorities Project (State by state breakdowns of the social costs of military spending and war) www.nationalpriorities.org

❑ Veterans for Peace www.veteransforpeace.org

❑ Harpers Magazine (Excellent reading) 666 Broadway, 11th Floor, New York, N.Y. 10012 www.harpers.org

❑ *The Guardian Weekly* (I subscribe to this weekly British newspaper that gives good coverage of international news you won't find in U.S. papers.) www.guardian.co.uk

❑ *C-SPAN* www.c-span.org

❑ Democracy Now (You can listen to the show on the Internet) www.democracynow.org

❑ Abolition Now Campaign (International network of groups to abolish nuclear weapons) www.abolition2000.org

❑ Nuclear Policy Research Institute (Dr. Helen Caldicott's organization working to shut down the entire nuclear industry) www.nuclearpolicy.org

❑ Yorkshire Campaign for Nuclear Disarmament (CND) www.cndyorks.gn.apc.org

❑ Space.Com (Best internet source for space industry propaganda) www.space.com

❑ Center for Voting & Democracy (Working on the important Instant Runoff Voting issue) www.fairvote.org

❑ POCLAD—Programs on Corporations, Law, and Democracy www.poclad.org

❑ *Washington Post* (I check their web site daily to see how the power structure is spinning their issues) www.washingtonpost.com

❑ Local Newsletters (I love to see what local groups are doing. I get many of these from all over the world. Great source of new organizing ideas.)

❑ Local cable Access TV (I started my own show called "This Issue" and I always enjoy seeing what local folks come up with on cable.)

# ACKNOWLEDGMENTS

This book was made possible by the strong support of the boards (Directors and Advisors) of the Global Network Against Weapons and Nuclear Power in Space. The Global Network covered the cost of the book, seeing it as an investment in our collective work. Proceeds from the sale of the book will go to the organization.

Nancy E. Randolph, owner of Just Write Books and Just Write Communications in Topsham, Maine, did the desktop publishing and reduced her normal fee by 50 percent. Her encouragement, initiative, and creativity helped make this project possible.

I slept, or daydreamed, during high school English grammar classes. Thus I needed a lot of help editing the book. I used three volunteer editors. My partner, Mary Beth Sullivan, did the first read of the book and made many suggestions for changes. Mary Beth's love and support helped wash away my doubts and insecurities about writing. Then our friend, and former Gainesville neighbor, Julie Netzer did the second read. Julie was instrumental in encouraging me to include the organizing tips section at the end of the book. The third, and final editor, was our new friend and neighbor Selma Sternlieb in Brunswick, Maine. Selma is a real professional and brought her editorial expertise to bear.

Long-time friend Karl Grossman did the forward to the book and offered many kind words of encouragement. Karl, a journalist by profession, kept telling me that the honesty of my writing would be appreciated by the readers. Many thanks go to Daniel Ellsberg, Ardeth Platte, and Helen Caldicott for giving their kind endorsements for the back cover. Each of them have been, and remain, major role models for me.

I must also thank all those who read my e-mail trip reports and for several years have given me positive feedback on them. The fact that so many people say they find the stories educational and uplifting triggered the idea to put many of them into a book. I must thank all of those about whom I have written while on my organizing trips. Your efforts to host me, teach me, and keep peace issues alive in your community have been an inspiration to me and many others who read about your work.

W.B. Park has been illustrating my work for the past 20 years. His art, shown throughout the book, has illustrated leaflets, posters, and newsletters that I've done while working for the Florida Coalition for Peace & Justice and the Global Network. I am a visual learner and have always felt blessed to have Will's art giving folks another way to "see" our message. Will and I had many great experiences together, including a trip to Cuba and regular BBQ lunches where we talked politics in conservative Central Florida.

The last piece of art in the book, the drawing of an Indian woman in prayer, was done by an old Florida friend named John Beardsley. John, a brilliant artist, helped me publish my first newspaper, called *This Issue,* in the early 1980's. John suffered from depression and unexpectedly took his own life 20 years ago. I honor his memory by finishing the book with his piece—saying to him that his beautiful spirit still lives in me.

Lastly, I must thank all the people who have supported my work as an organizer over the years. It has been a pleasure and an honor to work with all of you. You've made it possible for me to serve in a way that I promised myself I would after I got out of the Air Force in 1974. I also thank the United Farm Workers Union for teaching me how to organize. Without that training and valuable experience, I would not be the organizer that I am today.

Good luck to all and get organized.

Bruce K. Gagnon

# INDEX

Printed in the United States
43372LVS00005B/184-210

9 780976 653356